T5-BPZ-720

Workings of the Picaresque in the British Novel

by

Lars Hartveit

Solum Forlag A/S: Oslo 1987
Humanities Press International, INC.: New Jersey

823·08
H 336w

First published in 1987 in Norway by SOLUM FORLAG A.S
and in the U.S.A. by HUMANITIES PRESS INTERNATIONAL, INC.,
Atlantic Highlands, NJ 07716.

© Copyright 1987 Lars Hartveit.

Cover design: Radek Doupovec.

Financially supported by Norges almenvitenskapelige forskningsråd (The
Norwegian Council for Science and the Humanities).

Library of Congress Cataloging-in-Publication Data

Hartveit, Lars.
   Workings of the Picaresque in the British novel.

   Bibliography: p. 168
   1. English fiction—History and criticism.
2. Picaresque literature, English—History and criticism. I. Title.
PR830.P49H37   1987   823'.087'09   86-20840
ISBN 0-391-03477-4 (U.S.)
ISBN 82-560-0417-7 (Norway)

All rights reserved. No reproduction, copy or
transmission of this publication
may be made without written permission.

Printed in Norway by S. Hammerstads Boktrykkeri A/S, Oslo
Type-set by typo-service a-s, Oslo

88-8940

VOID

Library of
Davidson College

WORKINGS OF THE PICARESQUE
IN THE BRITISH NOVEL

Contents

Acknowledgements

The project from which this book has emerged dates back ten years to a seminar on the picaresque novel which professor Stein Haugom Olsen, then research assistant in this department, helped me to organize. The many lively discussions in this seminar convinced me that there was room for a book on the changing fortunes of the picaresque genre in the English novel. I would like to thank him for all his help at this decisive stage in the genesis of this work. I am also indebted to Maureen Jaunsen who decided to write her MA thesis on the picaresque novel while I was immersed in my research on the topic.

The Norwegian Research Council for Science and the Humanities has provided generous support over the years. Without their assistance this project could not have been realized. My thanks are due to the Editors of *ENGLISH STUDIES* and *PAPERS ON LANGUAGE AND LITERATURE PRESENTED TO ALLVAR ELLEGÅRD AND ERIK FRYKMAN* (Gothenburg, 1985) for allowing me to include formerly published material, in modified form, in chapters two and four of this book.

Finally I would like my colleagues to know how much I have appreciated the interest they have shown and for enabling me to concentrate on this work during my research leaves.

Bergen, 1987.

Chapter 1

The Perennial Appeal
of the Picaresque Novel

The picaresque novel has fascinated readers since its emergence in Renaissance Spain. Novels such as *Lazarillo de Tormes* (1554) by an unknown author, Alemán's *Guzmán de Alfarache* (1599-1604), and Quevedo's *La Vida del Buscón* (1626) share characteristics that mark them as belonging to a particular genre in opposition to the prevailing literary fashions of their day. Part of their appeal is their concern with the ordinary and trivial in contrast to the subject matter of traditional romance. Yet the everyday is given a touch of the extraordinary in that the picaro's circumstances and the vicissitudes of his wanderings are so extreme. The pathetic nature of the protagonist and his story stirs the reader's conscience, and the autobiographical mode adopted satisfies the demand for authenticity. At the same time, the reader gets his fill of exciting adventure: the picaro also seems through his misfortunes to have escaped from the monotonous uneventfulness of ordinary life. Besides, the trickster of fairy tales and popular humor appears to have survived in the picaro's makeup as resourceful rogue. The bestseller status, which novels such as *Gúzman* achieved, is evidence of the success of the picaresque formula.

The lasting appeal of the picaresque has something to do with its easily recognizable formula, which gives scope to the story teller, portrayer of the *comedie humaine,* and social critic alike. It focuses on individual human interest as well as on a panoramic social canvas. The hold it has had on the later English writers within the framework of this study may well derive from what Ralph Freedman calls the picaresque story's function as "a *paradigm* for the novel as a whole". Freedman goes on to describe the way the "picaresque [as] a paradigm (...) presents a space described entirely by interactions between heroes and their antagonists, between selves and others"[1]. During his journey — the basic plot formula of the picaresque novel — the protagonist is endlessly confronted with antagonists. Relationships are formed and interrupted, but he is always thrown back upon himself and his own inescapable loneliness. Alexander Blackburn stresses that the "fundamental situation of the literary picaro is the loneliness of an individual isolated *within* society."[2] Claude Guillén sees the theme of human alienation as a link between the early Spanish picaresque tale *Lazarillo de Tormes* and our time, while he also finds that they share the Jamesian "tangle" as well. As he puts it, the picaresque hero "is involved from the start in (…) a 'tangle', (…) an economic and social predicament of the most immediate and pressing nature. (…) The picaresque *novel* (…) offers a process of conflict between the individual and his environment, inwardness and experience (…)"[3] The picaresque encounter thus becomes a formula that suggests one component of the plot pattern of the novel, while it also furnishes sociological insight. In addition, it offers close-ups of the protagonist's mechanism of response to his environment.

The territory Guillén describes is shared by the novel as a whole, and by the novel of social criticism in particular. The somewhat elusive nature of a pursuit of the picaresque outside Spain, and after the seventeenth century, is due to the fact that the mode has mixed so successfully with other fictional traditions. With a "pure" nineteenth or twentieth century picaresque novel one is often left with an impression of pastiche, as in the case of Thackeray's *Barry Lyndon* or Nathaniel West's *A Cool Million*. This is rather puzzling as parody is one of the stocks-in-trade of the picaresque[4]. The answer is perhaps that the picaresque, like the novel as a whole, has always been both sensitive to tradition and critical of it. This ambiguity is at the heart of the process of continuity and renewal to which the novel has always submitted. In his book on the history of the novel, Walter L. Reed applies the insights of Russian Formalism in his view of the novel as "a long prose fiction which opposes the forms of everyday life, social and psychological, to the conventional forms of literature (…) inherited from the past. The novel is a type of literature suspicious of its own literariness." In seventeenth-century Spain, *Don Quixote* and picaresque novels are, according to Reed, "the first fully developed examples of an extended prose writing which opposes the fictions of everyday life to the fictions of a literary tradition". He then goes on to argue that "the moment (…) that the canon becomes identifiably canonical and the novel a critical departure from it (…)" occurs in late sixteenth- and early seventeenth–century Spain.[5] One of the most interesting aspects of this view is the insight it offers into the way the various modes may act as vehicles of transformation. A romance motif, for example, may be "defamiliarized" in the context of a realistic novel. It is part of the aim of the present study to trace the persistence of the picaresque in the English novel as well as its potential for renewal and transformation. The picaresque at times gives one the impression of being the picaro of the fictional universe, securing a family resemblance even in novels that seem far removed from the Spanish point of departure. Is the picaresque genetically dominant, like brown eyes? This may cause the genre-oriented critic a headache, unless he confines himself to

Spain or the seventeenth and eighteenth centuries. What appeals to the present writer is the circumstance Robert Alter describes so well in the preface to his book on the picaresque novel:

> It seems reasonable to assume that the picaesque novel is not simply a long-finished episode in Western literature but rather a permanent addition to the storehouse of literary resources, capable of regenerating and transforming itself in a surprising variety of new environments[6].

My main reservation about Alter's statement is the term "picaresque novel." Robert Scholes's preferable term, "picaresque mode," takes care of the mixed character of the novel as a genre, subsuming as it does a wide variety of narrative kinds. According to the scheme he sketches out in *Structuralism in Literature*, a novel may draw on a wide spectrum of fictional modes ranging from satire, picaresque, comedy, history, sentiment, and tragedy to romance. A particular mode may dominate, but others are not excluded. Thus according to Scholes: "If the novel began in the eighteenth century as a union of comic and sentimental impulses which we may call realistic, in the nineteenth century it moved toward a more difficult and powerful combination of picaresque and tragic impulses which we have learned to call naturalistic."

The "modal scheme" Scholes sketches out can, he hopes, "help to tell us where we are and to explain how we got there[7]". Such an approach, combined with attention to recurrent formulas, also enables us to chart the picaresque impulse and determine its role as catalyst of the sociological element in the novel with which we are concerned.

One of the recurrent concerns of the picaresque mode is what Wicks terms "the *essential picaresque situation*," which he describes as "that of an unheroic protagonist, worse than we, caught up in a chaotic world, worse than ours, in which he is on an eternal journey of encounters." The *"essential romance situation"* he sees as a contrast to this world: it "is that of a heroic protagonist in a world marvelously better than ours in which he is on a quest that confronts him with challenges, each ending in a moral victory leading toward a final ordered and harmonious cosmos[8]".

The journey in a picaresque novel appears in ironic contrast to that of the questing knight, but, as we shall see, there are also other ironic links between the two modes. Thus the suggestion of a pastoral heaven of harmony and security for which the picaro, like the wandering knight, is yearning, appears in contexts that make the pastoral seem like an elusive dream in the picaresque tale, while reflecting the ideology of a fossilized social system in tales of chivalry.

In both cases, the idea of an essential situation suggests a timeless element, that approaches both modes to the world of myth, reaching back

beyond historical time to the beginnings of the race. Picaresque and
romance both embody stories that are part of our common heritage, stories that are "already alive," according to Guillén, and have "been so for
many centuries[9]". They are, in other words, archetypal. One might, for
example, argue that the picaresque tale and the romance in their essential situations hark back to two stories in the Bible, Joseph's story in
Genesis and the story of Moses in Exodus. Joseph, thrown into a "pit in
the wilderness" by his wicked brothers and then sold as a slave "into
Egypt," experiences as traumatic a rejection and abandonment as any
picaro. He begins with nothing, being a complete outcast. It could be
argued that the story of his life shows how he adapts himself to circumstances and how he fights his way into society through his resourcefulness, to become a successful businessman and civil administrator—in
this respect he is more fortunate than the Spanish picaro. His essential
situation, however, must have been determined by his early experience
of shock and the resulting sense of engulfing chaos, further underlined
in his role as prudent guardian of limited resources. Through his fore-
sight, Egypt has corn while the surrounding nations starve. Joseph was
granted Goshen, which he may well have thought of as a very precarious
paradise.

Moses, too, begins with nothing, but he is not thrust to the bottom of
the social scale by his own family when too young to fend for himself.
On the contrary, he is the foundling whom fate—here the God of Israel—
rescues from certain death. Placed in a superior social position, he is
then selected by Jahve to lead his people out of Egypt through the wilderness to the Holy Land, which, however, he is only allowed to see in
the distance. These details in Moses's story place him within the essential romance situation: he shares many of the features of the questing
knight, and his journey is closer to that of romance than that of the picaresque tale.

Both these stories contain mythic features in their concern with fundamental, timeless human urges and needs. They both relate to humanity's yearning to belong, to be inside, safe and protected—a feeling which
is counterpointed by a sense of precariousness, a nightmarish obsession
with insecurity and lack of protection—the sum of anxiety centered in
the image of the lonely castaway in a bustling community. At the heart
of the continuing appeal of the picaresque is this emotional core of the
protagonist's response to the environment, which makes him express so
perfectly the mood and temper of a community in turmoil, in the throes
of change, or threatened with economic ruin. Suffusing the whole picaresque situation is the fear of moral chaos. According to Blackburn:
"This essential morality of the picaresque novels is contained in the
manner in which individual and society reflect each other; in fact, they
are each other. If society is morally astray, then the individual may go
morally astray, and vice versa.[10]"

The fear of going astray, of losing his bearings in a wilderness because he is without friends and helpers, is a recurrent aspect of the picaro's essential situation throughout the history of the English novel, although Alexander A. Parker feels that the "spirit of optimism and the scientific rationalism" of the eighteenth century made that period inimical to the picaresque novel[11]. It could be argued, however, that this optimism is qualified by the sense of social unrest and suffering, and, not least, the economic insecurity and moral corruption conveyed by writers such as Fielding and Smollett. Pope may celebrate the Great Chain of Being as the supreme symbol of order and harmony in *An Essay on Man*, but his vision is accompanied by a countervision of chaos and destruction:

> And, if each system in gradation roll
> Alike essential to the amazing Whole,
> The least confusion but in one, not all
> That system only, but the Whole must fall.
> Let Earth unbalanced from her orbit fly;
> Planets and Suns run lawless through the sky;
> Let ruling angels from their spheres be hurled,
> Being on Being wrecked, and world on world

> (*Essay on Man*, Epistle I, 11. 247–254)

The anxiety in these lines is an undercurrent in the novel of social realism that is such an important part of the eighteenth-century literary legacy. The recurrent image of social stability and security is surrounded by an atmosphere of precariousness and latent or overt violence. The resulting grey zone between order and lawlessness is the perennial domain of the picaro, the very emblem of social preacriousness.

The family likeness among Spanish picaresque novels can be expressed in a formula that can then be used in an investigation of the changing fortunes of the picaresque mode in the history of the English novel. Awareness of the basic formula, and of its persistence and transmutations, can also facilitate our approach to the social models that the novels under discussion present and help us discover whether the picaresque is a key to our undrstanding of these models and the authors' sociological awareness.

The following outline of the picaresque formula draws on the increasing number of critics who have devoted their attention to the picaresque since Frank Wadleigh Chandler's pioneer work at the beginning of the twentieth century[12]. The most systematic attention to the formulaic aspect of the picaresque, within limited scope, may be found in the works by Guillén and Wicks referred to above.

The picaresque prototype is a first-person account of a protagonist's life and adventures, beginning with his childhood and ending at some often vaguely defined point in his maturity when he can view his life retrospectively and often reflectively. His beginnings relate him to his family—he is shown as either the member of a family or an orphan. Common features are family consciousness and family pride. Despite his poverty and humble social position, the protagonist is at times intensely aware of his forebears and often imagines that he is of noble birth. This is part of the mock romance element in the picaresque novel. The picaro is born at the bottom of the social ladder or altogether outside of it. His parents tend to be disreputable, associated with crime and prostitution. Thus Pablo in *El Buscón (The Swindler)* discovers that two basic tenets in an honorable family's genealogical makeup, respectability and noble descent, do not apply to his parents, despite their pretensions. His father, a "respectable" barber, is a thief, and his mother, whose ancestors have such fine names, is a common prostitute.

This kind of discovery is part of the eye-opening process by which the picaro discovers his identity and the true nature of his environment. It is linked with the event which closes the first phase of the picaro's career, the moment of his dramatic ejection into the world—a traumatic experience that Wicks calls "the picaro's second 'birth'"[13]. The irrevocable nature of the picaro's parting from his family is made clear in the scene in which Lazarillo leaves his mother, who has been forced by necessity to enroll her son in the service of a blind man:

> I went to my mother and we both cried. She gave me her blessing and said: "I know I'll never see you again. Try and be good and may God guide you. I've raised you as best I know and I've put you with a good master. Now you must look after yourself."[14]

This is the juncture at which the picaro discovers that he is completely alone in a hostile or indifferent world. He is an outcast, completely abandoned to his own inadequate resources. The nightmarish nature of his experience is finely brought out in the incident that immediately follows Lazarillo's parting from his mother, when Lazarillo and his master pass a stone bull on their way into Salamanca:

> The blind man told me to go to it and then he said:
> "Lazaro, put your ear close to the bull and you'll hear a loud noise inside it."
> I was so simple that I did just that, and when he felt that my head was against the stone, he straightened his arm and gave me such a blow that my head crashed against that blasted bull so hard that it hurt me for three days and more.
> "You silly little nitwit! You'll have to learn that a blind man's boy has got to be sharper than a needle!"

And he cackled with glee. At that moment I felt as if I had woken up and my eyes were opened. I said to myself: "What he says is true; I must keep awake because I'm on my own and I've got to look after myself."[15]

The picaro's journey tends to begin with this kind of violent encounter with the world, initiating a process in which the picaro is transformed from inncoent victim to resourceful rogue. He soon discovers that he has to sink or swim. Thus Lazarillo learns to pay his master back in his own coin. Before eventually running away from him, Lazarillo makes the blind man undergo the same kind of experience to which he had been submitted: he directs "the poor wretch" to jump across a ditch straight into a stone pillar[16]. Lazarillo has lost his trustfulness, but he has learned how to look after himself. The picaresque novel tends to contain incidents that show the picaro's initial gullibility; his journey from innocence to experience takes him from credulity to cunning. *En route* he shows an amazing ability to adapt himself to constantly changing circumstances. His lack of strength is made up for by nimbleness and ready wit, which enable him to survive and advance in the struggle for a place in the sun, even if he is starving. Yet there is always a touch of the victim about the picaro: he is forever exposed to a merciless fate that may allow him to advance a notch or two up the social scale, but which without warning may thrust him down again. Wicks refers to this as the "Sisyphus" quality in the picaro, his refusal to give in and ability to endure the vicissitudes of fortune with equanimity and good humor[17].

The structure of the picaresque novel is episodic, a journey of unexpected encounters and incidents strung together in a haphazard manner. Nothing is predictable in the picaro's world. Nor can he avoid being tainted by the vicious environment through which he passes: his is, after all, the delinquent's progress, his territory, the land between respecatbility and crime[18]. Gradually adventures and comic episodes are enjoyed for their own sakes, but the panoramic social perspective is always present as the picaro, in Guilléns words, "moves horizontally through space and vertically through society"[19] His is a lonely journey: in a world where everyone is fighting for his own interest, he is generally without guidance and protection. His skill in surviving may give one the impression that he is leading a charmed life, but he only rarely manages to extricate himself from the sordid milieu into which he has been thrust.

The open, inconclusive ending of the picaresque novel nevertheless may imply a happy conclusion to the protagonist's wanderings. As in the case of the hero of the *Bildungsroman*, there is a suggestion that his wanderings are over, at least for the time being. His, too, is a story of growth from childhood through adolescence to maturity. Lazarillo does achieve a measure of success, although his claim to respectability is debatable. Pablo, in *El Buscón,* ultimately finds himself in America. Pablo's expectations of a happy ending, however, are soon defeated: "I thought things would go better in the New World and another country. But they went worse, as they always will for anybody who thinks he only has to move his dwelling without changing his life or ways."[20]

The mock-romance element is a persistent feature in the picaresque novel. The fragile, low-born picaro is, in his outcast state, a striking contrast to the handsome, aristocratic wandering knight. Both are exposed to the vicissitudes of the journey, but their aims, adventures, and circumstances belong to worlds that have nothing in common. Yet both may be seen as going through long periods in which their characters are tested, even though they represent contrasting codes of conduct. The knight's code of honour is, however, also part of the status of gentleman to which the picaro often aspires.

The insider-outsider opposition permeates the social model the picaresque novel contains. We meet a hierarchically arranged, stratified social system with a well-developed defense mechanism to keep outsiders out. There is also a suggestion of an alternative, classless society in the picaresque novel—occasionally the travellers along the road form a kind of gypsy brotherhood, and sometimes the childhood home appears by contrast as a happy place to the picaro. Normally, however, it is the picaro's aim to gain a foothold on the ladder into respectable society. His half-outsider status is caused by his need to operate within the established social system to survive. His chameleonlike skill in adopting the language and manners of the class he is trying to infiltrate is also evidence of the extent to which he has been bitten by social ambition.

Money and patronage constitute the gateway into this apparently closed world, unless a niche in the inside circle has been acquired by birth. The elite is surrounded by a bustling multitude of knights of fortune on the make in an acquisitive society. The wheel of fortune is an appropriate image of the power structure of this kind of society, suggesting a closed community. The force behind it is the system itself, which assumes a pyramidal structure with a master at the top, the source of an entirely erratically dispensed influence. The picaro is, at the outset, forced to resort to theft to obtain the money he needs to improve his lot, honest work appearing to be out of the question in a no-man's-land where he is best able to follow his predatory instinct. Honest work assumes a society in which you are locked within a niche. Along the road, in the numerous inns, and above all in the towns to which his journey takes him, theft enables the picaro to join the ranks of the parasites, the motley crowd of hangers-on who surround the privileged rich. Through his position as servant, which he often obtains with money acquired by shady practices, the picaro both benefits from and becomes a link in the patronage system. Without money and an influential friend, any appointment is beyond reach. Gambling, of which the picaro soon becomes a master, secures the pattern of quick reversals which characterizes the rogue's progress from rags to riches to rags. In the course of his wanderings, the picaro exposes a society which, paradoxically, is fluid and mobile and riddled with corruption, but which also presents a curiously fossilized facade to the upstart climber. The wheel of fortune either moves the picaro back toward his outsider beginnings, or leaves him in a backwater, as in the case of Pablo in America.

The social model in the picaresque novel contains a critical dimension, emphasized by the parodic/satirical tone it often assumes. The pseudoautobiographical, first-person mode of narration ensures, according to Guillén, that "life is at the same time revived and judged, presented and remembered"[21]. The protagonist is presented as the victim of circumstances fixed by historically determined necessity. Yet the same process turns him into an agent who, through his own acts, can make the most of a critical situation and in the process gain insight into the workings of the community. For instance the wisdom imparted to him by his father is at the heart of Pablo's cynical view of society:

"Being a thief isn't just a job, it's a liberal profession (…) If you don't thieve you won't eat. Why do you reckon the police and the mayor hate us so much? … It's because they don't want there to be any thieves except themselves and their lot. But if you are crafty you can get away with anything."[22]

Thieving is established as the central organizing principle in this society. By implication, the thief is established as the principal civil servant, and craftiness, in which the picaro is such an adept, is put forward as the supreme social virtue. The moral/satirical perspective is deepened when Pablo tells his parents that he wants "to learn to be an honest man" and therefore wishes to go to school[23]. In the context of the world of *El Buscón*, "honest" means the socially secure position of a gentleman, a position in which the picaro can reap the benefits of thieving and craftiness. The gentleman is not self-made by his own hard manual work, but by gambling and shady practices.

Formula as well as model suggest recurrent features that together constitute a structure which acts as a paradigm. The picaresque prototype provides a design that later practitioners of the craft of fiction may use; it also provides an interpretative approach which allows for continuity as well as change. Further, viewing the social content of the picaresque novel from a formulaic angle makes it possible to avoid the quagmire that a socially oriented critic may fall into—the view that literature reflects social reality. Instead, one may focus on the society that a particular novelist has constructed. Again a protoype-oriented

approach may bring out recurrent features and thus reveal the
conventional nature of the world the novel presents. "Conventional"
refers to the extent to which the novel in question conforms to the social
code the genre assumes, but also to its place in the ideological framework
of the time and class it represents and to which it belongs. The author
paints the social canvas of his or her time, but also interprets it. Besides,
since the author is often hostile to the established society he or she
portrays, in the course of a novel, an alternative ideal society may
emerge. Also, an author's assumptions about society and human intercourse are important elements in the ideological make-up of the novel
which a formula-oriented scrutiny may enable us to clarify. It is, however, important to bear in mind that formulas and models are of very
limited interest in themselves. The real test of their value is the extent to
which they throw light on the way the individual writer both absorbs and
transforms tradition.

An early example of this process is Alemán's *Guzmán de Alfarache*.
One is struck by its immediate as well as its lasting popularity. "Within
six years, it reached its thirtieth edition," rivaling even *Don Quixote*[24].
Furthermore, its popularity spread to other countries. James Mabbe's
English translation appeared in 1622, and four editions had been issued
by 1656[25]. In his short account of *Guzmán*, Harry Sieber shows how
Alemán both exploits and expands the formula established in
Lazarillo.[26]

Guzmán shares the first-person autobiographical perspective with
Lazarillo and *El Buscón*. The four-volume account of his life and
wanderings ends with his conversion and exile as a galley slave; the
reptrospective angle of vision has a clear didactic focus. The story opens
with the protagonist's disreputable origin. Having settled down in
Seville after a period in Turkish captivity, his father, a Genoese Jew,
marries a woman of doubtful reputation. He acquires wealth by shady
means after a life full of vicissitudes.

Guzmán's moment of ejection comes when his father dies, and he and
his mother are left penniless. With his only inheritance—the conviction
that he comes of a good family—he decides to go into the world and seek
his fortune, although he is only fourteen. His aim is to travel to Genoa
and claim kin there. But long before he is out of Spain, he becomes painfully aware of his lack of experience and knowledge of the world. Unable
to fend for himself and without friendly guidance, he is continually
tricked and has soon "lost all that little that I had"[27]. The passage, in which
we are shown Guzmán asleep on a bench in the porch after he has been
refused shelter even in the church is an emblem of the picaro's initial
state of complete abandonment and unrelieved loneliness (II,95). This is
the moment at which Guzmán becomes aware of his outcast state as a
picaro.

From then on his traveling is a matter of necessity. The story line is a string of random adventures and episodes along the road and in towns like Genoa, Rome, and Madrid. Exposed to harsh circumstances and the unpredictable whims of fortune, he learns the value of wit and resourcefulness. Soon he can hold his own with any rogue, and becomes adept in all branches of the picaro's trade; he is a master of begging and stealing as well as of gambling and card playing. His good looks and gallant manner make him a model gentleman's servant, particularly as a page. In this capacity, Guzmán moves up and down through polite society, an excellent hunting ground for the accomplished rogue who has replaced the innocent gull. His nimbleness and cunning along with his ability to make shift are evidence that he has graduated in the art of survival. Towns are the favourite haunts of Guzmán and his fellow rogues. The capital with its endless possibilities for parasitic infiltration is their paradise. Guzmán's multifarious career takes him from rags to riches but also shows how precarious his foothold is on the wheel of fortune. His wealth never lasts long; without warning he soon finds himself again reduced to poverty. Petty crime provides the money needed to keep off starvation, but it also enables him to gain access to the safe and respectable world of the gentleman. Petty crime, however, is also the gateway to corruption, leading eventually to a career of crime and wickedness, with prison or the galleys as the inevitable final stage—or the gallows. A promised sequel that will presumably deal with Gúzman as convert provides an open ending of a different kind from the one we find in *Lazarillo* and *El Buscón*. It suggests a new way of life as a result of the "absolute discharge" he was granted, enabling Guzmán to "put a full point to these my misfortunes" (V, 353).

Guzmán conforms to the picaresque formula by focusing on the fate of an orphan without family and protection, ejected at an early age into a hostile world. Through an endless series of encounters with the environment through which he travels, he is engaged in a Sisyphean struggle for admission to a society that is closed to him. Always ready to start from scratch with undaunted stoicism and energy, he only momentarily achieves an insider's status. The fine clothes he keeps acquiring are always in the end defiled and reduced to rags, his efforts to achieve the status of a self-made man are always defeated.

Guzmán is a *Bildungsroman* in which the protagonist relates and reflects on his career, as we have seen, from the point of view of the converted galley slave. His didactic aim is reflected in the structure of the novel which alternates between the narrative and moralizing commentary. The resulting double perspective joins concern with the moment for its own sake, embedded in sin, suffering, and excitement, to concern with the overall exemplary value of the string of moments the book as a whole contains. Moreover the two perspectives suffuse the novel with ambiguity, especially as the first one singles out the element of excitement for special attention. As fully demonstrated in Defoe's picaresque novels, the author may sometimes give one the impression of wanting to have it both ways: on the one hand, acting as the recorder of a rogue's progress who wants to satisfy his readers' appetite for criminal adventures, and on the other, acting as the reformer who attempts to turn them against these sinful practices.

The social model contained in *Guzmán* may be studied on three levels: the story, the moral commentary, and the level of the religious "world view," which dominates the book. The story level reveals a social structure dominated by the contrast between the haves and have-nots. The society outlined in the story is vulnerable to infiltration by picaros and their fellow knights of fortune, but it is also a closed community that keeps insiders in and outsiders out. The social structure has the shape of a pyramid which is possible to climb, but it is slippery, and the climber is more likely to tumble down than reach the top or any safe place. Egotism is the ruling social principle; the "claw me, claw thee" principle (II, 101) is at the heart of countless episodes in which the picaro is shown in a ceaseless struggle to elbow his way to success at everybody else's expense—sometimes succeeding, but as often failing. The protagonist is a lonely figure, deprived of the protection of his family or of a community where he has a well-defined place and a piece of property that would secure him an insider's status. Guzmán moves around in circles in a social void. Both the road and the city offer doors of opportunity for the resourceful Guzmán, but he finds again and again that they lead to anarchy and lawlessness rather than to social recognition. To achieve such a goal, he has to break the law which protects the insiders, and consequently, the law destroys him when he seeks to escape his outsider's position.

On the level of moral commentary, the social model within the story is clarified and expanded. The governing principle of social organization is shown to be injustice, which means that there is one law for the rich and privileged—the insiders—another for the poor and down-and-outs—the outsiders. Bribery is a universal form of theft, a recognized means of social advancement or of looking after one's interests. But the petty thief alone is punished for stealing, although this is the only way he can obtain the money he needs to buy himself a place, once his worst hunger is stilled. The pyramidal social structure is reflected in Guzmán's lengthy sermons on social malpractice: "Thus is it, in all your Officers of Justice, as well as with your royall Merchant, as your Retayler; your Alcalde, as your Alguazil; your Judge, as your Petty-fogger; with him that selleth in groosse, as him that selleth by retayle; your Justicer is the Merchant; your Petty-fogger, the Pedler." (II, 55).

All the representatives of these classes, high and low, practise bribery. We are given an inventory of a society in which there is an unbridgeable gap between the haves and have-nots. We are shown the unfairness of a system that punishes the outsider for what the insider takes for granted.

It follows that a friend is a wise investment. Guzmán gradually realizes that "to gain friends, is a putting forth of money to interest, and the sowing of seed in a fruitfull soyle" (III, 33). Money is the be-all and end-all of the community Guzmán aspires to. He experiences to the full the merciless turning of the wheel of fortune which underlines the precarious nature of wealth and social position for the upstart picaro. He recognizes that

> povertie is the poore mans portion, and riches, that of the rich. And therefore, where good bloud boyleth, and the Pulse of honour beats strongly, want is held a greater losse then life; death is not so hurtfull, nor seemeth half so terrible unto him, as Necessitie. For money warmeth the bloud, and makes it quicke and active (...) This is the course of the world (III, 129–30).

Consequently he goes on to argue:

> It is as common, as ancient in the world, for every man to love prosperitie, to follow after riches, to seeke for fulnesse, to procure preferment, to pursue plentie, and to hazard our lives to get where-withall to live, and to grow into money (which is the mother of abundance) (III, 131).

Thus, while he seems to assume a permanent division between rich and poor, he also assumes a society in which the pursuit of money is the dynamic principle which may also secure the rogue's progress from rags to riches. The passage quoted contains an inventory of ways in which riches can be achieved. Money and the principle of ownership are the cornerstones of society, and Guzmán defines his situation in relation to them. Yet there is nothing of the revolutionary in his increasingly critical attitude.

Indeed, Guzmán's attitude to the community he passes through is determined by the religious perspective he adopts in his memoirs. In retrospect, he sees his travels as a kind of pilgrim's progress: the various episodes recorded are stages on his journey toward the moment of conversion. His evil deeds and misfortunes are related to his upbringing and environment—circumstances over which he has no control. But gradually he is also shown in encounters that demand a choice between actions that are morally right or wrong. We are told that his "naturall disposition was good" (III, 62) but corrupted in the course of his wanderings. However, he cannot blame "Nature" because he has followed vice rather than virtue: "For I had no less abilitie for good, then inclination to evill. The fault was mine owne." (III, 258).

Despite Guzmán's well-developed sense of social injustice, his recurrent message is acquiescence and forbearance. It is this essentially conservative social view that makes Guzmán express so well the contrasting dynamic principle of social progress through the acquisition of money. This monetary principle is shown to be at the heart of the God-given socal system he invites the reader to accept and is part of the moral choice with which Guzmán is continually confronted.

The fact that Guzmán exposes the iniquities of the social system yet also teaches acceptance makes it difficult to assess the element of criticism in the social model that the religious perspective invites the reader to formulate. On the one hand, Guzmán expatiates on the universality of self-interest:

> Turne thine eye aside, and looke upon as many men, as now live in the world; (...) and thou shalt finde, that they all goe seeking to encrease their estates, to advantage themselves the best they can (...) The King, seekes to augment his State, and inlarge his Kingdome; The Gentleman, to raise his House; The Merchant, to encrease his wealth, and to drive such a trade, as may turne to his great profit; And the Trades-man, to gaine by his Trade. (IV, 259).

The system conforms to a Chain-of-Being model, which also invites misuse: instead of a well-regulated, harmonious society in which everybody has his or her place and operates within her or his allotted sphere, we are shown a community in which "every man lives for himselfe; get hee, that can get" (IV, 259). Injustice flourishes: the rich get away with theft of "the largest size," while the "poore rogues" are sent to the galleys or hanged, although they "neither have the wit to invent, nor the power to aspire to any great bootie, nor to undertake great matters" (IV, 259–60).

On the other hand, the principle of inequality is accepted as natural. The social model in *Guzmán* assumes a system of separate, but interdependent estates: "If a Noble man shall be a great spender, let a meaner Gentleman hold his hand" (III, 41). The ideal way for a rich man to spend his money is to be charitable to the poor (Cf. III, 168), while the ideal poor man is content with little, in contrast to "the rich man that walloweth in his wealth" (V, 148).

The spirit of acquiescence makes Guzmán accept the ferocious system of punishment to which he and his fellow galley slaves are exposed. In the last resort, punishment is not seen as an aspect of the social institution that the novel portrays in such a critical manner. It is the instrument with which God opens Guzmán's eyes to his spiritual plight. It leads to the epiphany which heralds his conversion, the final act of acquiescence, which determines the angle from which Guzmán narrates the story of his life and looks back on his social experience as a picaro.

1 Ralph Freedman, "The Possibility of a Theory of the Novel," *The Disciplines of Criticism*, eds. Peter Demetz et al. (New Haven: Yale University Press, 1967) 75.
2 Alexander Blackburn, *The Myth of the Picaro* (Chapel Hill: University of North Carolina Press, 1979) 19.
3 Claudio Guillén, *Literature as System* (Princeton: Princeton University Press, 1971) 79—80.
4 Cf. Ulrich Wicks, *The Nature of Picaresque Narrative: A Modal Approach*, PMLA 1974: vol. 89, 245.
5 Walter L. Reed, *An Exemplary History of the Novel* (Chicago: University of Chicago Press, 1981) 3-4; 12; 24.
6 Robert Alter, *Rogue's Progress* (Cambridge, Mass.: Harvard University Press, 1964) ix.
7 Robert Scholes, *Structuralism in Literature* (New Haven: Yale University Press, 1974) 137-138.
8 Wicks, 242.
9 Guillén, 99.
10 Blackburn, 21.
11 Alexander A. Parker, *Literature and the Delinquent* (Edinburgh: The University Press, 1977) 136.
12 Frank Wadleigh Chandler, *The Literature of Roguery* (1907, New York: Lenox Hill, 1974)
13 Wicks, 247.
14 Michael Alpert, trans. *Lazarillo de Tormes. Two Spanish Picaresque Novels* (Harmondsworth: Penguin, 1975) 27.
15 Alpert, 27-28
16 Alpert, 37.
17 Wicks, 243-244.
18 Parker, 4.
19 Guillén, 84.
20 Alpert, 214.
21 Guillén, 81.
22 Alpert, 86.
23 Alpert, 86.
24 Mateo Alemán, *The Rogue or the Life of Guzmán de Alfarache*, trans. James Mabbe (New York: AMS Press, Inc., 1967)ix.
25 Alemán, x.
26 Harry Sieber, *The Picaresque* (London: Methuen & Co., 1977) 17-23.
27 Alemán, II, 93.
Further references are included in the text parenthetically. Roman figures refer to volume, Arabic numbers to page.

Chapter 2

Picaresque Formula and Social Models in Daniel Defoe's *Colonel Jack*

"I have seen the rough side of the world as well as the smooth, and have in less than half a year tasted the difference between the closet of a king and the dungeon of Newgate."[1]

These words, uttered by Daniel Defoe towards the end of his extraordinarily full and varied career, could have been used by almost any of his principal characters. The wheel of fortune that dominates their lives may vary in velocity but its movement between luck and disaster takes the same inevitable course, even if the moment when an individual is hit is unpredictable. The formula contained in the statement covers the rags to riches to rags movement of the picaresque novel. It also shares with it a common tradition of fables about humankind's precarious position in a pyramidal society in which favour is the ruling principle. It expresses a mood of resigned acquiescence, but also conveys the anxiety of the individual who never knows when his or her luck may run out. In Defoe's novels, as in Spanish picaresque fiction, this feeling is closely linked with the experience of fighting for survival in a chaotic world in which everyone is left to her or his own devices. Defoe's sense of his own and his characters' "marginal existence"[2] is at the heart of his affinity with his Spanish predecessors. His own career as businessman, government servant, and journalist no doubt gives a personal dimension to his awareness, but it springs, above all, from his sensitivity to what was happening in British society at the time. The feudal pattern of order and stabililty was being replaced by a dynamic pattern in which the individual no longer merely inherited his position but could become one of the growing middle class who saw the whole world as his play-ground. He could acquire great riches and power but also lose all he had—even his fredom. The marginal situation of the individual on the make in this community made him feel that he was moving along the razor's edge between security and disaster, exposed to forces which he could not control. The harmonious and settled nature of the middle station which Robinson Crusoe rejects at the outset of his voyages is in

Defoe's fiction continually complemented by a venture-oriented view of the community. A venture might lead to unprecedented riches and the resulting princely state, but it could also fail and lead to extreme poverty—the worst horror of all. The merchant adventurer might, through his own efforts, create a thriving business and lay up stores against a rainy day, but the inscrutable rhythm of the economic laws that determine the wealth of individuals, as well as nations, is outside his sphere of influence. T. S. Ashton, for example, shows how the unpredictable cycle of good and bad harvests, of war and peace, shaped the curve of economic development in England in the eighteenth century.[3] The impact of these large, impersonal movements on individual lives was as unavoidable as it was arbitrary—constituting the power behind the wheel of fortune. But Defoe's fiction also shows how the moment of crisis could challenge individual and collective advancement. The disastrous wars of the seventeenth and eighteenth centuries also saw the birth of British mercantile and industrial hegemony.

Defoe's fiction, with *Robinson Crusoe* in the foreground, owes much of its appeal to the sensitive recording of a society and age in the turmoil of transition. But with his traditional dual aim of teaching and entertaining, Defoe also drew on the genres that were fashionable at the time. The picaresque novel became popular in England towards the end of the sixteenth century. Mabbe's translation of *Guzmán de Alfarache* was, as we have seen, a best-seller, and the history of the fate of the picaresque novel in seventeenth-century England illustrates the way a genre could be modified through fusion with others, merging with native traditions such as the rogue story, dating back to Thomas Nashe's *The Unfortunate Traveller* (1594), criminals' (auto)biographies, and travel literature. Sieber draws attention to an interesting development which the "English Guzman"—the protagonist of an anonymous novel from 1680—had undergone since Alemán's novel. For whereas Alemán celebrates the picaro's "poor hungry plot upon his penurous master's bread and cheese...", the English protagonist aims at commercial ventures, which were out of bounds for the Spanish picaro who "operated within an hierarchical society in which honour and status were defined by birth and lineage, by 'blood'."[4]Similarly, in one novel after the other, Defoe exploits the picaro's new domain. The essential picaresque situation is retained, as well as the picaro's salient characteristics and the basic elements in his journey-bound story. New perspectives are added, however, which broaden the social scope of the novels.

The present chapter focuses on a particuclar novel, *Colonel Jack*, in order to clarify the manner in which Defoe uses and modifies the picaresque formula to present what Earle calls his "mental image of his world and the way in which it worked."[5] Such an image relates to the social facts Defoe includes as well as to the ideology he expresses.

Colonel Jack conforms in many respects to the picaresque formula. It is the first-person retrospective account of a man's long series of encounters with the vagaries of fate as a traveler in Britain, on the continent, and in America. As a foundling, he is left to make his own way in the London underworld. He is one of the ragged boys whom necessity has forced to become pickpockets. After a spell in Scotland, where he tries to make a living in an honest way, he joins the army, deserts, and is kidnapped. As slave on a plantation in Virginia, he reaches the low point of fortune. His luck changes abruptly when he finds himself his own master and the owner of a plantation. A spirit of restlessness then leads to twenty-four years of wandering, which takes him back to England and then to the continent, where he joins the Jacobite army and becomes a colonel (a title he had been given when a child by his nurse). Both before and after his army period, he tries his luck in the marriage market, and returning to Virginia he remarries his first wife. But after a while he leaves again, this time to seek the king's pardon for his Jacobite activities. At the same time, he embarks upon a career as a merchant in the Caribbean. Despite pirates and hostile Spanish warships, he manages to acquire great wealth. The end of the story indicates that the time has come for retirement.

Defoe's novel goes beyond the picaresque formula in following the rags to riches story to a happy end. Furthermore, although Jack is exposed to the vicissitudes of fortune throughout his career, he gets out of the clutches of necessity when he becomes his own master in Virginia. From then on, he never again sinks to the picaro's level of subsistence. His fear of ruin, when troubled by his Jacobite past or interned by the Spanish toward the end of the novel, does not materialize; he always has capital in hand. Moreover, the peaceful and contented ending, where the hero is surrounded by princely luxury, is in striking contrast to the ending of *La Vida del Buscón,* where the protagonist finds that the New World can offer him no release from his want-ridden existence.

The contrast between the wealthy gentleman at the end of the story and the street urchin at the outset is contained in the opening incidents. Abandoned by his parents, Jack is a complete outcast. He represents "Nothing" on the social scale. His nurse tells him that he is, nevertheless, a gentleman by birth, and he never ceases to believe it. Indeed, this conviction inspires a code of conduct which increasingly sets him apart from his fellows.

The moment of ejection, which tends to close the picaro's first phase, comes in the case of Jack and his two brothers when the nurse dies, and they are left to fend for themselves. Like the Spanish prototype, they survive because of their resourcefulness and ability to adapt. Many phrases indicate how close Defoe is to the formula: the boys "were turn'd loose to the World"; they "made a shift (...) to keep from starving"; and slept among "the Ash-holes... in the Glass-house" with a "Gang of

naked, ragged Rogues like ourselves" (pp. 8–9).[6] What is more, the
Glass-house serves as an emblem of the picaro's state of Nothingness and
of his adaptability.

Also like the Spanish picaro, Jack moves from innocence to experience in the early stages of the story. Like Oliver Twist, he is to begin
with unaware of the wickedness of the pickpocket's trade (pp. 18–19). He
enjoys the agility involved and finds it an easy way to make money.
Necessity has forced him to steal in the first palace. Gradually, however,
Jack's notion of being a gentleman interferes with his prospects as a
thief. His increasing hoard of money is a source of worry. He bears the
picaro's stamp of being a victim and has his sense of precariousness and
loneliness, but he does not share his zest for adventure. He fears a fall
because the status of gentleman would then recede even further beyond
his reach. Associating the status of gentleman with money and fine
clothes, he is encouraged when a woman remarks on his good looks and
says that he might well have been a gentleman's son "if he was clean and
well dress'd" (p. 27).

As Jack grows apart from his fellow pickpockets, he is also soon at variance with his friend and tutor, Will. Success urges the others on, but
Jack holds back, especially after robbing two poor women (p. 64). The
incident opens his eyes to his wicked ways and fills him with anxiety and
remorse (p. 67). In a conversation between the two friends, Will speaks
for further adventures, which for him constitute a life worthy of a
gentleman, while Jack suggests that a gentleman is cautious and prudent,
ready to retire while the going is good:

Will: "We will take the Highway like Gentlemen, and then
we shall get a great deal of Money indeed…"
Jack: "…what then?"
Will: "…then (…) we shall live like Gentlemen."
Jack: "But (…) if we got a great deal of Money, shan't we
leave this Trade off, and sit down, and be Safe and
Quiet?"
Will: "(…) when we have got a great Estate we shall be
willing to lay it down."
Jack: "… but where … shall we be before that time comes, if
we should drive on this cursed kind of Trade?"
Will: "… never think of that … if you think of those things,
you will never be fit to be a Gentleman (…)"
Jack: "… do you call this way of Living the Life of a Gentle-
man?"

(p. 67).

Jack, too, takes to the road. But for him the road is a means of
extricating himself from what he has now come to regard as an insecure

and morally reprehensible existence. From then on, it is his brother Captain Jack who represents the delinquent element in the picaro's character, while Colonel Jack keeps his hands clean and aims at respectability. Captain Jack, in his crude way, and the nimble, quick-witted Will think of the road as the domain where the Artful Dodger in the picaro can gamble for high stakes. Jack, cast in the role of victim, and increasingly under the spell of his dream of becoming a gentleman, is a traveler exposed to a fate that teaches him to acquiesce. Even the threats of starvation and loss of liberty cannot shake him out of this passivity.

At the same time, Jack's situation in Edinburgh and the period leading up to his captivity illustrate the dilemma of the picaro who tries to extricate himself from his disreputable past. Initially brought to a life of crime by destitution, he bears a stigma. Jack trains himself for a job as clerk but fails, through no fault of his own, to get permanent employment. He would have starved to death in Edinburgh, if his brother had not relieved him of the onus of making an honest living. The only door open to Jack leads back to the world of crime. Without help from somebody within society, he cannot hope to acquire the respectability he yearns for. It is interesting to note that the criminal element saves Jack from a down-and-out existence.

This explains his relief when he joins the army: "Tho' I far'd hard, and lodg'd Ill ... yet to me, that had been us'd to Lodge on the Ashes in the Glass-House, this was no great matter." The main point is that he is "now under no Necessity of stealing, and living in fear of a Prison, and of the lash of the Hangman" (p. 104). He refers to his "inexpressible ease (...) that I was now in a certain way of Living, which was honest, and which I could say, was not unbecoming to a Gentleman" (p. 104).

This attitude, helped by his conviction that he "was born to better Things", which is also a magistrate's belief (p. 80), enables him to make a shift, even during his captivity in Virginia. He is able passively to endure, because he knows he is saved from his worst anxiety: reversion to a life of crime. Despite the fact that the slaves "work'd Hard, lodg'd Hard, and far'd Hard" (p. 119), Jack has a paradoxical sense of deliverance: "I might live without that wretched thing, call'd stealing" (p. 117). Besides, he can afford to bide his time, knowing he will be a free man after five years. He learns his new trade well and is a faithful, obedient, and diligent servant. Passive acquiescence, followed by making the best of his new situation, is Jack's ticket to respectable society. However, without the good offices of powerful helpers (the gentleman in London, his master in Virginia), Jack's skill and resourcefulness would have been to little avail. In contrast, his brother Captain Jack refuses to submit to circumstances on board the ship and later persists in the rogue's career he had been taught as a child. His adventures inevitably end in disaster, while Jack's career, after his success in Virginia, leads to prosperity, the life of a gentleman of means. Furthermore, while his merchant ventures may sometimes be at risk, he always keeps on the right side of the law. His only false step is his enlistment as a Jacobite in France and in the affair of 1715.

During Jack's twenty-four-year absence from Virginia, and also during his later spells of traveling, the plantation is simply there, under the management of his faithful steward, an investment which quietly builds up capital. Whatever Jack chooses to risk during his travels, he always carries with him the air of a retired gentleman of means. Although he turns out to be a shrewd and resourceful businessman, his approach to the world around him remains singularly passive. Even as a boy, when Jack has the reputation of being lucky (p. 21), luck increasingly comes to mean his ability to adapt. From early on, he has an uncanny talent for lying low and strategical planning even in the most difficult circumstances. His helpers, for instance, do not simply turn up: Jack prepares the ground with skillful posing, as a desolate outcast. He always makes the most of the situation he is in, whether as a London street urchin, slave, or marooned merchant in a remote corner of Mexico. Moreover, the picaro survives in Jack, the gentleman, whose strategic bent and aptitude for role-playing stand him in good stead as a merchant.

The story is told in retrospect. However, Defoe attaches a remarkable immediacy of experience to his episodes. This is particularly striking in the episodes from Jack's boyhood. Defoe has an uncanny gift for making us see what happened through a child's eyes. Later, it is above all the persistent sense of anxiety that lends authenticity to the narrative. Like Pip in *Great Expectations,* Jack can never get rid of the legacy of guilt from his boyhood. His traumatic experiences as a common thief pursue him relentlessly to the end of his career. The arrival of Jacobite prisoners on his plantation revives this deep-rooted fear. As he describes it, an abyss opens beneath his feet, and his position of power and wealth seems to rest on sand: "I was now reduced from a great Man, a Magistrate, a Governor, or Master of three great Plantations; and having three or four Hundred Servants at my Command, to be a poor self condemn'd Rebel" (p. 267).

The persistent undercurrent of fear and anxiety, arising from an irreducible sense of insecurity, is at the heart of the picaro's existence. For Jack, the road to escape lies in two directions: back to his down-and-out, Glass-house existence, purged of crime, or ahead to the gentlemanly retreat. "Nothing" and "Everything" seem to cancel each other out in Jack's Garden-of-Eden-like residence in the closing pages of the novel.

The dream of the safe retreat is in counterpoint to Jack's restless spirit, and evidence of the picaro in him. The successful plantation owner feels "Buried alive" (p. 172) and that he has not yet quite achieved the "life of a Gentleman" (p. 172). Feeling, as he says, that "I had nothing to hinder me from going where I pleas'd" (p. 172), Jack embarks upon his twenty-

four-year Grand Tour of Europe. The colonelcy he acquires in the
course of this tour is, in his eyes, the acme of success: "I us'd to say to
myself, I was come to what I was Born to, and that I had never till now
liv'd the Life of a Gentleman" (p. 207). As this was an appointment in
the Jacobite army, it turns out to be as compromising an achievement as
his performance as a thief. It remains, however, a climactic experience because here the notion of gentleman is wedded to the traditional view of
military adventure as noble and heroic.

From time to time, he is tempted to return to his Virginian retreat, but,
Jack confesses, "I had got a wandring kind of Taste (...) I could not live
in the World, and not enquire what was doing in it" (p. 233). The Grand
Tour aspect is in the foreground here: Jack, the upstart, feels the need to
be educated in the ways of the world so that he can cope with being a
gentleman.

Finally, Jack's restless spirit finds ample outlet in his activities as
freebooting merchant among the West Indian Islands and along the
Mexican coast. In this careeer, he can combine ambition, zest for
adventure and business aumen. Since rising to distinction in Virginia,
he has veered between the impulse to wander and the impulse to retreat
and consolidate. The final lines of the novel suggest at least a temporary
compromise. Released from Mexican captivity, Jack goes to London,
where he is joined by his wife, "leaving with full satisfaction the
Management of all our Affairs in *Virginia*, in the same faithful Hands as
before" (p. 309). So London, in the past a hunting ground for Jack and
his fellow street urchins, has now become a retreat from retreat, worthy
of Jack's well-established position as gentleman.

In the course of his career, Colonel Jack, like the traditional picaro,
"moves horizontally through space and vertically through society",[7]
according to Guillén's model. The social fabric is revealed from within
as well as from without: Colonel Jack always carries with him his semi-
outsider status. The retrospective didactic perspective makes the reader
see the social panorama as "reality", the matter against which existing
society can be assessed and an ideal community outlined. Thus Colonel
Jack's childhood career as pickpocket is related to the endemic social evil
of poverty—the necessity which forces people to steal to survive. Colonel
Jack's tutor tells him that "to be reduc'd to Necessity is to be wicked",
and goes on to declare that "Necessity is not only the Temptation, but is
such a Temptation as human Nature is not empower'd to resist" (p. 161).
Life as a slave on the Virginia plantation is a blessing because Providence
has in that way removed necessity.[8]

Unlike the author of *Guzmán*, who suggests that theft is closely related
to the power structure of society, Defoe sees it as an evil that people
might escape in a different environment. Colonel Jack's—and Defoe's—

dilemma is that while individual effort is futile when one is reduced to a down-and-out existence, help is either erratic or a matter of divine mercy. Providence may intervene through the established political and legal system, which, therefore, connects the laws of the land to God-given authority, so obedience is every man's duty. However, necessity may force the individual to use his latent resourcefulness and adapt-ability do dodge the law. Therefore, throughout *Colonel Jack*, Defoe is pulled between his sympathy for the outsider, the victim of a society that guards the interests of the insiders, and his equally strong interest in the mechanisms of that society.

Focusing on the protagonist's protracted process of transformation from outsider to insider status, the picaresque formula exploited in *Colonel Jack* shows the way the communities he encounters are struc-tured and, therefore, presents the reader with a hierarchy of social models.

The initial opposition in the novel between the state of Nothing and the state of Gentleman is a fablelike expression of the gulf between the have-nots and the haves in Jack's world as well as in Defoe's. Of that world Pat Rogers writes:

> The favoured twelve thousand in London shared in a round of genuine cultivation and sensitivity, with a real taste for the most exquisite objects of art widely evident. This was a truly metropolitan culture, second only to that of Paris in range and glitter. Yet there were at least six thousand dram-shops to satisfy the other half million inhabitants.[9]

The have-nots prey on the society from which they have been shut out. Jack's belief that he is of gentle birth is useless as a ticket to the world of the haves. Stuck among the outcasts, the "rabble" or "dregs" of society according to the contemporary way of thinking,[10] Jack is completely without credentials. His belief in his gentle heritage is only an elusive dream and cannot gain him access to the world of the haves. The gulf between the "two nations" is well expressed right at the beginning of the novel:

> ...as the Great rise by degrees of Greatness to the Pitch of Glory, in which they shine, so the Miserable sink to the depth of their Misery by a continu'd Series of Dissaster, and are long in the Tortures and Agonies of their distress'd Circumstances before a Turn of Fortune, if ever such a thing happens to them, gives them a Prospect of Deliverance. (p. 4)

32 THE PICARESQUE IN THE BRITISH NOVEL

The impression this passage gives of a widening chasm between rich and poor is qualified slightly in the final lines. In *Colonel Jack*, it soon becomes evident that the idea of survival in a world governed by harsh economic laws is inextricably bound with the idea of "Deliverance"— achieved through the help of people in power, or Providential intercession.

The prospect of deliverance also suggests that there is a latent impulse to improve one's position in Jack's community. The urge towards social improvement originates in Jack's discovery that he is a gentleman. The name "Jack" and the fact that all three brothers bear that name suggest a classless society.[11] Yet Jack is recognized by his community as a gentleman. A hierarchical structure based on officers' titles is introduced by Jack being given the highest rank. In the Glass-house, all the other ragged boys are below him. But on the surface, this is an egalitarian society, in which the organizing principle is the idea of sharing everything, such as food and booty. According to Novak, Defoe subscribed to the view that primitive man was solitary and isolated,[12] but in the early pages of the novel there are suggestions of an alternative view of man's original state. Basil Willey draws attention to the traditional distinction in the Christian concept of Natural Law between a prelapsarian state of liberty and equality and a postlapsarian state based on private property and "acquisitive impulses" (which came to a head after the Renaissance).[13] Seen in this way, there is in the Glass-house section a clear movement from classlessness—Jack and his fellow rogues are outside even the rudimentary social unit of the family, as Ian Watt points out[14]—to the embryonic beginnings of a system of social differentiation according to rank, influence, and talent.

John J. Richetti claims that Jack "is formally separate from the start, granted a secret and socially guaranteed apartness by his gentle birth."[15] His gentle birth certainly makes Jack feel apart form his fellows, and his sense of superiority leads to his increasing concern with the question of personal, as distinct from communal, identity. Moreover, Jack makes the crucial discovery that a communal name is inadequate. He needs to be able to define exactly who he is, to name his parents, and to give his address. Otherwise, he is a nobody. The problem first crops up in the scene where people remark on his "good Face" (p. 7). If it were not for his rags, he might have been a gentleman's son. He is then asked about his parentage. People wondered:

> what the Rogues Father and Mother was, and the like; then they would call me, and ask me my Name; and I would tell them my Name was *Jack*. But what's your Sir Name, Sirrah? says they: I don't know says I: Who is your father and Mother? I have none, said I. What, and never had you any? said they: No, says I, not that I know of. (pp. 7–8)

The scene shows that the two communities speak completely different languages, and that what one side takes for granted, is incomprehensible to the other. Jack is left with an intense feeling of his outcast state.

Another problem that leads to isolation and a sense of helplessness arises when Jack finds himself with more money than he can use. He is full of worry because he does not know what to do. Again the reader's attention is focused on Jack's unprotected urchin state. However, this time he is also intensely aware of his plight:

> I had really more wealth than I knew what to do with, for Lodging I had none, nor any Box or Drawer to hide my Money in, nor had I any Pocket, but such, *as I say*, was full of Holes; I knew no Body in the World, that I cou'd go and desire them to lay it up for me. (p. 22)

And he sees himself as "a poor nak'd, ragg'd Boy". Then follows the famous episode in which Jack tries to hide his money in a hollow tree, which, like his pocket, is no use because there is a hole at the bottom of the trunk (pp. 23–25).

The incident could serve as a fable about the transition from a society without to a society with banking facilities.[16] The transition from one socio-economic model to another is rendered in a dialogue between Jack and the Gentleman who eventually helps to bring about Jack's gradual transformation from urchin to gentleman. By now, Jack has advanced further in the pickpocket's trade. He has learned to use his "natural Talent of Talking" (p. 7) as the Gang's negotiator for stolen bills that can fetch ransom money. Jack's problem about surplus money is that he does not know where he can safely keep it. The encounter shows how well Jack is now able to play his cards, exploiting to the full the "Boy with a good face reduced to rags" formula to gain sympathy. And again the have/have-not opposition is brought into sharp relief. Jack is shown to be in the process of being alienated from his group by his hoard of money: he is convinced it will only be safe in the type of social organization the Gentleman stands for. Jack clearly associates personal identity with the status of gentleman, and the Glass-house world with complete anonymity, a state of "Nothing" which makes him feel lost and unprotected. Most of the dialogue is quoted to show how the transition from one model to the other is achieved through juxtaposition of the two:

Gentleman:	"What wilt thou do with this Money now thou hast it [the reward money]?"
Jack:	"I don't know."...
Gentleman:	"Where will you put it?"...
Jack:	"In my Pocket."

....

Gentleman:	"And where will you put it, when you come Home?"
Jack:	"I have no Home" ... *cry'd again.*
Gentleman:	"Poor Child! ...What dost thou do for thy Living?"
Jack:	"I go of Errands."...
Gentleman:	"And what doest thou do for a Lodging at Night?"
Jack:	"I lye at the Glass-House ... at Night."
Gentleman:	"... have they any Beds there?..."
Jack:	"I never lay in a Bed in my Life..."

....

Gentleman:	"...do they give you no Money, when they send you of Errands?"
Jack:	"They give me Victuals ... and that's better."
Gentleman:	"But what ... do you do for Cloths?"
Jack:	"They give me sometimes old things ... such as they have to spare."

....

Gentleman:	"Well ... now you have this Money, won't you buy some Cloths, and a Shirt with some of it?"
Jack:	"Yes ... I would buy some Cloths."
Gentleman:	"And, what will you do with the rest?"
Jack:	"I can't tell" ...and cry'd. (pp. 37–38)

The basic difference between the two communities lies in contrasting attitudes to money. Although Jack and his fellow rogues make forages into the society above them, their goal is not money for its own sake, but to satisfy their basic needs: food, shelter, and a minimum of clothing. Jack expresses the spirit of the Glass-house community when he claims that it is better to be given victuals than money. The Gentleman, on the other hand, assumes, in accordance with the common view of his community, that food and clothes are commodities purchased by means of money, and that there are ways of dealing with what is left over.

The Gentleman's questions and Jack's answers illustrate contrasting social models. Both are concerned with basic requirements, but they are at cross purposes as to what is essential. As in the incident where people tried to work out who Jack was by interpreting his good looks, a sense of frustration is conveyed because the two take different matters for granted. The Gentleman is faced with a case he cannot make sense of in the language of his class, while Jack's problem can be solved only by a practice not yet developed in his community.

The two communities are juxtaposed in the dialogue and represent two stages in socio-economic development. The Gentleman's society can offer two ways of absorbing Jack's spare money. One is consumption: Jack might, for example, buy clothes. The other is investment, for example, in business, when it can be left to look after itself as capital. Both ways are alien to the Glass-house community, but common practice in the community to which Jack aspires. By giving Jack a bill for his money, the Gentleman removes Jack from the communal Glass-house model.

In the rest of his London phase, Jack exploits the two modes of using money which his encounter with the Gentleman has taught him. He buys clothes, gets better lodgings, and increases his capital. As a consequence he is encouraged to "look higher" (p. 55). The dialogue between Will and Jack soon follows, where, as we have seen, the two represent opposing views of what a gentleman should do. The prudent line Jack takes is in keeping with his hoarding instinct. Although later in his career he tends to be torn between the dream of a safe retreat and the dream of wandering, it is noteworthy that he never touches invested capital, which is left to accumulate through the secret workings of trade and banking.

The rags-to-riches formula suggests a dynamic principle of social advance through one's own efforts. However, the main emphasis in *Colonel Jack* is on the patronage model. Jack's urge to become a gentleman can be consummated only with the help of persons in power, and Jack's main helper is his master on the plantation in Virginia. The society to which he is eventually admitted as a free man has the traditional shape of a pyramid with the gentleman at the top and with everyone else in his appointed place below. The plantation is a self-contained community whose structure corresponds to the secular and spiritual worlds which surround it. The Master is at the top of his kingdom as the king is of his, and Providence of his.

On first meeting with his master, Jack assumes the submissive manner of the slave. In response to the plantation owner's benevolence, Jack feels tied to him as his servant. The master-servant relationship is the basis for his social advancement. He is exalted through patronage. The servant's response of gratitude to his master for having raised him from the dust is a sign of health as well as a guarantee of progress in his society. As Novak writes, "for Jack, gratitude is good because it may be used advantageously in both public and private life as a dependable natural virtue."[17] Jack also experiences its benevolent effects on a national level when he receives the King's pardon, and he sees it at work among the Negro slaves on his master's plantation. As demonstrated in Jack's own case, the grateful servant's reward is success in business. Such success, however, is also dependent on skill and application, acquired through education or practical work. According to Earle, Defoe believed that "self-help was the means by which [man] got on in the world."[18] Success in Colonel Jack's world depends on diligence, good management, and resourcefulness. In his time as a servant, Jack displays all these qualities as well as honesty and moral integrity. As a result, he himself rises to the top.

When Jack becomes a merchant, the patronage model, which assumes a hierarchically arranged community of mutually dependent loyal members is replaced by one that is completely egocentric and stripped of communal elements. Jack finds himself in a world where he is released from every social obligation. The principle of free enterprise reigns supreme, and speculation has free play. The price is individual isolation, seen by Ian Watt as the symptom of extreme economic individualism.[19] On the other hand, even the merchant formula, as practised towards the end of the novel, depends on individual links beyond mere competition or the cash nexus. Much attention is given to Jack's activities as a patient and shrewd negotiator. His success as a trader as well as his comfortable retreat among the Spanish merchants have a firm contractual basis. Jack has not forgotten his skill in talking and his ability to inspire trust. The speculator and the negotiator are twin aspects of the merchant model.

The social models in *Colonel Jack* show how society may be organized. They also illustrate phases of social development which correspond to stages in Jack's journey towards socio-moral awareness. The Glass-house period, as well as the Mexican period at the end of the novel, carry pastoral overtones which may refer to the type of Arcadian society which is at times juxtaposed to the picaro's dismal environment. They are, however, also signs of Defoe's sense of living in an age of rapid socio-economic transformation. But this sense is set against a vision of order and stability which surrounds Defoe's picture of a community that is organized along rigid hierarchical lines. As a result, Colonel Jack's career is viewed with a certain ambiguity. Both his extensive traveling and the many social and professional levels he reaches could indicate a mobile soial structure. However, the reverse is in actual fact the case. He is only to a limited extent able to move up the social ladder on his own. He is liberated from his down-and-out existence by external influence. Jack is only mobile within the sphere he has been admitted to, although he may have bought the ticket with money his own efforts won him.

The image of a fluid social fabric within rigid limits is in keeping with the picture historians give of late seventeenth- and early eighteenth-century England. Hill shows how the "Glorious Revolution" of 1689 "helped to harden the formation of England into two nations," those with and those without property. "Liberties," Hill writes, "were for men of property."[20] The gulf between the two nations is illustrated by a late seventeenth-century estimate of the population of England in 1688. According to M. Dorothy George, the investigator, Gregory King, calculated, that "more than half the population (...) were 'decreasing the wealth of the kingdom', that is, their expenses exceeded their earnings, and the deficiency had to be made up from poor relief, charity,

or plunder."[21] Legislation protected the nation of property-owners
against the other nation by, for example, restricting their movements.
The 1662 Settlement Act thus tried to prevent the poor, reduced to
vagabond status, from becoming a burden on neighboring parishes.

An optimistic account of English society in the eighteenth century
claims that "this freedom of movement between the classes extended
right through the social scale", although the writer admits that "the
minute gradations in society made for the stability of the whole". Yet
according to him, it was possible to climb the pyramid from bottom to
top "and the rewards were enormous."[22] A more sober analysis of the
situation is given by W. A. Speck who documents "downward and
upward mobility" between and inside the various social classes within a
social structure that is essentially static and eclectic. The apprentice
system provided a bridge between the gentry and the merchant and professional worlds, but, otherwise, one is left with the impression that
people rarely managed to break away from the class into which they had
been born.[23] Defoe's emphasis on the role of helpers in Jack's process of
social elevation underlines how diffcult social advancement was in a
community geared to prosperity and profitmaking. Individual
endeavor was of little use until the heavily guarded border had been
crossed through the good offices of an insider.

James Sutherland sees *Colonel Jack* as "an amalgam of all the genres"
Defoe had tried. His metaphor does not tally very well with the charge
that the novel is incoherent and carelessly written.[24] But it is an apt
description of the way Defoe in *Colonel Jack* brings together a variety of
models related to genre as well as society. The various genres Defoe
adopts provide angles from which the critic may approach the world of
the novel. Thus, G. A. Starr traces the links between Defoe's novels and
the spiritual autobiography or memoir, which was such a popular
literary mode at the time. He demonstrates the way the retrospective
technique lends significance to particular episodes, however trivial, and
brings out a pattern of meaning in the events recorded from the vantage
point of conversion and repentance. The confessional and self-analytic
perspective focuses the reader's attention on the internal world of the recorder's mind.[25]

A concern with formula is one way in which Defoe lends significance
to his story. The retrospective technique accentuates this effect. Further,
Defoe is concerned with the didactic import of his tale. The event behind
Jack's decision to write his memoirs is his conversion, which apparently
took place during his exile in Mexico (pp. 307–308). This experience
enables him to see "how an invisible over-ruling Power, a Hand
influenced from above, Governs all our Actions of every Kind, limits all
our Designs, and orders the Events of every Thing relating to us" (p. 308).
His concern with Providential meaning and the act of repentance put

Jack's whole story into relief and give it coherence.

Another feature which is emphasized by comparison to the confessional element in spiritual autobiography is the sense of the precariousness of the human condition which pervades the whole novel. The picaro's daily experience is part of the protagonist's ordeal in an existential wasteland, closely related to the ups and downs of the surrounding world.

By approaching *Colonel Jack* from the point of view of the picaresque, emphasis is placed on society rather than on the soul of the protagonist. The novel then emerges as a record of the permutations of the two contrasting human impulses dramatized in the dialogue between Jack and his friend Will: the impulse to advance and the impulse to consolidate. These two impulses form the basic conflict between retreat and wandering in Jack's story. In the picaresque formula the opposition between victim and agent is subsumed in the dichotomy between advance and consolidation. The picaro veers as it were between Oliver Twist, asking for more, and the Artful Dodger, responding to fate with wit and resourcefulness. The two represent basic responses to the environment - endurance and challenge. Contrasting models for social organization follow from this dichotomy. *Colonel Jack* demonstrates the protagonist's encounter with various models that represent real as well as ideal ways of organizing society. In the course of the novel, Defoe interprets Jack's environment, but also provides blueprints for the communities Jack encounters. The blueprint that emerges from the novel as a whole is firmly rooted in the dichotomy traced above: it assumes patience and acquiescense as well as enterprise and strategic skill. It combines stability and adventurousness in a manner which recalls the Janus-faced existence of the eighteenth-century wealthy gentleman. The stately home of the benevolent landowner in a well-ordered, peaceful English village is the place of retreat for the mercantile adventurer abroad. Jack's career towards the end of the novel is thus in keeping with the spirit of the time.

1 Quoted in Peter Earle, *The World of Defoe* (London: Weidenfeld and Nicolson, 1976) 12.

2 Harry Sieber, 53

3 T. S. Ashton, *Economic Fluctuations in England 1700-1800* (Oxford: Clarendon Press, 1959) chapters 1-3, in particular.

4 Sieber, 52

5 Earle, ix.

6 References, included parenthetically in the text, are to the Oxford paperback edition (London: Oxford University Press, 1979).

7 C. Guillén, 84.

8 See also Maximillian E. Novak's discussion of Defoe's view of necessity and man's right of self-preservation in his *Defoe and the Nature of Man* (London: Oxford University Press, 1963) ch. III, "The Problem of Necessity in Defoe's Fiction." *Colonel Jack* is dealt with on pp. 74-78.

9 Pat Rogers, *The Augustan Vision* (London: Methuen & Co., 1978) 9.

10 See *OED* entries under the two words. According to Peter Earle, the poor were thought of as potentially wild beasts. If they were not tamed to become "humble, hard-working [and] god-fearing", they would turn out "lazy, vicious, and ungrateful". Earle, 217.

11 See David Blewett's discussion of the etymology of the word "jack" and its bearings on the theme of gentility in his *Defoe's Art of Fiction* (Toronto: University of Toronto Press, 1979) 94-95.

12 Novak, 23.

13 Basil Willey, *The Eighteenth-Century Background* (Harmondsworth: Penguin, 1962) 22-23.

14 Ian Watt, *The Rise of the Novel* (Harmondsworth: Penguin, 1963) 67.

15 John J. Richetti, *Defoe's Narratives. Situations and Structures* (Oxford: Clarendon Press, 1975) 147.

16 We are reminded of the emergence of the modern banking system at this time and of the South Sea Bubble scandal, which shook the nation in 1720. See Christopher Hill, *Reformation to Industrial Revolution* (Harmondsworth: Penguin, 1978) 183-184 and 244 (banks) and Dorothy Marshall, *Eighteenth Century England* (London: Longman, 1974) 123-127 (The South Sea Bubble).

17 Novak, 121.

18 Earle, 37.

19 Watt, 116.

20 Hill, 144-145.

21 M. Dorothy George, *England in Transition* (London: Penguin, 1953) 10.

22 E. N. Williams, *Life in Georgian England* (London: B. T. Batsford, Ltd.) 7 and 9.

23 W. A. Speck, *Stability and Strife. England 1714-1760* (London: Edward Arnold, 1963) 62-67.

24 James Sutherland, *Daniel Defoe. A Critical Study* (Cambridge, Mass.: Harvard University Press, 1971) 197-198.

25 G. A. Starr, *Defoe and Spiritual Autobiography* (Princeton: Princeton University Press, 1965) ch. I.

Library of
Davidson College

Chapter 3

The Picaresque Formula and the Sense of Socio-economic Precariousness in Tobias Smollett's *Roderick Random*

The social metamorphosis that Colonel Jack has undergone by the end of his wandering life and his accompanying concern with the precarious- ness of the status of gentleman, anticipate central preoccupations in the mid-eighteenth-century English novel, frequently embodied in the picaresque formula. Thus in Henry Fielding's *Joseph Andrews* (1742) and *Tom Jones* (1749), the protagonists travel through a familiar picaresque landscape of roads, stagecoaches, and inns, making the customary journey through a multilevel community between country and town and *vice versa*. The memorable scenes in which Joseph Andrews is first stripped of his servant's uniform and turned out of Lady Booby's residence in London and then attacked by highwaymen who leave him naked in the ditch become vignettes of the picaro's initial experience of ejection and abandonment. The moment of ejection is less dramatic in *Tom Jones* but a similar mechanism is at work: the protagonist is arbitrarily deprived of his protected place in Squire Allworthy's household and then, at the outset of his journey, the money he has been given is stolen because, like so many picaros at the moment of ejection, he is utterly ignorant of the ways of the world. After countless encounters with the whims of fortune, Joseph and Tom in the end are moved from the bottom to the apex of society, again through arbitrary acts. Their identities as members of the class from which they have been ejected is established from above. Their entries into the upper ranks of society constitute new births.

Money and influence rather than manners and social origin had shut them out from the class to which they naturally belonged and to which they could not be readmitted through the picaro's skill in climbing. The harmony and bliss of the happy ending cannot remove the persistent, nightmarish sense of precariousness which pervades these novels and which they share with the business-bound citizens among their readers.

The social scope of Fielding's novels is, therefore, wider than those in the Spanish novels that furnish the basis for the picaresque formula. We have seen how Defoe's protagonists also invade spheres that were closed

to Guzmán even when he was most successful, and this trend is con-
tinued in Smollett's fiction, perhaps most notably in his first novel,
Roderick Random (1748). By moving the emphasis in the picaresque
formula from the lower-class protagonist, who has become an outcast
through poverty and is trying to survive through climbing, to the upper-
class protagonist, who has been exiled from his class and is a picaro for
the time, Smollett, like Fielding, exposes the precariousness of the individual's foothold on the social ladder.

The picaresque formula was modified in a similar manner in the
French novel, most successfully in Lesage's influential novel *Gil Blas*,
which, in Chandler's view, "perfected the genre, and did more than any
other to develop out of it the modern novel".[1] *Gil Blas* was completed in
1735, the first volume appearing twenty years before, in 1715. Smollett's
translation appeared in 1749, so his mind must have been on it while he
was working on *Roderick Random*. Moreover, the preface to *Roderick
Random* shows Smollett's consciousness of his debt to Lesage. It is
therefore reasonable to consider *Gil Blas's* impact on the picaresque
formula as it was interpreted by Smollett and his successors in the
English novel.

The Spanish picaresque formula is modified from the start. Gil Blas's
origin is not disreputable. Although his parents belong to the servant
class, the uncle who raises him, is a canon. The moment of ejection is
tied up with concern for the boy's education, as it is in *El Buscón*. But in
the latter novel, education is seen by the boy as a means of escaping from
a disreputable milieu, while in *Gil Blas*, it is the respectable aim of respectable parents. Further, it is not destitution which sends Gil Blas off
on his wanderings, as tends to be the case with the picaro, but his own and
his guardian's feeling that "it is high time for a brisk lad of seventeen(…)
to push [his] fortune in the world…"[2] Believing that the boy has
sufficient "genius and learning" to get a "good post" in Salamanca (I,
3), his uncle gives Gil Blas money for his expenses on the road.

Gil Blas descends to down-and-out status soon after his departure
because he, like Tom Jones, is robbed of his money. He is kidnapped by a
gang of thieves who intend to teach him their craft. This happens partly
through misfortune, and partly through inexperience: Gil Blas is as
innocent at the outset as any picaro. Because of his sheltered, middle-
class background he is even more gullible than his predecessors in the
Spanish novel, who also start their travels at an earlier age. The element
of social displacement in *Gil Blas* anticipates Fielding and Smollett.
From then on, Gil Blas shows the usual adaptability and resourcefulness. He thus manages to find his way out of captivity on his own
initiative. He learns that, in the world he has encountered in such a
dramatic manner, survival is a matter of using one's wits and any
available resources. The art that matters is the art of fending for oneself.
He soon discovers not only that fortune is a fickle mistress, but also that

opportunities for improving one's situation are always at hand if you are ready to exploit them. At an early stage, Gil Blas decides to "to turn gentleman, and endeavour to make my fortune in the world" (I, 66). He finds that service offers the widest scope for an outsider who wishes to get in. He is certainly, as Guillén puts it, "a servant of many masters,"[3] but in the course of the novel he covers a far greater social range than the Spanish prototype could hope to. The picaresque is only an interlude in his career which, despite the rise and fall rhythm of a wheel-of-fortune-dominated narrative, leads Gil Blas further and further away from the outsider's status.

The picaresque formula in *Gil Blas* thus undergoes what Parker characterizes as "the most astonishing transformation in the whole history of the picaresque *genre*, which has by now come to foster the aristocratic cult of propriety, decorum and social gentility in literature."[4] The panoramic view that the picaresque novel develops through its endless chain of episodes and encounters up and down the social hierarchy is extended in *Gil Blas* to include top levels within the Church and the state. The society the satirist Lesage exposes is built on the principles of patronage and bribery. The picaro's process of corruption reaches its climax in *Gil Blas* with the protagonist's activities as servant and favorite to the King's ministers. Gil Blas acquires great wealth, but he also discovers how fickle fortune is on this level. After a spell in prison, he decides to become honest, a very unpicaresque choice, which emphasizes the point that poverty may drive anyone to theft.

The picaresque formula and its accompanying view of society are also developed through the numerous inserted stories in the novel. One of them is the account that Scipio, Gil Blas's servant, gives of his life. At the beginning a picaro by necessity, he eventually chooses the career of a servant and the prospect of honesty. In turn, by acquiring a servant, Gil Blas moves further away from his own picaresque past.

With Gil Blas, honesty is part of his vision of a pastoral retreat from a corrupting world. Through one of his virtuous aristocratic helpers—another example of the way Lesage has transformed the picaresque formula—Gil Blas acquires an estate in southern Spain, where he enjoys a short period of marital bliss and to which he returns at the end of his story. There is also a pastoral vision at the outsider's end of the social spectrum. Instead of the picaro's bleak and down-and-out domain, we are given, in the master thief Don Raphael's story, a glimpse of a gypsy paradise, as far removed from the cares of intriguing society as Gil Blas's estate. At one stage in his career, Gil Blas is offered the kind of Lotos-land escape that Don Raphael's retreat represents, but he continues his climbing. In Don Raphael's version of the picaro, one may perceive the contours of the outlaw of the Romantic period.

Gil Blas thus extends the picaresque formula and exploits it as a means of portraying and criticizing a society which is far more complex than that of the Spanish picaresque novels. At the same time, rejection of the picaresque mode of life as dishonest and corrupt is central to the moral of the novel. Gil Blas refers to the fact that although "Scipio in his childhood was a real *picaro*, he has corrected his conduct so well since that time, that he is now the model of a perfect servant" (III, 196). Gil Blas's own career makes his noble employer, the Duke of Lerma, remark that "I see you have been in your time a little upon the picaro (...) I am astonished that thou wast not undone by ill example" (II, 263).

We shall now turn to Smollett's *Roderick Random* and examine the way the picaresque formula is used to articulate Smollett's sensitivity to socio-economic precariousness. A passage in a letter of 1761 to Garrick, which Smollett wrote when he was at the height of his literary career, refers to a classical view of the uncertainty of the human condition, but also bears the stamp of personal experience:

> I am old enough to have seen and observed that we are all playthings of fortune, and that it depends upon something as insignificant and precarious as the tossing up of a halfpenny whether a man rises to affluence and honours, or continues to his dying day struggling with the difficulties and disgraces of life. I desire to live quietly with all mankind.[5]

These words could have been uttered by a Gil Blas or Roderick Random after they had acquired the peaceful gentlemanly retreat which terminated their years of wandering. The halfpenny may be taken to refer to the invested capital which was the eighteenh-century gentleman's bulwark against the chaotic multitude of have-nots. If the gentleman had retired from a merchant career, he might have been one of the sources for the following observation by a foreigner writing from London in 1736: " 'Here are continually such ups and downs and various turns of fortune (...) that the winds and waves are not more uncertain than the circumstances of the merchants and tradesmen of the City of London.' " After quoting this passage, W. A. Speck goes on to comment that

> the vicissitudes of fortune, buoying people up one day and breaking them the next, forms one of the major themes in the novels of the period, from *Robinson Crusoe* to *Roderick Random*. Crusoe and Random had their counterparts in real life. ... Banking broke as well as made men (...) whether individuals fared well or ill would depend upon accidents of personality (...) However, there were more impersonal forces at work, forces which some were inclined to call providence, making trade more hazardous than farming.[6]

The halfpenny in Smollett's letter might also refer to this power. Trade is of little importance in *Roderick Random*, but the unpredictable conditions which determined the outcome of a business venture are part of the lifeblood of the novel, and the view we are given of the system and principles of government certainly contributes to the sense of precariousness both novelist and historian convey.

The experience of ejection from the parental home is short and dramatic in the Spanish picaresque novel. Circumstances suddenly force a boy to take to the road. In *Roderick Random*, ejection is a long, drawn out process rather than the act of a moment of crisis. The novel starts with the protagonist's genealogy, a feature it shares with romance and the picaresque tale. In the latter, the information we are given tends to be vague or bogus, and it is often part of the mock-romance strain in the genre. But in *Roderick Random*, there can be no question of the protagonist's social bearings. He is the grandson of an irascible Scottish laird "of considerable fortune and influence".[7] The moment of his birth is, in actual fact, the moment of his ejection. Without his grandfather's consent, his father had married the housekeeper, "a poor relation", and had consequently been disinherited. Roderick is born in a miserable garret in the laird's house, where a kind servant has hidden his mother who is turned out as soon as her father-in-law discovers she is still under his roof. She dies soon afterwards, her husband vanishes, and Roderick is left on his grandfather's estate as an orphan. He is "the darling of the tenants" (p. 13), but neglected and resented by the rest of the family as a rival in the merciless fight for the old man's favor and money.

Throughout childhood, Roderick hovers between half-insider and half-outsider status on the land he might have inherited. At school or on the estate, efforts are continuously made to push him out into the cold; ejection is the sword that might fall at any moment. But the boy early learns to fend for himself. The school is his main battleground. Roderick survives because of his intelligence and strong fists, and not through any financial assistance from his grandfather. Surrounded by ejectors, he is, however, not without helpers. Apart from his friends among the tenants, there is his uncle, the sailor Tom Bowling, who suddenly turns up and takes up the cudgels for his nephew. His efforts at persuading the laird to do his duty by Roderick are futile, although he proves an invaluable ally when the moment comes for revenge upon the schoolmaster, who for years had tormented Roderick and his fellow pupils.

The process of ejection is completed when it becomes clear that Roderick is left with nothing in his grandfather's will. The only items he inherits are his name and his family pride. His status as gentleman is thus an inalienable right, not a vague dream as in the case of Colonel Jack. The final act of ejection does not leave Roderick in the state of shock, which accompanies the picaro's initial sense of abandonment. He has not been turned loose into the world because of his family's destitution, but because the resources he feels entitled to are withdrawn from him. This is the essence of ejection in his case, and it produces a feeling of resentment which persists throughout his wanderings. His sense of abandonment is related to his sense of the injustice done to him by those who should have protected him. Thus the initial focus of the picaresque formula is shifted again to the aristocratic outcast.[8]

The first stage in what Lewis M. Knapp calls Roderick's "picaresque obstacle race"[9] is the college in the neighbouring town, where he is a student at his uncle's expense. He "resolved to apply myself with great care to my studies..." (p. 27). With greater justification than Pablo in *El Buscón*, he sees education as a means of social advancement, an opportunity he is determined to exploit. Roderick is clearly capable of making the most out of the situation in hand. He quickly establishes himself as a good-looking, well-bred, and well-read gentleman about town. There is, perhaps also a touch of his uncle's light-heartedness about him, although he is not capable of living up to his uncle's carefree code of behaviour. Tom Bowling can console himself and his nephew after their disappointment about the laird's will with a song that defies the riches which have disrupted the Random family: "Why should we quarrel for riches," he sings, "A light heart and a thin pair of breeches goes through the world, brave boys" (p. 23). But for Roderick and for the picaro, proper money is the irreplaceable means of gaining access to and of retaining a position in polite society.

Roderick's first discovery of the power of money in society is the result of the uncle's sudden loss of his fortune. He is forced to leave college, and he is quickly abandoned by all his "friends". Instead of flocking to his side, they reject him, teaching him that loss of money inevitably discredits a person in the eyes of the world. At the end of his wild goose chase for assistance among his acquaintances and those he had helped, he feels "deserted to all the horrors of extreme want, and avoided by mankind as a creature of a different species, or rather as a solitary being, nowise comprehended within the scheme or protection of Providence" (p. 33). This is the first of a series of encounters which open the inexperienced Roderick's eyes to the ways of the world. Picaro-like, he has to pass through a phase of being the victim of circumstances that are unexpected and, thererfore, beyond his control. And also like the picaro, he has to learn to distinguish between forces that can and forces that cannot be tackled through his own resorcefulness.

His long trek toward experience and a place in the sun begins when Roderick is able to stave off destitution by apprenticing himself to a local surgeon. Like Gil Blas, he enters upon a career as a servant out of necessity, but as his aspirations as a gentleman are more justified, the proud Roderick's adaptability is even more striking. His intellectual superiority is shown by the manner in which he gains a certain power over his employer despite his inferior position as a mere servant who sleeps in the garret. As when he was s student, he exploits the opportunity his apprenticeship offers for professional knowledge, which can improve his chances in the world. As he says, he gains "knowledge (…) by a close application to the duties of my employment (…) and (…) my care (…) was wholly engrossed in laying up a stock of instruction that might secure me against the caprice of fortune for the future" (p. 36). At the same time, "I began to cast about for an opportunity of launching into the world" (p. 36).

For a while he is "in the utmost perplexity" about how to break out of his dependent position (p. 37). Suddenly, however, "a small accident" occurs which places the apothecary in his power. Roderick is able to help his employer out of a domestic dilemma and, in return, is furnished with enough money to "maintain me comfortably in London until I should procure a warrant for my provision on board of some ship" (p. 38). We are reminded of the comfortable start of Gil Blas's wanderings, although the latter's uncle and the apothecary are worlds apart.

The formula that emerges from Roderick's first encounter with the world after his loss of family support is a paradigm for similar encounters later on. For Roderick shares the picaro's eye for the opportunity a moment offers and his readiness to grasp it. He also shares his strategic skill, while he exceeds the picaro in prudent calculation, being far more concerned with thinking ahead. Roderick's formula takes him from a state of frustration, through periods of resignation, adaptation, apprenticeship, and consolidation, followed by new encounters with fortune in which he can exploit what he has learned.

At first glance, Roderick appears to leave for London in the spirit of his uncle's song. Necessity forces him to travel light, but he is as frugal and calculating as Defoe's Moll Flanders, who is obsessed with making inventories of her possessions, revealing her skill in insuring herself against a rainy day. There is a similar strain in Roderick's temperament, as shown in the following list of his possessions at the outset of his journey:

> My whole fortune [consisted] of one suit of clothes, half a dozen of ruffled shirts, as many plain, two pair of worsted, and a like number of thread stockings, a case of pocket instruments, a small edition of Horace, Wiseman's *Surgery*, and ten guineas in cash (p. 38).

Roderick may be poor, but he is not the destitute outcast that the picaro tends to be in his opening situation. His clothes are those of a gentleman, and he carries the rudiments of his profession with him. From now on, his credentials in both capacities will be continually tested, particularly in London.

The fairly short account of Roderick's journey to London exploits the episodic structure of the picaresque novel to highlight the manner in which Roderick, encountering the customary vicissitudes of travel, is the butt of fortune who has sufficient resilience to "bounce back".[10] The most important event during his journey, however, is his meeting with his old school friend, Strap, a cobbler's son who becomes Roderick's servant, like DonQuixote's Sancho Panza and Gil Blas's Scipio. Strap, who is now a barber, boosts Roderick's self-respect as a gentleman by taking on menial tasks and looking after his needs. One as poor as the other, they act as a parody on the traditional gentleman-servant relationship. Besides, Strap is ready to assume the traditional roles of the picaro on behalf of Roderick. In fact, Strap declares: "I'll beg for you, steal for you, go through the wide world with you, and starve with you" (p. 78). Although the spirit of sacrifice behind the offer is not a part of the picaresque formula, the activities listed are.

By the time Strap makes this statement, Roderick is facing destitution in London. Furnished with a servant, Roderick has moved up the social ladder, but without money or recognition this improvement is of no use. He has not added one iota to his credentials. From the moment he enters London, the focus is on the outsider-insider conflict: Roderick's main obstacle is the wall that surrounds the professional status he aspires to and that prevents him from being recognized as a gentleman. It is the barrier he graphically describes in the scene where he waits for an audience with his member of Parliament, Mr. Cringer:

> In this place I continued standing for three-quarters of an hour, during which time I saw a great many young fellows, whom I formerly knew in Scotland, pass and repass, with an air of familiarity, in their way to and from the audience chamber; while I was fain to stand shivering in the cold, and turn my back to them, that they might not perceive the lowness of my condition (p. 79).

Roderick and Strap are already painfully aware of their outsider status as ignorant rustics in a great city where they are complete strangers. The reception they are given provides them with the "shock of experience" that initiates the picaro into the ways of the world, akin to the stone bull incident in *Lazarillo de Tormes*.[11]

The two Scots' outsider status is further emphasized by Strap's desperate attempt to gate-crash into Mr. Cringer's closed world by throwing a stone against a streetdoor in response to the most humiliating of the series of acts of repulsion with which the "insiders" welcome them (p. 74). His action is as futile as Bowling's attempt to force old Random to do his duty by Roderick. Roderick and his companion have to learn that survival in the city depends on adaptability rather than brute force. New clothes and a new wig are better weapons than fists when it comes to fending for oneself in a society where no one can be trusted. The most important lesson Roderick learns is that power and position can only be acquired through bribery; qualifications and merit are of no consequence.

Smollett keeps close to the picaresque formula in his account of Roderick's innumerable encounters wih the London world and the merciless struggle for admission in which only the strongest swimmers will survive. It is above all, a question of money. Thus Roderick, forced to "dance attendance every morning at the levee of Mr. Cringer" (p. 80) and of the whole insider hierarchy to achieve his position as surgeon's mate, finds his money dwindling away as he is forced to pay for every step in the intricate system of patronage. The traditional openings for a gentleman in distress—gambling and a rich heiress—only lead further into the financial quagmire.

Fortune reduces Roderick once more to servant status. He is forced to seek menial employment, this time as journeyman to an apothecary. Ironically, he gains his modest position through patronage—through the good offices of a schoolmaster, a relative of Strap's—but his favor does not cost Roderick anything. His lodgings are in keeping with his outcast state:

> Strap conveyed my baggage to the place allotted for me, which was a back room up two pair of stairs, furnished with a pallet for me to lie upon, a chair without a back, an earthen chamber-pot without a handle, a bottle by way of candlestick, and a triangular piece of glass instead of a mirror (p. 103).

The formula of the disinherited gentleman reduced to servitude is repeated. Roderick is quick to respond to the opportunity that his new position offers. He displays the equanimity with which he tends to respond to misfortune, although his inherent "pride and resentment" may be difficult to curb (p. 104). These qualities set him apart from the common picaro, and also give him a sense of his own importance, which helps him to endure. However, we have seen that the Colonel Jack-type of picaro also seeks support, encouraged by his conviction that he is a gentleman by birth, a circumstance which draws attention to the crucial importance of the individual's sense of his heritage in the battle of survival, as well as his concomitant sense of precariousness.

Adaptation, consolidation, and advance are again the stages by which Roderick overcomes his degrading position. The twin resources of "industry and knowledge" are exploited to gain "the good will of my master" (p. 105), and then counteracted by the ill will and animosity of his employer's daughter and her lover, Roderick's old school mate, Squire Gawky. Meanwhile, Roderick also learns the ways of a gentleman about the town: "I shook off my awkward air by degrees, and acquired the character of a polite journeyman apothecary" (p. 109). Imperceptibly, he thus begins to climb the social pyramid, displaying the intrepidity as well as the vitality of the picaro of old. He exceeds, however, the latter's readiness to pay back prank with prank. He may have shed his clumsiness and gullibility, but he still responds to violence with the same zest for violence which made him get his own back on his schoolmaster in the village in such a vicious manner. According to Boucé, "Roderick has need of a centre of hostility in order to canalise all his aggressiveness"[12] This is demonstrated by the scene in which Roderick avenges a violent attack on himself with almost boundless inventiveness and cruelty:

> We rushed upon him all at once, secured his sword, stripped off his clothes even to the skin,which we scourged with nettles till he was blistered from head to foot (...) When I was satisfied with the stripes I had bestowed, we carried off his clothes (...) and left him stark naked (p. 111).

The unfortunate O'Donnell is hardly the theme of the Good Samaritan kind of social satire that marks the corresponding incident in *Joseph Andrews*. However, although violence is cultivated for its own sake in an incident like this, rather in the manner in which Pablo is mobbed by his class-mates in *El Buscón*, it is also shown to be endemic in the community described. As Alter suggests, Roderick's precarious situation is aggravated by the "monstrous conspiracy",[13] operating through chance, that is latent in the environment through which he passes.

The supreme example of the way this hidden force may erupt at any moment is the press gang incident which brings Roderick's London period to such an abrupt conclusion. Roderick has been fired by the apothecary. Like the picaro, he is immediately reduced to outcast status, a circumstance which is further accentuated by the circumstance that Strap has left him and has gone abroad as the *valet de chambre* of a gentleman. In his desperate situation, Roderick contemplates joining the army or navy. Although "reduced to a starving condition," his resilience keeps him going. In his own words, "my spirit began to accomodate itself to my beggarly fate," when he is suddenly thrust as low as Colonel Jack at the nadir of his misfortunes. He, too, is press-ganged and brutally "thrust down into the hold among a parcel of miserable wretches" (p. 143). From now on violence is his and his fellow victims' daily food. The low-water mark of his fortunes has been reached, deprived as he is of his freedom and banished from his country—the ultimate act of disinheritance.

The dungeon-like, claustrophobic atmosphere of its opening passage clings to the long navy section throughout. The descending movement began with Roderick's dismissal from service and continues in the Miss Williams interlude, which opened his eyes to the seamy side of London

existence. It reaches its lowest point, however, when Roderick is taken to
the cockpit, the dungeonlike quarters he and his fellow surgeon's mates
share. From "this dismal gulf" (p. 14) he gate-crashes into the sick bay,
and finds himself in another inferno, arriving as awkwardly as he did in
London. However, Roderick's landlubberly behavior underlines the
mixture of absurdity and horror which permeates these chapters (p. 154).

The scene indicates Roderick's state of bewilderment in a situation he
has not been taught to master. This state leads, however, to his first faint
advances up the social ladder. Although he has acquired a mortal enemy
in the midshipman, Crampley, he lives "tolerably easy, in expectation of
preferment" (p. 157). Ironically he finds himself doing the kind of work
he would have done had he acquired his commission in the first place.
The nightmare of the sickbay is a situation he can learn to handle.
Again, he develops the professional skill he needs to be recognized as a
gentleman, and he lives up to his earlier reputation as a conscientious
worker. His advance—this time from lower down the social scale than
ever—is, as usual, accompanied by consolidation: he resolves "to submit
patiently to my fate, and contrive to make myself as easy as the nature of
the case would allow" (p. 165).

He is, however, like his fellow crew, "under the dominion of an
arbitrary tyrant" (p. 165), and this is a situation with which he cannot
cope. Like the rest of the men, he has to endure the captain's wrath. He is
imprisoned without trial "and carried to the poop (...) where I was
loaded with irons and stapled to the deck, on pretense that I was a spy
on board, and had conspired against the captain's life" (p. 169). The Pro-
methean note deepens into horror and absurdity in the battle scene.
Roderick is still chained to the deck and fully exposed to enemy fire
without being able to defend himself. At the height of the battle "the
head of the officer of the marines, who stood near me, being shot off,
bounced from the deck athwart my face, leaving me well-nigh blinded
with brains" (p. 170). Roderick emerges as the emblem of suffering
humanity in a senseless campaign, the helpless victim of a crazy system.
At the outset of his captivity, he curses his "capricious fate" (p. 169), but
after the ordeal he urges his fellow sufferers to "take an example from me
of fortitude and submission, till such time as we could procure redress"
(p. 171). In this incident, Roderick's "sense of outrage"[14] is channeled
into a sense of fellowship. He sees himself as spokesman for and example
to the oppressed crew and is not merely concerned with getting his own
back.

This episode is also the point in his career when Roderick moves
closest to "the *essential picaresque situation*." He certainly is reduced to
the lowest of outcast states—formally a criminal, if not in fact—and
"caught up in a chaotic world".[15] His nightmarish situation is deepened
by the fact that his helpers—decent members of the crew—are as helpless
as he, or even worse off. They can, at most, alleviate his suffering, but can

do nothing to release him from it.

Fortune is as chance-bound in *Roderick Random* as in any picaresque novel, but chance appears to work through some hidden plan. For instance, when Roderick happens to be shanghaied into his uncle's old ship, and the first man he meets is one of the former's old friends. When Roderick eventually thinks he is on his way to better days in England in a new ship, he discovers that his old enemy Crampley is its captain. This discovery is the customary moment of abrupt reversal, which thrusts Roderick from happiness to misery. The transition is the more abrupt this time because he has enjoyed a spell of tranquil happiness on a plantation ashore. This pastoral interlude, reminiscent of Gil Blas's retreat in Southern Spain, is the result of another chance meeting—this time with one of the surgeon's mates who had escaped from the miseries on board. The interlude shows another side of Roderick's adaptability: provided by his friend with "half a dozen fine shirts, and as many linen waistcoats and caps, with twelve pair of new thread stockings (...) with money, and all the necessaries for the comfort of life, I began to look upon myself as a gentleman of some consequence, and felt my pride dilate apace" (p. 207).

The precariousness of Roderick's state as a gentleman soon becomes evident on board ship. The captain may not be able to deprive him of his professional position, but he can terrorize him and ostracize him from the society of the ship's officers. He is again an outcast, "fain to eat in a solitary manner by myself" (p. 209). His return to England is as dramatic as his departure. About to get his own back on Crampley in a desperate fight on a beach in Cornwall, Roderick is struck down and abandoned to his fate, "alone in a desolate place, stripped of my clothes, money, watch, buckles, and everything but my shoes, stockings, breeches, and shirt" (p. 211). He is again without credentials. No one is prepared to help him in his friendless state except an old woman, who is herself an outcast, considered by her neighbors as a witch because of her eccentric ways.

Like the picaro, Roderick has to begin from scratch again. As before, poverty forces him to become a servant, this time to a rich lady, under a false name. Fortune again changes for the better, but not much, although his period of service turns out to be another oasis-like interlude. Roderick falls in love with his employer's beautiful niece, Narcissa, and seeks to establish his real identity as a cultured and well-read young gentleman—in fact, a nobleman in disguise. This interlude, too, ends with a brutal act of exclusion. Roderick wounds a neighbouring squire in his brave attempt to defend Narcissa and is forced to run away.

Reduced to the uncertain state of an impoverished fugitive, he is once more kidnapped and carried out of his country, to France, against his will. His situation is closer to that of the picaro than ever. Chance again confronts him with a futile helper, this time his uncle, whom he meets in

Calais. The latter has just enough money to take him to England, so Roderick's only option is the road. He is intensely aware of his outcast state, which he expresses in conventional picaresque terms: "I found myself reduced almost to extreme poverty, in the midst of foreigners, among whom I had not one acquaintance to advise or befriend me" (pp. 235-236). Patience and resentment—this time toward the English nation which has so consistently rejected hm—as usual keeps him going. He is exposed to the vicissitudes of the road, and finds to his dismay further evidence of the unreliability of his fellow travelers. Left at last "a prey to famine (...) in a foreign country, where I had not one friend or acquaintance" (p. 242), he is taken care of by a company of ragged soldiers who, "far from the hospitable haunts of man,... formed a ring and danced around me" (p. 243). He is invited to share their "banquet" and the carefree "pleasures of a soldier's life" (p. 243), which he accepts, and is "admitted into the regiment of Picardy" (p. 243).

Roderick has entered another oasis, this time outside society, and his luck again brightens, however modest his progress. He is infected with the soldiers' high spirits, reveals his old patience and endurance, and becomes a good soldier. His natural propensity to feel resentment helps him to endure the horrors and absurdity of war. Despite his competence as a soldier, he scarcely moves above starvation level. The camp at Rheims represents the nadir of his miserable army career: "I found myself in the utmost want of everything," abandoned to his "old remedy, patience" (p. 249).

Again his luck, operating through chance, changes. Strap, metamorphosed into a rich gentleman, turns up and immediately changes places with his old master: he resumes his position as servant, and Roderick is once more able to try his luck as a gentleman. He re-enters society disguised as a well-dressed gentleman with great expectations, seeking a rich heiress—an enterprise financed by Strap's slender resources. Roderick's situation when they settle down in London, is, therefore, still precarious. The contrast between their first and second arrival in London underlines the way in which dress and manners—all the paraphernalia of pretended wealth—open doors that would have been closed to real merit.

Seeking the best company in town to pursue his scheme, Roderick joins the army of fortune hunters who lead a parasitic existence on the fringes of London high society. This is one of the higher-class picaro's favourite domains. Impoverished, these people depend on gambling, fraud, and the prospect of catching a good match for survival. Wit and cunning are essential qualities in a battle in which only the fittest survive. The keynote is precariousness. The curse of this community is money, which Roderick discovers to his dismay as he flits up and down the social ladder. Continually threatened by "the prospect of approaching want (...) [he] posted, in a thoughtless manner, towards poverty" (p. 297). *Roderick Random* rivals the panoramic sweep of *Gil Blas* in this section, which includes taverns, coffeehouses, playhouses, the haunts of gamblers and other practicers of shady businesses, and their clientele.

This is a milieu in which the helpers are themselves parasites and climbers. The precariousness of life in such an environment is partly due to the fact that no one can be trusted: each climber is on his own. It is a milieu in which it is difficult to retain one's honesty and sense of integrity. Roderick's main problem is that his ruthless pursuit of an heiress collides with his dream of Narcissa, whom he is apt to forget. He is shown to be easily tempted by the women about town. In fact, throughout the novel, Strap is a foil to his master, standing for honesty and simple decency. Roderick's moral sense is, by contrast, blunted, which is shown in his rather callous behaviour to Strap. The impression that he lacks the charm that is often a redeeming feature in the picaro is above all the result of his behaviour during this period.[16]

Gradually Roderick moves away from the picaro's sphere of interest. He becomes increasingly concerned with the problem of establishing his identity as a gentleman. However low his fortunes, he does not again resort to menial work. When recourse to gambling, speculation on the rich-heiress market, or the bottle are of no avail, he contemplates adopting the career of a highwayman. Strap's offer to support them by honest work is countered by Roderick's boast that "I should never want a resource while I had a loaded pistol in possession" (p. 365). This is never more than a tempting thought, which does not keep his debtors away, and the outcome of his quandary is the notorious Marshalsea, where an impoverished writer emerges as the emblem of down-and-out existence: he had, like Miss Williams earlier in the novel, been "turned (...) out into the streets naked, friendless, and forlorn" (p. 389). For all his claim to being a gentleman, this is the fate that threatens Roderick.

The irony of his situation in London is that he has to rub shoulders with upstart gentlemen who are trying to force their way in—if possible, at his expense; he is, after all, a genuine gentleman by birth. Worse still, he has to resort to upstart status and means to regain his birthright. The absurdity of the situation is brought home to him when he is faced with the problem of establishing his identity as gentleman to Narcissa and her brother. To his chagrin, Roderick realizes that he would "find it a very hard matter to make good my pretensions" to the status of gentleman "by birth, education, and behaviour" (p. 337).

As so often before Roderick's luck changes abruptly through no efforts on his part. In *Roderick Random,* the formula of the picaresque wheel of fortune is replaced by the battle between two converging antagonist forces, which, in the end, signifies victory of benign over hostile force. The disinherited Roderick is in the first place liberated from prison by his uncle, who is now a rich man. He is, naturally, "utterly confounded at this sudden transition", but is quick to submit to the process which transforms him from beggar to gentleman: "Having performed the ceremony of ablution, I shifted, and dressing in my gayest apparel, waited for the return of my uncle, who was agreeably surprised at my sudden transformation" (p. 392).

From now on, it is smooth sailing for him. The final stages on his journey back to his birthright take him to the West Indies as a promising young merchant, where he meets and recovers his lost father, and then back to England, where he is now able to marry Narcissa, although she, in turn, has been disinherited. Money and a well-established social position are firm bulwarks against the tribulations of a vagabond existence. The happy ending focuses on the kind of secure and tranquil existence Roderick should have had in the first place. The ending cancels out the injustice that has been done to him, and also the possibility that fate may strike again—as the open ending of the picaresque formula implies. The return of the lost father has restored order to chaos.

In *Roderick Random,* Smollett carries on the autobiographical tradition which the picaresque writer shares with other narrative genres, most notably the spiritual autobiography and travel memoir, which enjoyed great popularity in the days of Defoe and Swift . The picaresque formula with its indefatigable traveler within, yet excluded from, society, came in handy for the great novelist-portrayers of mid-eighteenth-century England. They reflect the age that, according to Rogers, was the first "consciously to cultivate the art of travel". They were also quick to see the potential of the picaresque mode for a panoramic, satirically tinged rendering of a complex social reality.[17] The memoir approach is by definition concerned with past experience. Even the worst-off picaro must have experienced a lull in his misfortunes when he sat down to record his life and adventures. Thus Guzmán finds the peace he needs during his time as galleyslave. Roderick Random, on the other hand, has been restored to his family estate by the time he becomes a writer. His picaresque career can thus be viewed from his safe side of the gulf that separates the haves from the have-nots. Gil Blas and Colonel Jack have acquired a similar congenial environment for their writing. Roderick and these two travelers have features in common, yet the emphasis chosen by the authors differs. A brief comparison may illuminate the particular use Smollett makes of the picaresque formula in his effort to produce "a large diffused picture" of the individual and society.[18]

Roderick is, like his fellow picaros, the victim of events and circumstances over which he has no control. He, too, learns patience and endurance; *Roderick Random* is indeed "a chronicle of resilience."[19] The power that keeps him going, however, is different from the instinct for survival that enables Colonel Jack to keep his head above water. In Roderick's case, a twin instinct, gentility, derived from his aristocratic birth, is at least as vital for his strength to defy a hostile fate as the energy that impending starvation instills into him. In *Colonel Jack*, the state of gentleman is merely a vague dream at first. Only gradually does it become the consideration that makes him choose honesty even when starvation is the alternative. The status of gentleman he can achieve at a later stage. The same is the case with Gil Blas, who we have seen deliberately chooses the ways of a gentleman, which means giving up the life and habits of the picaro. His reward is insider status in polite society. Roderick has no social status to win because he already has the natural right to call himself gentleman. The journey in Roderick's case is partly a matter of necessity, but partly also a series of encounters in which he is up against forces which threaten his reputation as gentleman, or in which he must strive to establish his real identity under the most untoward circumstances. Roderick is not, like the picaro, an outsider who is striving to get into the social hierarchy. He has been thrust out of a niche which is his right by birth. The goal of his journey is to get back into the system. The increasing feeling he has of descending into an inferno is not only his natural response to physical horrors or to the picaresque situation of abandonment. It is also the result of his perhaps unconscious feeling that the disinheritance, passed on to im by his father at birth, is repeated in the major disasters that confront him on his journey: the press gang incident, his being kidnapped and sent to France, his imprisonment for debt, and all the occasions when he is met by closed doors.

Fate in *Roderick Random* is thus not merely related to the wheel of fortune movement of the picaresque novel. The maliciousness of fate in Smollett's novel gives it a flavor of Scottish predestinarianism. There is also something Scottish about the sense of injustice and resentment which we have seen is such an important ingredient in the boy's fortitude. In this case, too, Roderick is supplied with an instinct that qualifies him for a different type of survival than the picaro's. Given the chance, the picaro may reveal hidden resources as leader or businessman, as Colonel Jack does on the plantation, or Rebecca Sharp does in *Vanity Fair*. Roderick's sense of injustice deepens into a sense of social wrong in the Navy chapters and while he is a soldier on the Continent.[20] Up to a point, he is a *Bildungroman* hero whose social consciousness matures as he becomes increasingly entangled in his own and his fellow human beings' buffetings with man-made misfortunes. The "chip on his shoulder"[21] that Roderick carries around is, however, part of his idiosyncracy and may well stem from his childhood experience of repulsion in his native village. The underlying sense of insecurity makes him stiffen into a particular social image, out of keeping with the picaro's repertoire of aristocratic roles.

In *Roderick Random*, the journey focuses on moments of disruption rather than on moments which offer opportunities for the picaro's climb-and-fall career. The initial episode shows the reader two people bent on dissolving the bonds which hold the family together—the son, by defying the father's traditional rights, the father, by withdrawing the financial support his son is entitled to. The two move to extremes which disrupt the mini-society that the family and the tenants constitute—the laird, by giving full rein to his despotic tendencies, the son, by simply vanishing from the scene after the death of his wife. The crimes of grandfather as well as father are visited on Roderick, who is reduced to the status of a vagabond on the estate that might well have been his. The squabbles among the relatives over old Random's will serve to highlight the state of disharmony that the disruption within the family has caused. The happy ending which sees Roderick restored to and happily married on the estate of his ancestors appears in striking contrast.

The act of disinheritance and the accompanying spirit of strife and divisiveness in the family leads to the breakdown of discipline and order in the handling of Roderick. "Ragged and contemptible" (p. 13), he runs wild in the village, exposed to the schoolmaster's arbitrary cruelty, but also ready to fight back when he can. The schoolmaster is a petty tyrant, the worthy counterpart of old Mr. Random. We are a long way from the Scottish village ideal, in which the enlightened schoolmaster spends his days detecting and nourishing "lads of pairts" and getting them ready for a university education. The poorest has a chance because the laird or some other well-off person is ready to give talent a chance. The tenants may be partial to Roderick because he is so like his father in appearence, but otherwise he has "the character of a vagabond" (p. 14), and neither the schoolmaster nor anybody else encourages the obviously talented boy. One cannot tell if Smollett had this village model in mind, but it is at the heart of the pre-Industrial Revolution Scottish national education system.[22]

This ideal helps to give depth to Smollett's portrait of a family and village that have gone to pieces. No wonder Roderick leaves Scotland with a chip on his shoulder, his "thoughts being engrossed by the knavery of the world" (p. 54).

On his grandfather's estate, at school, in the little town where he is apprenticed to the surgeon, and on the road to London, Roderick experiences a series of displacements. The first stages in his picaresque career open his eyes to the power of money in society, and how friends and protection are commodities to be bought and sold. But the sense of displacement is, above all, due to Roderick's feeling that he is continually being demoted to ranks where he can make a go of it professionally or physically, but where he would not have been if it had not been for his grandfather's willful use of power.

The road in *Roderick Random*, as in the traditional picaresque tale, is a source of endless adventure, affordig the down-and-out the opportunity to make easy money, but also leading him further into misery. It represents the lowest rung on the social ladder, but also where luck may change most suddenly, and where the unfortunate may escape from disaster, at least for a while. It is also through traveling that the haves and have-nots meet, and the former's power, as well as vulnerability, are continually displayed. Roderick's displaced position is brought out in his plan to walk to London, like a friendless and ragged urchin, which is out of keeping both with his temperament and his aristocratic heritage. By the time he approaches London, he has improved his social standing by acquiring Strap as a servant, and traveling by coach. The boys nevertheless arrive in the metropolis with no other status than that of being Scots.

This is, however, hardly a recommendation. The self-portrait Roderick draws of himself looks like the caricature an Englishman might draw of a "needy" Scot, one of the army of fortune hunters who had been crowding to London since the Union.[23] By making Roderick see himself as a caricature, Smollett exploits the gullible rustic youth tradition, but he also heralds the next phase in his perennial confrontation with forces of disruption and displacement:

> My hair, which was of the deepest red, hung down upon my shoulders, as lank and straight as a pound of candles; and the skirts of my coat reached to the middle of my leg; my waistcoat and breeches were of the same piece, and cut in the same taste; and my hat very much resembled a barber's bason, in the shallowness of the crown, and narrowness of the brim (p. 68).

Only by donning a wig and the clothes of a man about the town can Roderick start his laborious task of gaining admission to those with influence—servants and masters. Only by modifying his Scottish tongue can he make himself understood. In this, Roderick conforms to the protagonist in the picaresque formula; he is always ready to adapt his behavior to circumstances. It must, however, have been an eye-opener to him that his appearance, which in Scotland was his passport to society, now was merely bizarre. In the eyes of London society, all Scotsmen were "needy", and Roderick, whose "pride and resentment (...) were two chief ingredients in my disposition" (p. 104), may well have found the English contempt for his nation hard to swallow.[24] One of the reasons for the general discontent in Scotland prior to the 1745 uprising was, according to J. H. Plumb, that "many of the minor Scottish aristocracy envied and distrusted the way of life of the English aristocracy who despised them, and never bothered to conceal it."[25]

Roderick shares the picaro's problem of finding a door that will open into the hierarchically arranged social system. He soon discovers that the

London warren is the home of parasites and timeservers. It also offers endless vain opportunities for anybody seeking anything as definite as a decent livelihood. With his lack of money, and with neither a name nor reference to make up for this lack, Roderick is the victim of a socio-economic process that disrupted the feudal tenant-landlord relationship of the old community, which was replaced by "a gradual stiffening in the system"[26] and, thus, a deepening gulf between the insiders and outsiders which London epitomized. The influence-ridden, closed society that offers such insurmountable obstacles to Roderick is the system Walpole perfected in his twenty years as Prime Minister. "The secret of political success in normal times," Christopher Hill writes, "was assiduous application to the day-to-day questions of patronage and place."[27] Favoritism is a traditional satirical target, but in his account of Roderick's buffetings with the world of Mr. Cringer or the Navy Office, Smollett also reflects a movement which was gaining momentum in the middle of the century: as Hill describes it, "external public opinion was beginning to express the moral repugnance which the system of corruption and family graft roused in those outside the charmed circle."[28] No doubt Smollett did much to arouse this resentment in his drastic descriptions of the system in *Roderick Random*. The universal belief in the sesame effect of influence in the right places and the manner in which the patronage formula assumes a closed, hier-archichal system are clearly developed in a passage which is both satiri-cal and poignant. Roderick's sailor uncle, reduced to extreme want, nevertheless believes he can tap the system and get a commission:

> I shall steer my course directly to London, where I do not doubt of being replaced, and of having the R taken off me by the Lords of the Admiralty, to whom I intend to write a petition setting forth my case. If I succeed, I shall have wherewithal to give you some assistance (...) I may have interest enough to procure a warrant appointing you surgeon's mate (...) For the beadle of the Admiralty is my good friend; and he and one of the under-clerks are sworn brothers, and that under-clerk has a good deal to say with one of the upper clerks, who is very well known to the under-secretary, who, upon his recommendation, I hope will recommend my affair to the first secretary; and he again will speak to one of the lords in my behalf: so that you see I do not want friends to assist me on occasion (p. 234).

Roderick may well laugh indulgently at his uncle for his confidence in the system, which by then he has found is as baffling and frustrating as Dickens's fog-bound Chancery, but its corrupting effect cannot be laughed away. Despotism combined with bureaucracy creates the state of absurdity and horror of which Roderick is both victim and witness on board the *Thunder*. As a result of his repeated collisions with a society which keeps on rebuffing him whatever his rights, he is completely alienated and cut loose from any social function. He finds himself in a community where professional skill only counts far down on the social scale. The commanding officers have not been selected for their qualifications but for their connections. They are fops or bullies—caricatures of the principles of arbitrary whim and cruelty with which Roderick has been surrounded since his birth. Roderick never comes forward as the advocate of an influence-free society. However, he has in mind a community in which individual merit counts and in which there is room for the sense of responsibility and fellowship which characterized the landlord-tenant relationship at its best in the feudal system, and which still lingered on in Scotland.[29]

This is the message of the ending of the novel, in which Roderick is restored to his birthright. The circular movement of the novel's plot structure is well described by Richard Bjornson, who also points out an important difference between *Roderick Random* and *Gil Blas*:

> Unlike Gil Blas's retirement to Lirias, Roderick's happiness represents a young nobleman's victory over the general wickedness of the world, rather than an old man's long career of faithful service in subordinate positions. Where Gil Blas succeeds, Roderick Random triumphs.[30]

The ending is, however, also an alternative opening to the novel, in that Roderick appears in the kind of community his grandfather might have presided over. Throughout the novel, as an undercurrent to the dominant disruptive movement, a social impulse gathers momentum that harks back to the days before the fall, but also forward to the reign of the enlightened landlord during the Age of Improvement.

Although the forces of disruption are in the ascendance at the outset of Roderick's adventures, there are also early signs of a countermovement. Roderick may be neglected, but he is recognized by the tenants as his father's son, although at this stage "their favour was a weak resource against the enmity of my cousins" (p. 13). His "boldness of temper, and strength of make", together with his haughtiness and pronounced sense of justice (p. 14) reveal his heroic potentialities. He may look like a vagabond, but his latent gifts for leadership push him into the foreground, making him the head of a "confederacy" of thirty boys, "the teror of the whole village" (p. 15). The resulting gang wars are seen as more than the usual games of boyhood. The atmosphere of lawlessness is related to the general situation of rivalry and strife on the estate. Roderick's skill as organizer and leader may be seen as the first stage in the countermovement against the forces of disruption.

Roderick's meeting with Strap on the road and the resulting servant-master relationship is an even more significant event. There is nothing to choose between them as far as money goes. If anything, Strap is better off because he has a job. The two sign what amounts to a social contract defining their relative positions according to birth rather than according to personal and professional qualifications. In this, they conform to the social structure of the community they have left. The contract foreshadows the restoration scene at the end of the novel. The social reality behind their contract is their lonely and unprotected state in a chaotic world. The ideology behind it is in keeping with the chain-of-being, station-oriented view of man's place in the community, as expressed in the following manner by Strap:

> "Mr. Random, you are born a gentleman, and have a great deal of learning—and indeed look like a gentleman; for, as to person, you may hold up your head with the best of them. On the other hand, I am a poor but honest cobbler's son (...) I know a little of the world (...) though you be gentle and I simple, it does not follow but that I who am simple may do a good office to you who are gentle" (pp. 100–1).

The "contract" between Roderick and Strap and the way it is expressed in this passage reflect their attempt at coming to grips with the chaotic world with which they are confronted.

The image of the honest and faithful servant which is established in *Gil Blas* receives in Strap its supreme prototype. His "diligence, sobriety, and affection" (p. 252) and his contentment with his position as servant (p. 255) appear in striking contrast to the picaro's view of service as a means of enriching himself at his master's expense. The latter turns servant in order to be admitted to insider society and thus gain a foothold from which he can advance. This is, as we have seen, also the aim of the parasites Roderick has to vie with for the favor of the great in London, while Strap always remains "simple" and has no wish to advance socially.

The fact that Roderick is "gentle" means, however, that he is confronted with a dilemma when poverty threatens. Sooner or later he is forced to earn his own livelihood, although his "gentle" station makes service entail a loss of social status. We have seen how impossible it is for him to prove his identity as gentleman when he wishes to marry Nacissa. In the eyes of her family, he is a mere servant. On the other hand, the customary ways a penniless gentleman had to stave off destitution—gambling, borrowing, or securing a wealthy match—are shown to be equally futile and dishonorable. Each time Roderick is forced to take on a job, however, he is quick to adapt, and he gains both professional skill and pride. The alternative to the parasite's mode of existence which his first landlady sketches out is closer to Strap's domain than to Roderick's, but the spirit behind it may also be perceived in the professional world he is made to enter: "She wished I had been bound to some substantial handicraft, such as a weaver, or a shoemaker, rather than loiter away my time in learning foolish nonsense that would never bring me in a penny" (p. 29).

The landlady is referring to Roderick's career as a student, but she might just as well have in mind his education as a gentleman about town. At the back of her mind is the Calvinistic horror of idleness, which is also an undercurrent in the satirical picture Smollett gives of a patronage-ridden society. Throughout his first London period, Roderick is up against the intricate system of patronage which blocked professional skill unless it was combined with money and influence.[31] One of the most horrifying aspects of life on board the *Thunder* is the way favoritism leads to arbitrary and inefficient government. Professionalism is up against ignorance and senseless tyranny. On the other hand, Smollett is taking us to the period in English history when professional skill and pride gradually transformed the status for the professions of lawyer, doctor, and officer. By the end of the century, the medical profession had thus become a highly respectable and well-trained class, not least because of the high standing of the Scottish medical schools.[32] *Roderick Random,* like the rest of Smollett's work, contains satirical portraits of medical practitioners, but it is noteworthy that men like Roderick and his fellow surgeon's mates anticipate the age when professionalism ousted favoritism.

Roderick is only a professional man when he cannot keep up his appearance as a gentleman. It is nevertheless clear that he comes to accept the status of medical man as being in keeping with his position as a gentleman. In both capacities, he is exposed to charlatanism, just as in both he has problems in establishing his identity. Roderick shares this kind of precariousness with similarly placed young men in mid-eighteenth-century Britain. There was a certain fluidity along the borders between the lower reaches of the upper and the higher reaches of the middle stations of society.[33]

Thus, the social contract between Roderick and Strap does not exclude some rubbing of shoulders with the professional classes. Nor does Roderick's apotheosis as wealthy laird at the end of the novel exclude links with the mercantile world. On the contrary, he is released from prison through the good offices of his uncle, the newly rich sailor-turned-merchant, and Roderick himself passes through a brief period of apprenticeship as a merchant. When he meets his father in the West Indies, the latter is a well-off, retired gentleman. After a somewhat picaresque career he has made his fortune in trade (p. 409), thus repeating Colonel Jack's success story, although not his inglorious past.

In the process of being restored to his station, Roderick is continually being elevated from lower to higher positions through the influence of helpers with money and power. In return, Roderick is capable of elevating Narcissa from her disinherited state to that of a Scottish laird's lady. Narcissa takes this to be the final evidence of Roderick's identity as a true gentleman: " 'Sure the world will no longer question your generosity when you take a poor forlorn beggar to your arms' " (p. 421). Strap's two-part model is repeated: the opposition between gentle and simple corresponds to the one Narcissa suggests between benevolent master and beggar or slave. The underlying social model assumes a chain of dependency based on love and fidelity, a state of harmony and order which appears in striking contrast to the disrupting tyranny-based state of dependency in the early and middle parts of the novel.

Generosity is a central feature in this community. Generosity is also at the heart of two incidents which mark the decisive stages in Roderick's progress towards his position as wealthy and humane landlord. The first incident occurs when Roderick, a complete outcast from polite society, saves the life of an another outcast, Miss Williams, reduced by poverty to the state of common prostitute. His generosity makes him forget his own wretchedness, and he is filled with "sympathy and compassion" when listening to her story. In return, she assumes the role of humble servant. Again a "social contract" is formed which removes the parties from the domain of the down-and-out: "I found in her not only an agreeable companion, whose conversation greatly alleviated my chagrin, but also a careful nurse, who served me with the utmost fidelity and affection" (p. 121). From then on she is, alongside Strap, Roderick's most faithful helper.

The other incident occurs in the Marshalsea while Roderick is imprisoned for debt. Again he "breaks out of his self-centredness to pity the fate of another human being"[34] This time the story that releases his compassion is that of a wretched playwright, Melopyn. It is to Roderick final evidence of the way "the knavery and selfishness of mankind" ignores "uncommon merit" (p. 390). After his sudden metamorphosis into wealthy and well-dressed gentleman he takes leave of his prison-mates in a princely manner, but handing out his guineas with truly Scottish prudence. Roderick is ready to take up his superior position in society both financially and humanly.

The ending of *Roderick Random* has a princely quality about it. Indeed, throughout the novel Smollett exploits the motif of the lost heir or beggar prince, a feature which is further underlined by his use of chance-dominated plot sequences. The fairytale is common ground between romance and picaresque tale. Seen from the perspective of the picaresque, the prince-in-disguise theme and the view of a chance-ridden existence focus on the unpredictable and insecure nature of the human condition: the road from rags to riches to rags is as tortuous as it is inevitable—and it is never ending.

Just as a fairy tale has a beginning and an end, the ending here seems to liberate Roderick from his peregrinations. He is no longer random. The stories of his fellow sufferers along the road modify such an impression by focusing on the friendless and unprotected state that leaves them naked and helpless by the roadside. Roderick can avoid such conditions on his estate, but he cannot avert them in the world at large. Similarly, the realism and satirical power of Smollett's portrayal of the society through which Roderick moves reveal a sick community. However, despite his awakened social consciousness, Roderick inherits rather than revolts against the diseased system. He is at the summit of a social pyramid that is, if anything, more rigidly hierarchical than that of contemporary Britain. The final lesson of *Roderick Random* may well be that wealth rather than birth is the great divide between the insiders and outsiders. Roderick may have his "social contract" as evidence that he is gentle and Strap simple. But only money can buy him back his birthright. Basil Williams lists as one of "the most marked characteristics [of the period] (...) the great cleavage between the well-to-do 'persons of fashion and fortune' and the poor or 'lower order of the people.' " Only the former counted, the latter "were thought lucky to be protected by the rich".[35]

The precariousness that *Roderick Random* brands into the reader's consciousness has something to do with the sense Smollett conveys that not even the most ancient social position is immune to the ravages of economic change. At the heart of the anxiety he conveys, is Pope's fear that a link in the chain will break and cause chaos. However, by making excursions into the picaro's favorite hunting ground and at least partly identifying with him, we are also taken to the meeting places between haves and have-nots, above all, in the great city, but also in the micro-community of the ship.

Civilization is shown to be only a thin veneer, and violence and cruelty are rife. This is the gulf into which the poverty-stricken tumble, like the victims of South Sea Bubbles, the very emblem of precariousness. There is also a persistent fear that the have-nots—the "rabble"—will break loose and threaten the stability and order from which they are excluded. This is one of the horrors latent on board ship: what would happen if the crew rose against its tyrants? Roderick's advice to his fellow sufferers to bide their time does not lead to any rising, but it underlines the feeling that a small spark would be sufficient to set off a conflagration. It is in keeping with the picaresque formula that we may be taken to the edge of a fire, but not into it. The picaro exploits the chaotic situation to get into the social fabric rather than to tear it apart.

The anxiety that is at the heart of *Roderick Random* and that counterpoints the zest for adventure which fills the novel is related to the tension between disruption and restoration. It stems, above all, from the feeling that order is being threatened both from within the system and from below. The picaresque formula focuses on the chaotic experience, while the ending suggests the withdrawal that finds its supreme symbol in the rural retreat. The pastoral atmosphere of the final phase is in itself evidence of precariousness—the precariousness of a literary and social convention.

[1] Chandler, 22.
[2] Lesage, *The Adventures of Gil Blas of Santillane*, trans. Tobias Smollett (London: Walker and Co. et al., 1823) I, 3. Later references are included parenthetically in the text. Roman figures refer to volume, Arabic figures to page.
[3] Claude Guillén, 83.
[4] Parker, 121.
[5] As quoted in Paul-Gabriel Boucé, *The Novels of Tobias Smollett* (London: Longman, 1976) 31.
[6] Speck, 75
[7] Tobias Smollett, *Roderick Random* (London: J. M. Dent & Sons, 1975) 9. Later references are included parenthetically in the text.
[8] The process of "aristocratization" which Parker claims the picaresque is undergoing in *Gil Blas* is even more evident in the early pages—and later—in *Roderick Random*. Parker, 121.
[9] Lewis M. Knapp, *Tobias Smollett. Doctor of Men and Manners* (Princeton, N. J.: 1949) 316.
[10] Cf. Alice Green Fredman, "The Picaresque in Decline: Smollett's First Novel," *English Writers of the Eighteenth Century*, ed. John H. Middendorf (New York: Columbia University Press, 1971) 196 and 200.
[11] Guillén, "Toward a Definition of the Picaresque," *Proceedings of the Third Congress of the International Comparative Literature Association* (Utrecht: Mouton, 1962) 258 and note 13.
[12] Boucé, 106.
[13] Alter, 65.
[14] Richard Bjornson, "Victimization and Vindication in Smollett's *Roderick Random*," *Studies in Scottish Literature*, vol. XIII (1978) 198.
[15] Wicks, 242. Vide supra, p. 5.
[16] See Fredman, 190.
[17] Rogers, 63–64. See also George M. Kahrl, *Tobias Smollett Traveler-Novelist* (Chicago: University of Chicago Press, 1945) xix–xxiii.
[18] Smollett's prologue to *The Adventures of Ferdinand Count Fathom*.
[19] Rogers, 295.
[20] See Bjornson, 198.
[21] Fredman, 193.
[22] See Douglas Myers, "Scottish Schoolmasters in the Nineteenth Century: Professionalism and Politics," *Scottish Culture and Scottish Education 1800-1980*, eds. Walter M. Humes and Hamish M. Paterson (Edinburgh: John Donald Publishers, 1983) 76 and 80. The ideological implications of this model are dealt with in another article in this collection, by H. M. Patterson, "Incubus and Ideology...," 197 ff.
[23] The rush to London from Scotland apparently started when James I ascended the throne. Scott gives a graphic accont of a young Scottish nobleman's encounter with London, somewhat reminiscent of Roderick's, in *The Fortunes of Nigel* (1822).
[24] See J. D. Mackie, *A History of Scotland* (Harmondsworth: Penguin, 1979) 187. See also Kahrl on English "animosity toward the Scots" which was at its peak in the 1760's, 65–66.
[25] J. H. Plumb, *England in the Eighteenth Century* (Harmondsworth: Penguin, 1972) 107.
[26] Rogers, 11.
[27] Hill, 219.
[28] Hill, 220.
[29] See the account of Roderick's—and Smollett's—belief in social degree, rooted in their Scottish social milieu in M. A. Goldberg, *Smollett and the Scottish School* (Albuquerque: University of New Mexico Press, 1959) 31.
[30] Bjornson, 207.
[31] See Robert Giddings, *The Tradition of Smollett* (London: Methuen & Co., 1967) 84-85.

[32] See W. A. Speck, 50–53 and Basil Williams, *The Whig Supremacy 1714–1760* (London: Oxford University Press, 1962) 389–393.

[33] See John B. Owen, *The Eighteenth Century 1714–1815* (London: Nelson, 1974), 139–140.

[34] Paul-Gabriel Boucé, 111.

[35] Basil Williams, 128.

Chapter 4

The Picaresque Formula and the Mechanism of Socio-economic Change in Sir Walter Scott's *Rob Roy*

Rob Roy: I am but a poor man; but wit's better than wealth.[1]
Francis Osbaldistone: I welcomed the company of the outlaw leader (...) and was not without hopes, that through his means I might obtain some clew of guidance through the maze in which my fate had involved me (pp. 320–321).

The two quotations sum up two contrasting personalities. Rob Roy is active, outgoing, and bent on carving out his own fate. Francis Osbaldistone is introverted, acquiescent, and dependent on helpers. Rob's resourcefulness is a foil to Frank's bewilderment. Both wanderers in a community where most people are on the move, they also embody central features in the picaresque formula as it was developed in sixteenth- and seventeenth-century Spain. Like Frank, the picaro may find himself imprisoned in a maze of circumstance, but he can, like Rob, use his wit to adapt and make the most of his situation. The picaresque mode expresses two basic responses to the onus of existence: challenge and acquiescence.

At first glance, *Rob Roy* may seem very different from the picaresque novel. It is indeed steeped in the lore of the romance tradition. Scott was, however, as A. N. Wilson argues, "the happy prisoner of the literary traditions of his times, and drew on them all indiscriminately."[2] Besides, according to Northrop Frye, "no genre stands alone"[3], or remains static. Thus, filtered through the work of writers such as Lesage, Defoe, Fielding, and Smollett, the picaresque was no "pure" impulse by the time it reached *Rob Roy*. Moreover, in English fiction from Fielding onwards, it tends to merge with a powerful Quixotic strain. Scott makes clear his allegiance to *Don Quixote* at the outset of his first novel, *Waverley*.

We have seen how in the work of Defoe and Smollett the sense of the precariousness which characterizes the Spanish picaro deepened into the feeling of social and economic insecurity that pervaded the rising middle class in eighteenth-century Britain. The protagonist of their novels has become, in Alter's phrase, a "bourgeois picaroon".[4] Frank Osbaldistone, the protagonist of *Rob Roy*, is even more bourgeois than his immediate predecessors. He has also been infected with the late eighteenth-century bacillus of sentiment, and is, therefore, more susceptible to the traumatic impact of his experiences as a traveler.

In Scott's synthesizing imagination, a wide spectrum of narrative modes have been fused into a kind of novel that could express his awareness of the plight of the individual in a time fraught with social and economic change. It is the aim of this chapter on *Rob Roy* to study the manner in which Scott draws on elements in the picaresque formula to channel the protagonist's experience of existential anxiety and social turmoil. The discussion will focus on three central features in the formula: the inital act of *ejection* into the world, the resulting *journey*, and the sequence of *encounters* that constitute the protagonist's social experience.

The act of ejection with which *Rob Roy* begins is similar to that of *Roderick Random*, where the hero is forced to take to the road because his branch of the family has been disinherited. Destitution is the result of a deliberate act by the head of the family and not endemic in the milieu, as it is in the case of a Lazarillo or Colonel Jack at the outset of their careers. Frank is banished from London because he refuses to follow in his father's footsteps to become a merchant. His ambition is to be a poet. Frank's cousin Rashleigh takes his place in the firm, while Frank is exiled to his uncle's estate in Northumberland. Ironically, history appears to have repeated itself: Osbaldistone, senior, had been disinherited by his father when he insisted on going his own way. There must have been a touch of the picaro about young William Osbaldistone. Starting from scratch, he had achieved, through thrift and resourcefulness, commercial success. He could have adopted Rob's words—"Wit's better than wealth"—as his motto. Frank himself admits "you will find in my father a man who has followed the paths of thriving more for the exercise they afforded to his talents, than for the love of gold with which they are strewed" (p. 106).

William Osbaldistone and his father, a Northumberland squire, represent successive phases of socio-economic development. By sending Frank to Northumberland, old Osbaldistone initiates a journey back to his own starting point. The bustling business world of London fades into the background and is replaced by a community which is still in the throes of change. However, Frank, as a traveler, displays none of his father's resourcefulness. Like the typical Waverley hero, he is the one to whom things happen, although he never surrenders his stubborn moral integrity.

Frank's sense of freedom when he starts on his journey is the result of release from parental control: "I was lord of my person, and experienced that feeling of independence which the youthful bosom receives with a thrilling mixture of pleasure and apprehension" (p. 26). In addition, unlike the picaro proper, he has no economic worries: "My purse, though by no means amply replenished, was in a situation to supply all the wants and wishes of a traveller" (p. 26). Despite the vicissitudes he suffers later on, Frank is never, like Roderick Random, brought face to face with sheer want by the withdrawal of family support.

Nevertheless, Frank's sense of freedom evaporates almost immediately. His relief as he sees the towers of London recede behind him is replaced by a state of bewilderment. He shares the picaro's sense of being lost and abandoned, but because of his age and circumstances he is more acutely aware of his own inability to cope: "No schoolboy (...) could feel himself, when adrift in a strong current, in a situation more awkward than mine, when I found myself driving, without a compass, on the ocean of human life" (pp. 24–25). Shocked by the "unexpected ease in the manner in which my father slipt a knot, usually esteemed the strongest which binds society together," Frank feels degraded by having been treated "as a sort of outcast from his family" (p. 25). His self-confidence has been shaken. The pealing churchbells remind him of Dick Whittington. It is not, however, Dick's rags-to-riches story—rather like his own father's—that appeals to Frank. He does not see Dick as a poor boy who has still to make his way with his resourcefulness. He sees him as the Lord Mayor, the epitome of the world of comfort, wealth, and culture that he is now leaving behind (p. 25).

The journey takes the picaro from innocence, that is ignorance, to experience which is roguery and crime. Ignorance is at the heart of Frank's plight as a traveler. Traditionally, the journey involves encounters with lawlessness along the road. Frank has read about high-waymen and their exploits, but he has not been prepared for the real road. Despite his conviction that he "was born a citizen of the world" (p. 31), he has no idea of the real identity of fellow travelers like the pedlar Morris who later turns out to be a government agent, or Campbell, the illustrious Rob Roy. Least of all can he have any knowledge of the way these men are connected to his own fate.

Throughout, Frank's bewilderment is enhanced by his being utterly in the dark about the purpose of his journey. Convinced that there must be one, he feels more and more frustrated because no clear directives are ever given, nor are the motives of those who appear to guide him ever properly explained. After their last meeting in London, there is no direct communication between father and son. An impenetrable veil of mystery surrounds his father's movements. Later, we associate this mystery with Rashleigh's intrigues, but this circumstance heightens rather than resolves the oracular atmosphere that surrounds Frank's maze.

This element is part of the romance heritage which Scott exploits in the novel. Frank is cast in the role of the questing knight whose movements are guided by riddles. Old Osbaldistone's reference to "further instructions" (p. 24) is in the spirit of the Gothic romance, as is the whole plot of the novel. The problem is that these instructions never materialize, so the romance element in *Rob Roy* contains a touch of parody. If it is Frank's knightly mission to recover the lost heritage of his family, the bizarre reception he receives on his arrival and his own clumsiness soon surround him with a Don Quixotic aura. Although he is represented as a strong and agile young man, he nevertheless puts up a poor figure in the "dinosaur"[5] feudal milieu on his uncle's estate. He makes a fool of himself both as a sportsman and as a drinking companion. When Diana Vernon teasingly asks him, "'What *can* you do?'" he has to admit, "'Very little to the purpose.'" (p. 43).

Frank's journey from ignorance to experience involves a process of disillusionment. As in the picaro's case, this process has its roots in the experience of ejection. The process is complicated in Frank's case by the odd nature of his illusions: despite the fact that he appears to be utterly ignorant of his family in the north, his discovery that they are a bunch of buffoons is shocking to him. Like Lockwood in *Wuthering Heights,* he arrives with his middle-class London notions of behavior, and his cousins simply do not behave in the way he expects cousins to behave. His armor of conventionality cannot protect him, least of all when his self-confidence has already been undermined. The initiation ceremony through which Frank might have found his way back to his ancestral past is entirely abortive. Frank feels, if anything, more apart from his relatives when he leaves than when he arrived. His mission, if he had one, simply peters out. But even more frustrating is Frank's feeling of being surrounded by mysteries he cannot get at. He has no means of knowing that these mysteries are of a political nature. (The Northumberland estate is a Jacobite hiding place.) His outsider status is accentuated by the unwillingness of others to explain anything to him. He is never given more than hints, which he has no means of interpreting. Surrounded as he is by people who know but who cannot speak, and in love with Die Vernon, the very embodiment of mystification, he feels understandably frustrated and depressed as he continues his journey across the border and into the Scottish Highlands.

As when he started out from London, Frank gives the impression of being impelled to undertake a journey that is potentially futile because he has not been given any information at all. He is merely instructed to go to Scotland, first to Glasgow, and then to the Highlands, Rob Roy's country, to retrieve his father's fortune. He is completely ignorant of his father's difficulties beyond vague rumours that Rashleigh is behind them. He is equally in the dark about the forces behind this development as he was about the mysterious activities at Osbaldistone Hall. In addition, he has no idea what to do once he reaches his goal. It is as if willingness to serve is the only response that is required of him, a sign of faithfulness he shares with the hero of romance and fairy tale. In folktale fashion, he is provided with helpers and foes, but he is not called upon to do anything except venture into the wilderness. He is placed in situations that test his endurance and loyalty, but his ordeals, (for example, the midnight tryst on the bridge and in the prison in Glasgow), do not lead him anywhere, except into the Highland wilderness. In the manner of romance Frank has been furnished with a talisman, Diana's letter to Rob Roy, which he is to use in an emergency. Through this letter, the House of Osbaldistone is saved from Rashleigh's evil influence. But again, an atmosphere of futility surrounds the picture of Frank as a questing knight about to prove his manhood. The only thing he is requested to do is to burn the letter—the trivial action of a secret agent. The sequence of acts that release old Osbaldistone from the curse that is on him are beyond Frank's ken and control.

The sense of futility that pervades Frank's experience in the Highlands is akin to the picaro's sense of precariousness. The picaro and Frank share a state of anxiety because they have been thrown into a chaotic world. In *Rob Roy,* this feeling is deepened by continuous references to the bleakness of the landscape and its impenetrability to those without a guide. The unpredictable nature of the guides—the bizarre Andrew Fairservice and the flamboyant Rob Roy—adds to the nightmarish atmosphere of the novel.

The sense of moving through a topsy-turvy world on the borderline between dream and reality is particularly strong in the Glasgow section. The key of mystery is struck during Frank's visit to the Cathedral when an elusive stranger calls him to a meeting on the bridge at midnight. Then, the eeriness of the nightscene is deepened by the feeling one is given of moving through a silent world, with people passing to and from, without seeing Frank. Finally, there is the prison itself, like that in *The Heart of Midlothian,* a world of its own enclosed by the city. The sense of unreality is deepened by the manner in which Frank is conveyed into the prison through channels that work outside the law. The normal —law and order—has been suspended; the prince of the outlaws reigns supreme. An unbelievable meeting takes place between Rob Roy and Bailie Nicol Jarvie, normally the city's chief guarantor of peace and order. The prison is turned into a no-man's-land where the affairs of the House of Osbaldistone are discussed and a course of action, beyond Frank's reach, is decided upon.

Occurring as it does at the heart of the novel, the prison becomes the central image of Frank's precarious situation. The dreamlike quality of his sojourn in Scotland is deepened in his nightly encounter with Diana Vernon and her mysterious fellow traveler in the wilds of the Trossachs on the eve of the 1715 Jacobite rising. His recent dramatic escape from captivity, his futile love for Die, and his increasing sense of being dogged by mystery give Frank an eerie feeling of being imprisoned within elusive barriers. Significantly, the incident is followed by his decisive encounter with Rob, through whose resourcefulness and agility he is led back to normal, daylight society. The anxiety which accompanied Frank during his banishment from London deepens into the melancholy that seems to be his settled state of mind at the end of the novel. His eventual marriage to Diana Vernon, only mentioned in a brief sentence (p. 382), does not provide the haven that traditionally marks the end of the hero's vicissitudes.

In the course of his memorable Scottish interlude Francis Osbaldistone moves close to "the *essential picaresque situation.*" He is the unheroic protagonist-narrator of his own encounters with the chaotic world that he shares with the picaro. According to Wicks, the latter is alternately "victim of the world and its exploiter,"[6] but in this respect Frank and the picaro differ. In Scott's protagonist, the trend towards passivity, which we have detected in the heroes of Defoe and Smollett, culminates. Colonel Jack dissociates himself from the Artful Dodger approach to his surroundings because of his aspiration to be a gentleman, while Roderick Random's consciousness of being a gentleman by birth limits the scope of his activites drastically. Frank's class and upbringing form an even more insurmountable barrier between him and the down-and-out, but resourceful protagonist of *Lazarillo* or *El Buscón.*

The encounter, which is such an important element in the picaresque formula, is also prominent in traditional romance. Scott draws on both. The encounters in *Rob Roy* are important stages in the suspense plot of the novel. They are also signposts along Frank's road of development from adolescence to manhood, establishing the book's affinity with the *Bildungsroman.* But the encounters are no less important in bringing into focus impulses and forces at work in a community in the throes of socio-economic transformation. The nature of this process emerges in Frank's journey through bewilderment to social consciousness.

Frank's involuntary exile in the north coincides with a period of uncertainty in Scottish history. The Union of 1707 led, in the first place, to a rush to London by fortune hunters. As Defoe saw it, the "great men are posting to London for places and honours (...) I never saw so much trick, sham, pride, jealousy and cutting of friends' throats as there is among the noblemen",—so it was basically a situation in which picaros of the most resourceful kind thrive. Defoe's words are used by Christopher Harvie to illustrate the general trend in Scotland after the Union: "The ideal of austere independence had few takers; aristocrat and merchant alike looked south, the first attracted by political power and patronage, the second by an expanding English market (...)"[7] Henry Hamilton shows that Glasgow was quick to take the chance of establishing trade with Virginia and Maryland, thus initiating a "connexion [which] (...) enriched many houses in Glasgow", and paved the way for a period of rapid commercial expansion.[8] Resourcefulness might be the ticket to unprecedented wealth—or ruin, as was also the case for the adventurers portrayed in *Colonel Jack* and *Roderick Random*. The Union opened for Scottish merchants the door to the British trading empire, which by 1715 was well on its way to greatness. London merchant bankers had already the world as their playground.[9] Yet the future heralded by the Union had not yet taken shape when Francis Osbaldistone crossed the border into Scotland on the eve of the 1715 Rebellion. The wealth and stability that Scott felt were among the blessings of the Union were still only distant prospects.[10] Frank's feeling of being in a maze is therefore appropriate. The future was still in the balance, a circumstance which is underlined by the imminent Jacobite rising and the economic stagnation that prevailed in Scotland for quite some time after the Union.[11]

Frank carries with him from London the image of the businessman as a respectable pillar of society, who also has a streak of the adventurer in him. His father's firm is for him the symbol of stability and authority, yet it is endangered by scheming and speculation. It is this circumstance that sends Frank off as a wanderer to Scotland. The chain of mysterious happenings that pursues him on his journey through the northern part of the kingdom are rooted in the ambiguous nature of the activities and influence of the House of Osbaldistone. The firm has traditional links with Scotland through its Glasgow agents and their role as Government bankers. Even before the Union, "expatriate Scottish merchants" had settled down in London,[12] perhaps providing the network of contacts that the Osbaldistones needed for their activities in Scotland. In the hands of a plotter such as Rashleigh, the firm has become entangled in subversive activities, operated through the firm's far-flung, semi-secret network of business transactions. The very obscurity of all these matters gives the reader a feeling that forces are at work which threaten the old order (cf. pp. 239–241). It is intimated that capital is replacing muscular strength as the basis of power. The anonymity of the process contributes to the atmosphere of anxiety, which, as we have seen, pervades the novel.

A major source of anxiety is the Jacobite plot, which is tied up with the fortunes of the House of Osbaldistone. The sense of conspiracy contributes to Frank's feeling of being an outsider on his uncle's estate. He is rebuffed by mystery wherever he turns. Frank throughout is made to play the role of an ordinary young man suddenly transferred to a community where the individual seems to be exposed to the machinations of an inscrutable fate. As in the business mystery, we are given the illusion of watching one era evolving and another receding. The decisive turning point has not yet been reached; we are watching history in the making.

The year 1715 is only of marginal interest in the book since the act of rebellion takes place off stage at the end of the novel, but the possibility of a Jacobite rising is a real cause of anxiety. Even an outsider like Frank fears that "the Jacobites were on the eve of some desperate enterprise" (p. 170). Bailie Jarvie prophesies that "there will be an outbreak for the Stewarts" (p. 239) as a consequence of the new king's (George I) change of policy toward the clans. Economic problems are, significantly, shown to be at he heart of the unrest. It becomes increasingly clear that the Jacobites, through their links with an outmoded society, are clinging to a sinking ship. The 1715 uprising is shown to be entirely abortive: it "exploded prematurely, and in a part of the kingdom too distant to have any vital effect upon the country, which, however, was plunged into much confusion" (p. 354).

The role of the House of Osbaldistone in this affair is highly significant. In the hands of Rashleigh, who uses its resources to advance his own position of power, the firm might have come out in support of the Jacobites. As soon as Frank has been reconciled to his father and the firm is once more on safe ground, however, its resources are placed at the disposal of the Hanoverian government. After all, what could an obsolete party have achieved in the face of the "formidable body of monied interest" (p. 354) mustered by the London bankers? It is also a sign of the coming of a new dispensation when Frank is again sent to Northumberland, this time to take over his dead uncle's estate. A new order based on the alliance between land and trade has in the case of the Osbaldistones, as in many eighteenth-century aristocratic and upper-middle-class families replaced the old feudal community pattern. *Colonel Jack* reflects the successful merchant's dream of a pastoral retreat on an estate in England. In *Rob Roy*, the fusion between landed and monied interst is an image of the process which, after Culloden, led to the blossoming of "Scotland's golden age of intellect, invention and industry," resting on an "expanding middle class" and the Age of Improvement in agriculture.[13].

The nightmarish quality, which, as we have seen, is such a pervasive feature in the novel, is the product of Frank's encounters with a world in which the accustomed is forever exposed to attack from hidden sources of power and influence. A deepening sense of evil and lawlessness attaches to the story, adding a Gothic flavor of undefinable fear. Part of the power of the Glasgow chapters resides in the premonition of evil they convey to reader and protagonist alike. The presence of an actively operating principle of evil is increasingly associated with Rashleigh. Cast though he is in the traditional role of demonic villain, he derives his importance as an agent of terror from the circumstance that he is the link between the crisis in the firm of Osbaldistone and the process of transformation that the community as a whole is undergoing.

The sequence of encounters that constitutes the plot of the novel also marks the stages on a journey of discovery through contrasting types of social organization and experience. As a traveler and an outsider, Frank, like the picaro, traverses the country both geographically and socially. He may not be a gatecrasher[14] into the communities he visits, but he is made to enter one closed world after the other. In the course of the few months that his journey lasts, he moves from a state of baffled incomprehension to a state of sympathetic, though limited, understanding. He, like his colleagues among the Waverley heroes, is the "average English gentleman" who, according to Lukács, is such "a perfect instrument for Scott's way of presenting the totality of certain transitional stages of history".[15] In Frank's case, the picaresque situation of being outcast through rejection, together with the inability to respond to unfamiliar circumstances with an open mind, form psychological barriers which he often finds almost insurmountable.

This is most clearly seen in his relationship to Diana Vernon. In her he is confronted with a person brimful of vitality and whose "overfrankness of (...) manners" (p. 45) continually offends his sense of decorum. Furthermore, she persists in breaking out of the limited role he has been conditioned to expect from a lady, for example by insisting on being his guide. And she takes no notice of his stock response: "It is not proper, scarecely even delicate, in you to go with me on such an errand [to the Justice of the Peace] as I am now upon" (pp. 64-65). Through Diana, he is made aware of the dilemma of a woman of intelligence and independent spirit placed in a social and historical situation which provides no outlets for her energy and interests. Intensely aware of belonging to "an oppressed sect and antiquated religion" (p. 88), she is, like Flora McIvor in *Waverley*, prevented by her sex from standing up to its defence. Her special situation has probably made her particularly sensitive to the limitations fate has imposed on her as a woman: " 'I am a girl, and not a young fellow, and would be shut up in a madhouse, if I did half the things that I have a mind to; and that, if I had your happy prerogative of acting as you list, would make all the world mad with imitating and applauding me' " (p. 87).

Ironically, Frank is as much the prisoner of his temperament and upbringing as she is, being hardly ever able to wield his "happy prerogative". Diana is in the paradoxical situation of being out of step with history by being politically behind her times, but ahead of them as a woman. As it is, the only active role open to her is that of protectress and inspirer of action. Appealing to the conventional male response of sympathy for " 'a creature, motherless, friendless, alone in the world' " (p. 120), she urges Frank to action when he is faced with his father's ruin: " 'Every thing is possible for him who possesses courage and activity,' she said, with a look resembling one of those heroines of the age of chivalry, whose encouragement was wont to give champions double valour at the hour of need" (p. 148). Unfortunately, Frank does not have the

stature of a hero of romance. Her words underscore his powerlessness
rather than release manly action.

Through most of the novel, Rob Roy belongs to a world which is at
least as incomprehensible to Frank as that of Die. His community is as
inaccessible to the outsider as that of the Jacobites. From the outset, Rob
is the very exponent of dynamic activity. He is the noble outlaw who
comes and goes according to his own will and inclination, impervious to
the laws and demands of established society. At first glance, he appears
to represent an escape route from the exigencies with which the ordinary
mechanism of law and order seems unable to deal. Rob releases Frank
from the onus of vindicating his own and his family's interests by always
turning up at critical junctures. In the end, he, and not Frank, kills
Rashleigh as he is about to hand Diana, her father, and Frank over to the
authorities as Jacobite prisoners. Rob comes to represent justice *vis à vis*
intrigue and the letter of the law. However, through his wife we are also
made aware of the problematic nature of Rob's practice of taking the law
into his own hands. He acts as he does according to an outdated mode of
government. As chief of his clan, he considers it his prerogative to
punish his subjects, also with death. By 1715 this is the responsibility of
the state through its courts.[16] When Helen Macgregor, as Rob's deputy,
has the government agent Morris killed, it is thought of as cold-blooded
murder, the consequence of unrestrained violence. The ancient rights of
the head of the clan are rejected as morally inadmissible.

Frank's encounters with Rob and Bailie Jarvie during his sojourn in
the Highlands are means of evaluating contrasting phases of social
development. The two show remarkable awareness of the links between
the individual and his environment at a critical period.

Jarvie combines a prominent position in the city of Glasgow with that
of successful merchant. Indeed, the Bailie's breakfast table is evidence of
the thriving commerce between Glasgow and distant lands (p. 217).[17]
Through prudence and shrewdness, he carries on and expands the business activities of his father. The harmonious growth of the House of
Jarvie appears in striking contrast to the Osbaldistones' record of disharmony between the generations. His famous vision of an agricultural
paradise in a drained Loch Lomond (p. 347) is firmly rooted in his
pragmatic temperament and also in keeping with the improving spirit
of the times. "Let Glasgow flourish!" is his, as well as the city's, motto. In
his view, credit is superior to honour as man's guiding virtue (p. 231).
William Osbaldistone has similar priorities: arithmetic is to him more
important than "all the blazonry of chivalry" (p. 94). Jarvie is, however,
akin to Rob Roy. He admits that " 'the Hieland blude o' me warms at
thae daft tales' " of Rob's feats as an outlaw (p. 238). In his conversations
with Frank, he displays knowledge as well as understanding concerning
the circumstances which had made Rob and his clan outlws. At their
first meeting, he explains that " 'the agriculture, the pasturage, the

fisheries, and every species of honest industry about the country, cannot employ the one moiety of the population' " (p. 234). Rob, once " 'a weel-doing, pains-taking drover' ", (p. 236) became, according to the Bailie, an outlaw through necessity (p. 237). The feeling that Rob belongs to an oppressed race is further underlined in conversations between Rob, Jarvie, and Frank. Rob has turned down Jarvie's offer of training his sons in business with contempt—" 'My sons weavers!' " (p. 330). Yet he admits to Frank that he is " 'vexed for the bairns—I'm vexed when I think o' Hamish and Robert living their father's life' " (p. 335). However, he has been " 'forced to become (…) what I am (…) branded as an outlaw,—stigmatized as a traitor (…) hunted like an otter' " (pp. 334–335). He speaks for his people in a passionate appeal to Frank for sympathy and understanding:

> "But Remember, at least, we have not been unprovoked—we are a rude and an ignorant, and it may be a violent and passionate, but we are not a cruel people—the land might be at peace and in law for us, did they allow us to enjoy the blessings of peaceful law. But we have been a persecuted generation.' (p. 338).

The Bailie shows his instinctive sympathy by adding: " 'And persecution (…) maketh wise men mad!' " (p. 338).

The kinship and latent sympathy between Rob and the Bailie indicate that they "carry within themselves the healing balm of reconciliation"[18] which may well herald a future state of peaceful coexistence between Highlands and Lowlands.[19] In Scott's view, such a state had been achieved by his time. However, the book does not end on such a note. The feudal remnant that Rob heads cannot survive through amalgamation with the Glasgow community of weavers and merchants. Nor can Rob be reconciled to the government. In the eyes of the authorities, he is a criminal, while they are oppressors in his. The most he can achieve is "the connivance of government to his self-elected office of Protector of the Lennox" (p. 383).

Rob's resourcefulness enables him to survive. In his continous battle with necessity through his prowess and wit, he resembles the picaro more than any other character in the novel. Jarvie, equally ready to grasp the chance that the moment offers, possesses a vitality of spirit which enables him to survive as well a as advance within the framework of a society at the threshold of a new age. The spirit of adventure is in Jarvie's case kept in check by his prudence, humanity, and tolerance. With him as a guide, Frank returns to sanity, the House of Osbaldistone recovers from its South Sea Bubble period, and a strife-torn nation may at least dream of the reconcilitation Scott felt the Union eventually achieved.

We are given a sense of withdrawal from the world of chaos and turmoil that fills most of the novel, suffusing it with a persistent sense of uncertainty and fear. A. O. J. Cockshut refers to "the anarchic and romantic strain" in Scott which penetrates his conventional Tory makeup and makes him respond with sympathy to the victims of harsh social circumstances, for example, the gypsies in *Guy Mannering*. With his banishment from his customary environment, Frank is given the shock he needs to move through existential anxiety to social consciousness. The process involves a perception of the abyss of chaos[20] as well as a dawning understanding of the mechansm behind socio-economic change.

The sense of withdrawal is deepened in the final reference to Rob Roy. He survives as a legend, being "still remembered in his country as the Robin Hood of Scotland, the dread of the wealthy, but the friend of the poor" (p. 383). As a fairy tale figure, Rob has survived the process of change, which, by the time the novel was written, had transformed Glasgow, from the "large stately and well-built city ... one of the cleanliest, most beautiful and best built cities in Great Britain "that Defoe saw in the early years of the eighteenth century into a neglected and slum-ridden city of vast proportions, the victim of unbridled industrial expansion.[21]

The perennial appeal of Rob Roy relates to the haves/have-nots conflict, which by Scott's time had deepened into the gulf between the two nations which the "Condition of England" writers were to deal with in the 1840s. The dynamic principle which Rob stands for merges with the disruptive force of social injustice in the epigrammatic final lines of the novel. Stressing Rob's role as a legendary figure, they also bring into focus "the impossibility of the old life in the new world"[22].

By exploiting the resources of the picaresque formula Scott "defamiliarized" the time-honoured genre of romance. He was thus able to respond to historical change in all its kaleidoscopic magnificence, while at the same time paving the way for the heyday of social realism.

[1] Sir Walter Scott, *Rob Roy* (London: Dent [Everyman's Library], 1976) 209. All further references, included parenthetically in the text, are to this edition.

[2] A. N. Wilson, *The Laird of Abbotsford. A View of Sir Walter Scott* (Oxford: Oxford University Press, 1980) 75.

[3] Northrop Frye, *The Secular Scripture* (Cambridge, Mass.: Harvard University Press, 1976) 4.

[4] Alter, 35 (the title of chapter III).

[5] Wilson, 10. Wilson uses the phrase to describe characters in the Waverley novels who refuse to accept the idea of change.

[6] Wicks, 242. Vide supra, p. 11.

[7] Christopher Harvie, *Scotland and Nationalism* (London: George Allen and Unwin, 1977) 63-64.

[8] Henry Hamilton, *The Industrial Revolution in Scotland* (London: Frank Cass & Co., 1966) 4.

[9] Cf. Christopher Hill, 159-160, 244.

[10] See Avrom Fleishman, *The English Historical Novel* (Baltimore: John Hopkins University Press, 1977) 69-70; T. C. Smout, *A History of the Scottish People 1560-1830* (Glasgow: Collins, 1975) 195-196.

[11] See T. M. Devine, "The Scottish Merchant Community, 1680-1740," *The Origins and Nature of the Scottish Enlightenment*, eds. R. H. Campbell and Andrew Skinner (Edinburgh: John Donald Publishers, 1982) 26.

[12] Devine, 32.

[13] John Prebble, *The Lion in the North* (Harmondsworth: Penguin, 1973) 302.

[14] Parker, 5.

[15] Georg Lukács, *The Historical Novel* (London: Merlin Press, 1965) 33, 35.

[16] According to Smout, the transfer of jurisdiction from chieftain to the state was a slow process. Private courts persisted, "but the rights of this jurisdiction (...) did not extend any longer to executing the guilty". Smout, 314.

[17] Smout, 358. See also Henry Hamilton, Vide supra, pp. 72-73.

[18] E. M. W. Tillyard, *The Epic Strain in the English Novel* (London: Chatto & Windus, 1958) 101.

[19] Duncan Forbes underlines Scott's concern with "the progress of civilization,"" in the spirit of Montesquieu and the eighteenth-century "philosophical historians". "Scott's stories," he writes, "do not hinge on psychological conflict, but on the contrast between different 'degrees of civilization' and 'states of society', especially between Highland and Lowland." "The Rationalism of Sir Walter Scott", *Cambridge Journal*, vol. 7 (1953) 28 and 31-32.

[20] A. O. J. Cockshut, *The Achievement of Walter Scott* (London: Collins, 1969) 33, 39-40.

[21] Cf. T. C. Smout, 355-356. I am also indebted to Smout for the Defoe quotation.

[22] David Daiches, *Literary Essays* (Edinburgh: Oliver and Boyd, 1956) 113.

Chapter 5

The Picaresque Formula
and the Struggle for Socio-economic
Survival in William Makepeace
Thackeray's *Vanity Fair*

Defoe's intense awareness of his career as fortune's plaything no doubt
contributes to the reader's sense of authenticity and sympathy in his
encounters with Moll Flanders, Colonel Jack, or Roxana. Both Smollett
and Scott also experienced the vicissitudes of fortune in their own professional lives. They must have felt that they were emotionally on a wavelength with characters who suddenly find that they are faced with an
uncertain future, without money and protection. Thackeray, too, found
himself in an economically precarious situation after his carefree and
secure life at school and university. As a young man, ready to embark
upon the world, he, like many a picaro, lost his fortune through
gambling and the unpredictable fluctuations of the money market. A
similar anxiety and a deep sense of precariousness are recurrent features
in the novels with which we have been dealing. They also provide an
emotional substratum in *Vanity Fair*.

Sixty years ago, Percy Lubbock chose *Vanity Fair* as example of the
panoramic novel in which character and action are shown against a vast
social and historical background. "Thackeray saw [his novels] as broad
expanses, stretches of territory, to be surveyed from edge to edge with a
sweeping glance."[1] Gordon Ray refers to Thackeray's "profound inno-
vation" as a novelist, who used "fiction to convey a comprehensive vision of the social organism", something no one had tried to do since Fielding.[2] Indeed, the title *Vanity Fair*, the term "panoramic", and the puppet
theatre machinery all underline the visual, theatrical lay-out of the book.

This feature is countered by a dynamic element that can be traced to
the storyteller's traditional preoccupation with the interaction between
character and environment. The picaresque formula helped Thackeray
to focus on the manner in which contrasting characters respond to their
circumstances. Their behavior is determined by their background in
institutions within the community, but they also illustrate the scope of
individual action within power structures that are rigid as well as fluid,
but which favor insiders. Money rather than birth is the secret weapon
that gives the outsider a foothold on the social pyramid. Thackeray thus

illuminates the change of emphasis which took place in England during the Industrial Revolution. At the same time, he reveals the tenacity of the old class system, acting as a barrier to keep insiders in and outsiders out.

Vanity Fair demonstrates the vitality of the picaresque formula. It assumes situations and movements that reveal the structure of the social instutions portrayed in the novel. It shows the reader the mechanism behind the process which turned England into a "ready-money" society.[3] The puppetmaster and his show display universal aspects of the code of human behavior. The picaresque impulse takes the author to a period in history when the old order lingered on, while the new was still in the making. The resulting instability may hit the outsider severely because he has no reserves, but it also provides him with opportunities for climbing. It is the aim of this chapter to explore the use Thackeray makes of the picaresque formula in *Vanity Fair* to reveal the way that the facade of the social system was cracking and the extent to which this resulted in social mobility. In his dual concern with the puppet and the picaro, Thackeray takes the reader to the heart of a bitter struggle for socio-economic survival.

The explorer of the picaresque mode has to cover a lot of stony ground as he moves into the world of Victorian fiction. The interest at the time in stories about rogues and criminals (the Newgate novels), as well as the growing concern with social realism would seem to predispose writers for the naturalism of the picaresque tradition. On the other hand the moral squeamishness of the period and the appeal of a wide range of narrative modes tended to modify and dilute the picaresque element. The erosion of "the formal and thematic distinctions between the Quixotic and the picaresque" in nineteenth-century criticism and fiction had, however, as Walter L. Reed points out, been started in eighteenth-century fiction.[4]

No writer was more conscious of his literary heritage than Thackeray. He saw himself as the successor of writers such as Fielding, Smollet, and Scott. And these writers, along with the Spanish and French influence behind them, constitute a literary filter through which the picaresque impulse passes into Thackeray's fiction. They also act as a standard of perfection toward which he strives in his work. His sensitivity to the manner and style of his predecessors was a useful instrument when he wrote such historical novels as *Barry Lyndon* (1844), written in the manner of an eighteenth-century picaresque novel *á la* Smollett's *Ferdinand Count Fathom*. The book is, however, of less interest as a clever pastiche than as evidence of Thackeray's grasp of the picaresque formula.

Barry Lyndon conforms to the picaresque prototype by being the first-person retrospective memoir of an Irish vagabond rogue. Recurrent in the novel is Barry's emphasis on his initial poverty and outcast state, and on the manner in which he reaches wealth and power through his own talents and energy. His hold on success, however, is as precarious as that of any picaro. Luck is a fickle mistress, and again and again he is left to his own wit and resources. In a manner which anticipates *Vanity Fair*, Barry Lyndon is shown moving through a society in turmoil as a result of the disrupting impact of war, and having lost its moral bearings, it provides a hothouse atmosphere for parasites of every description. The reader is, however, never allowed to forget the pastiche element. We see *Barry Lyndon* as a novel that recreates a bygone age and imitates a genre. Despite the puppet-theatre paraphernalia of *Vanity Fair*, we are made to feel that in this novel Thackeray uses his literary heritage to blaze ar trail into the jungle of his own society.

Vanity Fair opens on a picaresque note. The doors of a new world are about to open as those of the old—the apparently secure world of childhood and adolescence—are closing. Two young ladies are ready to enter a waiting carriage. The contrast between them is striking. One is gentle and rich, and made much of by everybody; the other is poor and friendless, but steals the show with her act of defiance. The two girls are the famous pair, Amelia Sedley and Rebecca Sharp, whose fortunes form contrasting plot structures in the novel. Becky is from the outset cast in the mould of the traditional picara, while Amelia is akin to the social stereotype which embodies the ideal middle-class young woman in best-selling fiction of the time. In the course of the novel, she moves close to the dilemma which faces the protagonists of *Roderick Random* and *Rob Roy*: how to survive when hit by dire necessity. Amelia and her nearest family are reduced to poverty, but she never has to fend for herself like Becky and her fellow rogues. She is cast in the role of victim, while Becky is of the Artful Dodger brood. In his two heriones Thackeray completes the dichotomy between rogue and honest poor which was started in eighteenth-century fiction, perhaps under the influence of Lesage's *Gil Blas*. This development highlights two complementary trends in nine-teenth-century literature and society: on the one hand, there is the dream of achieving prosperity and social advancement through one's own talents and efforts, on the other, there is the dream of the retreat, the respectable but inactive status of gentleman.

Chapter one is an interesting variation of the initial stage of ejection in the picaresque formula. Attention is focused on Becky's situation on the fringes of respectable middle-class society. When she throws Dr. Johnson's *Dictionary* back at the well-meaning giver, Miss Jemima, Becky is getting her own back on Miss Pinkerton, who has already rejected her and is now trying to ignore her. In chapter two, we are told that Becky had been admitted to the Academy because Miss Pinkerton thought the school might benefit from the orphan's proficiency in French and music in return for a garret room and "scraps of knowledge" (p. 49).[5] Gradually she realizes that she has found more than her match

tuning- the
. ignoring.

in Becky, who in the end refuses to be used. The leave-taking scene between the two is a subtle ceremony of mutual rejection. Ushered into Miss Pinkerton's august presence, Becky immediately gains the upper hand by speaking French to her:

> Miss Pinkerton did not understand French (…) but biting her lips and throwing up her venerable and Roman-nosed head (…) she said, "Miss Sharp, I wish you a good-morning." (…) she waved one hand, both by way of adieu, and to give Miss Sharp an opportunity of shaking one of the fingers of the hand which was left out for that purpose.
>
> Miss Sharp only folded her own hands with a very frigid smile and bow, and quite declined to accept the proffered honour; on which Semiramis tossed up her turban more indignantly than ever. In fact, it was a little battle between the young lady and the old one, and the latter was worsted. "Heaven bless you, my child," said she, embracing Amelia, and scowling the while over the girl's shoulder at Miss Sharp (pp. 44–45).

Chapter one nevertheless ends on a note of exclusion: the leave-taking ceremony is over, and "the drawing-room door closed upon them for ever.… The carriage rolled away; the great gates were closed; the bell rang for the dancing lesson. The world is before the two young ladies; and so, farewell to Chiswick Mall" (p. 45). The sense of exclusion is, however, balanced by a sense of escape. We are reminded of Pip's feelings in *Great Expectations* when he sets out on his journey from village to metropole. The difference is that by the time he sits down to write his memoirs, the world he left behind has become an irrevocably lost Garden of Eden, while Becky always thinks of Chiswick Mall as a prison. After years of humiliating submission, she now has the chance of securing herself a place in respectable society, first as Amelia's guest and confidante in her comfortable London merchant family, then as governess in the service of Sir Pitt, one of the landed gentry.

Becky thus embarks upon her wanderings through a process of ejection which is as irrevocable as that of Alemán's and Quevedo's protagonists. Besides, she is an orphan, left to fend for herself in an indifferent and hostile environment—a familiar situation in picaresque novels. She is, however, very different from Lazarillo and Colonel Jack in their first phase. They are pathetic figures when we first meet them because they have not yet lost their innocence and are thus unable to look after themselves. Despite Becky's small size and childlike appearance, she is already well versed in the ways of the world: we are told that "she had the dismal precocity of poverty (…) she never had been a girl (…) she had been a woman since she was eight years old." Her father "was very proud of her wit"—the weapon she became such a master at wielding (p.

49). Her bohemian environment had corrupted her by the time she was admitted to Miss Pinkerton's Academy.

The orphan is the supreme image of the picaro's outcast state, but he also exploits it to hold his own in the world. In the same way, Becky both is and poses as an orphan picara. The picture we are given of the woman who has never been a child is one of Becky's self-portraits. Her play-acting is from the beginning a major channel for her resourcefulness. With this gift, she gains admission to circles which would otherwise have been closed to her. The skill with which she plays on the orphan image to gain access to respectable society is demonstrated in the chapters about Becky's adventures in London.

Becky strikes the orphan pose the moment she enters the Sedley household. She "said, with perfect truth, 'that it must be delightful to have a brother,' and easily got the pity of the tender-hearted Amelia, for being alone in the world, an orphan without friends or kindred" (p. 54). She follows up this pose with that of a conventionally brought up middle-class girl, whose proficiency in knitting is a major asset. While she thus fulfills respectable society's expectations by pretending to be a well-brought-up-angel-in-the-house kind of girl, she is busy scheming her own social advancement through marriage to Joseph Sedley. As she has no mother to do the job for her, she has to take on the "task of husband-hunting" herself (p. 57). Mrs. Sedley suspects Becky of trying to catch her son, and warns her husband that she is up to something. But they are easily duped when Becky next puts on her orphan act:

> One day, Amelia had a headache, and could not go upon some party of pleasure to which the two young people were invited: nothing could induce her friend to go without her. "What! you who have shown the poor orphan what happiness and love are for the first time in her life—quit *you?* never!" and the green eyes looked up to Heaven and filled with tears; and Mrs. Sedley could not but own that her daughter's friend had a charming heart of her own (p. 63).

In the end Becky's scheming is of no avail, and she leaves the Sedley household as an outcast. She has been deserted by everybody—"high and low" — except Amelia. Not even her appeal to Mr. Sedley to be "her kind, kind friend and protector" (p. 100) can change the course of events which take her into yet another new world, that of Queen's Crawley.

By now it is clear that a new world to Rebecca, as to the picaro, means new opportunities as well as starting all over again. The wheel of fortune has not brought her further up the social ladder, but it has offered her another chance in a double-or-quit kind of game. When Becky and Amelia leave Miss Pinkerton's Academy, they are both conscious of entering a new world. The phrase has, however, different meanings to them: "For Amelia it was quite a new, fresh, brilliant world, with all the bloom upon it. It was not quite a new one for Rebecca (…) At all events, if Rebecca was not beginning the world, she was beginning it over again" (p. 53).

There is this same feeling of starting from scratch with undaunted energy about the passage that gives us a close-up of Becky in Sir Pitt's gloomy London flat after her departure from the Sedleys. Sir Pitt and his premises are very different from what she had expected from a family belonging to the gentry. Despite her lonely and outcast state, she appears quite cheerful: "Rebecca lay awake for a long, long time, thinking of the morrow, and of the new world into which she was going, and of her chances of success there" (p. 107).

Becky's stoic and cheerful acceptance of what fate offers her are in accordance with the picaresque formula, as is the resourcefulness with which she faces her new milieu. The image she now presents to the world is that of competent governess who knows her place and behaves according to the rules. Again she poses as an outcast orphan, who sees it as her "duty to make herself (…) agreeable to her benefactors, and to gain their confidence" (p. 125). We are shown "the friendless girl" reflecting on her essentially picaresque situation: "'I am alone in the world (…) I have nothing to look for but what my own labour can bring me (…) Well, let us see if my wits cannot provide me with an hourable maintenance" (p. 125), and she repeats her determination to be her own mother.

Becky shows great skill at adapting herself to her new environment. She soon makes herself indispensable, first to Sir Pitt, then to his sister, the rich Miss Crawley whose favor everybody seeks to secure because of her money. Becky exploits her inferior social position to the full, but she also hints that she belongs to an impoverished branch of an ancient French noble family. She thus plays a double role — that of Cinderella and that of princess in disguise—both with great potential appeal in a rank-oriented society. Becky usurps the position of companion in Miss Crawley's London household and shows "indomitable patience" during her illness. The self-control she displayed at Miss Pinkerton's as long as she could benefit from such behavior is again in evidence: "During the illness she was never out of temper; always alert (…) she was always smiling, fresh and neat" (p. 173).

Becky's success in the Crawley family is the result of careful calculation: "Nothing escaped her; and, like a prudent steward, she found a use for everything" (p. 173). As in the Sedley interlude, she seeks to gain access to the class to which she is attached as an outsider through marriage. She selects Rawdon Crawley, Sir Pitt's younger son, as her prey because he seems most vulnerable and, above all, because he appears to be in line for Miss Crawley's money. Her secret marriage to Rawdon is, however, also evidence of Becky's limitations as a strategist. She had not anticipated that her scheming and charm had won her Sir

Pitt as well as his son. What could have been her greatest hour — when Sir Pitt proposes to her—is the beginning of her decline in the Crawley family. Her next miscalculations are running away with Rawdon and confessing her secret marriage to him. She had not expected Miss Crawley to disinherit Rawdon and refuse to be reconciled to her nephew. Instead of marrying into an ancient aristocratic family, and thus achieving social and economic security, she finds herself married to a penniless, outcast husband. Despite her skill in learning the language and manners of the class to which she aspires, Becky is still an outsider, at best considered as an upstart who pretends to a rank she has not got. The incident reveals a streak of impulsiveness beneath Becky's mask of cool calculation which was also in evidence when she flung the dictionary back at Miss Jemima. The way she made her marriage to Rawdon known indicates a certain urge to throw caution to the wind. The "limitations" in Becky's character to which Barbara Hardy refers, her "ineffiencies and her failures"[6] may be the result of a certain devil-may-care strain in her, perhaps part of her bohemian heritage, leading to unexpected eruptions of carelessness and playfulness. This untamed gypsy quality is also part of the lawless strain in the picaro.

Becky may have regretted that "a piece of marvellous good fortune should have been so near her, and she actually obliged to decline it" (p. 192). But her picaresque equanimity prevails: "Rebecca was a young lady of too much resolution and energy of character to permit herself much useless and unseemly sorrow for the irrevocable past; so (...) she wisely turned her whole attention towards the future" (p. 193). Therefore she, like the picaresque prototype, "surveyed her position, and its hopes, doubts, and chances" (p. 193), and acts accordingly.

So far Becky has, like the picaro, achieved geographic mobility through her forays into respectable society, but she remains socially displaced. From now on, her efforts are aimed at establishing her family credentials. Her marriage to Rawdon may not have improved her position financially, but she now can claim the benefits of his genealogy instead of spending so much energy on establishing her own doubtful claims to nobility. She can concentrate on the long-term plan of achieving reconciliation with Rawdon's family. In the meantime, she turns him into her obedient and admiring tool. Then she exploits the social and political turmoil of the Waterloo period to flirt her way into high society. While thousands of soldiers are dying on the battlefield, a merciless fight for survival is taking place among the parasites who followed the troops to Belgium. Becky's proudest moment so far is her entry into Brussels:

> In the midst of a little troop of horsemen, consisting of some of the greatest persons in Brussels, Rebecca was seen in the prettiest and tightest of riding habits, mounted on a beautiful little Arab, which

she rode to perfection (...) and by the side of the gallant General Tufto (p. 333).

Cinderella has been replaced by the princess in the image Becky presents to the world.

However, Becky has to fight tooth and nail for her position—the eternal fate of the upstart. Significantly, her royal manner is combined with her obsession with hoarding money and valuables. She is as proud of her prudence and thrift as Moll Flanders. The reward for her social triumph in Brussels appears in the inventory of her fortune that she makes after her husband has gone with his regiment to fight Napoleon in the battle of Waterloo. She sells her horses to Jos Sedley at an exorbitant price. The sum of money she got from him was

> so large as to be a little fortune to Rebecca, who rapidly calculated that with this sum and the sale of the residue of Rawdon's effects, and her pension as a widow should he fall, she would now be absolutely independent of the world, and might look her weeds steadily in the face (p. 378).

Becky's callous, calculating behavior is in keeping with the picaresque formula which assumes that self-interest takes precedence in the fight for survival. Becky is, as Kathleen Tillotson reminds us, "the triumphant knave in a world of knaves and fools." Our enjoyment of her skill "is not complicated by pity for the less successful knaves (...) nor yet for the fools."[7] Thackeray may strain our sense of enjoyment in this and later scenes, but one should bear in mind the merciless nature of the world of intrigue in which she moves, where one must either sink or swim.

This becomes increasingly clear as Becky seeks to consolidate her foothold in high society in the post-Waterloo world. She turns her marriage to Rawdon into a perfect rogues' union, in which he is the professional gambler and she the queen of every ball and social gathering. She "had a little European congress on her reception night" in Paris, out-maneuvring Lady Bareacres and "the chiefs of the English society [who] (...) writhed with anguish at the success of the little upstart Becky" (p. 413).

Rebecca, like the picaro, shows the world that it is possible to "live well on Nothing a Year" (p. 426), first in Paris and then in London. She is eventually reconciled to the Crawley family, although this does not lead to any financial improvement. Above all, she fights her way into the highest circles of society through her wit and charm. She is more ruthless than ever. Her greatest hour is when she is received at court, but to get there she has had to ride rough-shod over anybody foolish enough to let themselves be used. Basically as alone as she has always been, she is prepared to pay any price for a secure position as high up in society as possible. The precariousness of her situation is underlined by her quick transition from royal splendor—her departure from her residence in the Crawley family coach, when everybody shows her deference—to rags— her being stripped of her jewels after her husband has detected her affair with Lord Steyne.

Becky has practised every art in her possession to reach the summit from which she is so violently pushed. She had exploited the orphan image and the role of the loving and thrifty wife and mother to ingratiate herself with Sir Pitt and his family, while she used her royal manner to qualify as a leading lady. But like the occasion that precipitates her fall from favor in the Crawley household, the Steyne affair reveals the strain of carelessness in her character which at critical moments defies her cal- culating spirit. Critics have tended to take Becky severely to task for her heartless behavior toward her son and husband.[8] It could be argued that Thackeray loads the dice against her by transforming Rawdon from a rogue to a decent and hen-pecked husband. Yet Becky is, in fact, consist- ent in her behavior toward her fellow human beings, however close they are to her. She continues her habit of hoarding valuables to achieve the economic and social security she lacked as an orphaned outcast. Abject poverty is the nightmare behind the history of her arduous social climbing.

However, Rebecca also carries with her from her bohemian childhood the picaro's cheerful defiance of rules and conventions. Her compulsive pursuit of security, the circumstance that "to be, and to be thought, a respectable woman, was Becky's aim in life" (p. 556), are at the heart of her scheming. Her secret weapon is her ability to deceive and put on a show: "she got up the genteel with amazing assiduity, readiness, and success" (p. 556). But her skill as a performer is not only an expedient she uses to secure her position as respectable lady. She enjoys her role, and yet tires of it, which is in keeping with the bohemian strain in her. At the height of her social success in Paris, she feels bored (p. 432). When "she moved among the very highest circles of the London fashion [her] success excited, elated, and then bored her" (p. 587). Becky imagines herself in a number of roles that are all subversive in relation to the high society position to which she aspires: "'I would rather be a parson's wife, and teach a Sunday School than this; or a sergeant's lady, and ride in the regimental waggon; or, O how much gayer it would be to wear spangles and trousers, and dance before a booth at a fair' " (p. 587). It is not difficult to imagine which of these roles Becky would prefer: The role of parson's wife may not seem to be quite her cup of tea, but it is quite close to the pastoral dream which she at least affects when she visits Queen's Crawley. All the roles represent a simple way of life in which scheming and intrigue are of little consequence.

However, alternative modes of life in Becky's case are available only after a fall. She may toy with bohemianism in her affair with Lord

Steyne and prove herself to be a brilliant actress in the tableaux she puts on. However, only for brief moments does she allow herself to forget her main goal of social advancement. The bohemian existence we see her lead after the collapse of her marrige to Rawdon Crawley is not of her own choosing. Her exile is preceded by the scene in which Rawdon rejects her. Total rejection follows, on all social levels: by Lord Steyne, by the Crawleys, and by the servants, who desert her, taking all the valuables they can lay their hands on. Becky, now a complete outcast, vanishes from the scene, to where, no one knows, or cares (p. 647).

When we meet Becky again in Pumpernickel, the bohemian strain in her has supplanted, but not eradicated, the urge to be a respectable lady. In a series of short flashbacks, largely provided by Becky herself, we are shown the downhill course of her fortunes, but also her indomitable spirit. Again she practises the art of making "a little money go a great way" (pp. 647-648). We hear of her poverty and degradation, and of her endless struggle to be readmitted to respectable society. The princess in her survives in the "boarding-house queen" we glimpse in Paris (p. 747). Yet her triumphs are always short-lived: "Whenever Becky made a little circle for herself with incredible toils and labour, somebody came and swept it down rudely, and she had all her work to begin over again. It was (...) very hard; lonely and disheartening" (p. 744). In incidents like this one, we move close to the Sisyphus rhythm of the picaresque novel.[9] She tries hard at one point to keep "in the paths of virtue and good repute" under the guardianship of a rich old lady, but, as one would expect, "the life of humdrum virtue grew tedious to her before long." Although she sinks further down the social scale, she prefers the boardinghouse world because she "loved society, and, indeed, could no more exist without it than an opium-eater without his dram" (p. 745). Her growing "taste for disrespectability" (p. 747) draws her towards a bohemian way of life, which excites her, despite its vagabond, unpredictable character. When Amelia and her company meet Becky in Pumpernickel, she strikes them as a lady who has come down in the world. She has, however, retained her vitality, and she has not forgotten her old tricks. In Pumpernickel, she appears to have reached a point of equilibrium between the schemer and bohemian in her character:

> Becky liked the life. She was at home with everybody in the place, pedlars, punters, tumblers, students and all. She was of a wild, roving nature, inherited from father and mother, who were both Bohemians, by taste and circumstance; if a lord was not by, she would talk to his courier with the greatest pleasure; the din, the stir, the drink; the smoke, the tattle of Hebrew pedlars (...) the songs and swagger of the students, and the general buzz and hum of the place had pleased and tickled the little woman, even when her luck was down, and she had not the wherewithal to pay her bill (p. 755).

This is as close to Paradise as Becky ever gets. The novel closes on a much more sordid note. With her marriage to Jos Sedley, Becky achieves the respectability she has yearned for all her life. Soon afterward, her husband dies under suspicious circumstances, which are suppressed by the family. Our final view of Becky shows her posing as a well-off widow, isolated from her family, who "busies herself in works of piety. She goes to church, and never without a footman. Her name is in all the Charity Lists" (p. 796). Despite her conventionality, she is as controversial a figure as ever.

The wheel-of-fortune arc described by the Becky plot has that of Amelia as its foil, as the two characters are compementary figures. Amelia's story and personality are of less interest than Becky's, but are nevertheless of vital importance to the texture and meaning of the novel. Tillotson refers to the structural balance between the two "heriones" in the novel.[10] Lord David Cecil shows how the contrasting curves of their careers bring out the manner in which the inhabitants of *Vanity Fair* are "slave[s] of circumstance" with no chance of escape.[11]

Becky's lifelong attraction to Amelia is rooted in the dichotomy in her character between the respectable and the bohemian. Becky, the "young misanthropist", is, in contrast to Amelia, convinced that "all the world used her ill" (p. 47). She fastens on the merchant's daughter to escape from her inferior social position and to avenge herself on this vaguely defined enemy. Becky's ambiguous feelings towards Amelia and the society she represents surface in Becky's dream at Queen's Crawley of the day when she can show "Miss Amelia my real superiority over her. Not that I dislike poor Amelia: who can dislike such a harmless, good-natured creature?—only it will be a fine day when I can take my place above her in the world (p. 125).

A major reason for Becky's contempt for her friend is Amelia's impenetrable passivity, which Becky sees as stupidity and the result of her privileged social position. Becky's restless energy is juxtaposed to Amelia's lethargy. During their last half hour at Miss Pinkerton's, for instance, Becky's response is to move from one dramatic action to another, while Amelia's trivial dilemma is that "when the day of departure came, between her two customs of laughing and crying, Miss Sedley was greatly puzzled how to act" (p. 43).

Amelia has simply been born into safe and comfortable circumstances, and she has been brought up to serve a purely ornamental function as the bride-to-be of George Osborne, the son of another well-to-do London citizen. This feature is epitomized in another vignette of the two friends: "While Becky Sharp was on her own wing in the country (...) Amelia lay snug in her home at Russel Square" (p. 150).

When things start going wrong for old Mr. Sedley, Amelia is invariably seen as the mute victim whose one response is stoic endurance. The avalanche that hits her father sweeps Amelia from her safe little shelf.

Old Osborne's ban on the proposed marriage between his son and Amelia is for her an unavoidable disaster: she cannot do anything actively to secure her hold on George—she can only wait and suffer. Becky accepts failures and setbacks once they have happened, but she never gives in. A new situation offers new challenges, and she acts accordingly. Amelia merely allows herself to be moved from one place of residence to another. When the men go into battle at Waterloo, Amelia joins the other waiting women, while Becky, as we have seen, is busy feathering her own nest, thus improving her chances of survival in a world where heroism counts for nothing.

In Brussels, Amelia's wheel of fortune descends to its lowest point. We see her sitting "quite unnoticed in her corner," while Becky, whose fortunes are ascending as she flirts with George and the other officers during the ball on the eve of the battle, surrounds herself with royal splendor (pp. 342-343). Then and later loneliness is Amelia's lot, as it was Becky's when she was down in her luck. But this circumstance turns Amelia into a pathetic figure who merely suffers and endures: "how pure she was; how gentle, how tender, and how friendless!" (p. 346). Appropriately, this is the image of his wife that George carries with him to the front.

Back in London, Amelia has to endure the pettiness to which poverty has reduced her parents and the claustrophobia of a tiny house, and she does so uncomplainingly. The only action which is open to her is the sacrifice of her own son. She surrenders him to old Osborne, who refuses to be reconciled to her, in return for economic security for her parents. Becky, too, sacrifices her son, by sending him away to school, which leaves her free to flirt with Lord Steyne, the instrument of her final social triumph. Becky's act of rejection, however, paves the way for her eventual fall, while Amelia's genuine sacrifice starts the upward movement of her wheel of fortune. Amelia's reward for her one spurt of action is in the long run reconciliation with old Osborne, reunion with her son, and marriage to Dobbin, her long-suffering lover. Amelia never again has to act: she is merely called upon to receive and give in when the time is ripe. When Becky and Amelia meet again at Pumpernickel, they are in many ways back where they started. Amelia is restored to a safe, respectable social position, ready to take up her role as conventional wife and mother, with no economic worries in the world. Becky, on the other hand, is still on the move through a potentially hostile society from which she shrinks, but which she also yearns to join. Amelia, at the outset, attracts the attention and homage of society because of her wealth and prettiness. She is, however, soon overshadowed by Becky, who steals the show. At the end, as at the beginning of the novel, Amelia's passivity is no match for Becky's wit and vitality.

Vanity Fair is remarkable for the scope and depth of its social canvas.
Like Scott, Thackeray deals with a period in the recent past which
clearly had a decisive bearing on the present. Waterloo, the great
watershed in the novel, is also a watershed in English history. "At the
time of Waterloo," David Thomson writes, "Britain was midway
through the most far-reaching social transformation in her whole
history."[12] The fascination of the Regency period for a writer like
Thackeray was that its links with the social order of eighteenth-century
England were so strong, while the forces that were to change it so
fundamentally could be perceived as the laws of nature operating behind
the scene. Becky, along with the high-society ladies and gentlemen
whose company she seeks, are the products of a period when "the old
order changeth, yielding place to new"[13] Their ability to survive depends
on their skill in exploiting the resulting social fluidity. Becky thrives in
the old society in which patronage could ensure social advancement. But
with her lack of money, she is at a disadvantage in the new society that
was emerging.

The panoramic method lends itself to the kind of social portrayal and
analysis that Thackeray attempts to present in *Vanity Fair*. Like his
great predecessor and teacher, Fielding in *Tom Jones*, Thackeray, in
Vanity Fair presents an inclusive view of society and a wide range of
perspectives. Both writers chose protagonists who move close to the
picaro's world and share more than a touch of his temperament and
situation. Unlike the mainstream picaresque novelist, however, they
exploit the omniscient third-person point of view to achieve ironic
distance from protagonist and reader alike.

Both Tom Jones and Rebecca Sharp experience the vicissitudes of a
precarious existence in the grey zone between inside and outside status in
established society. Tom makes the typical eighteenth-century
picaresque journey from security, through chaos, back to security, while
Becky's hold on society is always precarious — much more in keeping
with the picaresque formula. Her vitality matches Tom's zest for life, but
they represent contrasting attitudes to the individual in society. Becky
does not share Tom's innate goodness. He has to learn to detect
hypocrisy and deceit before he can fulfil his obligations as Squire
Allworthy's heir. Thackeray's view of the individual as a social being is
far more cynical. Becky's guiding principle is self-interest, and no real
alternative is put forward to what appears to be the primary social
instinct. In her ceaseless struggle to escape from her insecure status and
achieve security at any cost, Becky emerges as Thackeray's Everyman, a
suitable vehicle for a sociologically oriented vision of the individual and
the community in a transitional period. What Arthur Pollard terms
"accuracy of awareness"[14] balances the puppet master's skill as
performer in Thackeray's art. Hardy sees him as "the great sociologist of
nineteenth-century fiction, the great accumulator of social symbols of

class and money".[15] He is also the great scrutinizer of the manner in which the individual conforms to or deviates from the ideology and pattern of behavior that has been codified by her or his community. The inside-outside opposition is at the heart of the vision, as well as the performance.

The initial chapter focuses on the insider-outsider opposition in its account of Amelia and Rebecca's contrasting behavior, which is rooted in their temperament and character-type and bears the stamp of their circumstances and background. The supporting characters add to the flavor of the stereotype, which *Vanity Fair* has inherited from the allegorical/satirical fable tradition. The concern with the typical is also an important element in the kaleidoscopic view the reader is given of a many-layered society. Dorothy Van Ghent draws attention to an important consequence of Thackeray's concern with the typical. According to her, through the "multitude of individuals" Becky meets in the course of her career, she forms "relationships with large and significant blocks of a civilization"—the various middle-class blocks, "the aristocratic Crawley block", and the "ambiguous Steyne block".[16] These blocks refer to the old hierarchical social structure as well as to the class-consciousness of the new. Like the picaro, Becky crosses the barriers between these blocks and tries her luck within each, with only temporary success.

Becky's journey thus exposes the basic structure of a society that is both rigidly compartmentalized and fluid. From the beginning, the classical concern with rank and degree is the first clause in the ideological framework. George Osborne expresses a well-worn view when he objects to a match between Jos Sedley and Becky on the following grounds:

> "Who's this little schoolgirl that is ogling and making love to him? Hang it, the family's low enough already, without *her*. A governess is all very well, but I'd rather have a lady for my sister-in-law. I'm a liberal man; but I've proper pride, and know my own situation: let her know hers" (p. 96).

George is here the spokesman for an antiquated feudal social model according to which there is no escape from the station into which you were born. The reader easily detects the false note in George's clichés. Either he is unaware of the falseness in what he is saying, or he ignores it. In actual fact, the Osbornes, like the Sedleys and many of their city colleagues, have made their way to wealth and respectable social positions from humble beginnings, their ultimate aim being the splendor of even higher social spheres. Thus old Osborne's ambition is, as in the case of many a contemporary Nabob, to gain admission to the aristocracy through his son by means of his wealth. The truth is therefore that George Osborne is an upstart, although not a first generation one like Becky. The snobbishness that George and many of the inhabitants of *Vanity Fair* suffer from, and which Thackeray never tires of satirizing in his early work, is symptomatic of the state of flux which characterized English society in the first half of the nineteenth-century. According to J. Y. T. Greig:

> No student of Victorian England in the forties will dispute that snobbishness (...) needed scourging. The comparatively stable society of the previous century had been thrown off balance. The Industrial Revolution had produced, and the Reform Bill of 1832 had enfranchised, a vast body of manufacturers, tradesmen, merchants large and small, apothecaries, surgeons, physicians, lawyers, and speculators who were elbowing their way up the crowded steps of the social pyramid, aping the manners of the older landed gentry.[17]

A community such as the one described in *Vanity Fair* is of this transitional kind. A jostling crowd of characters who "are or have been on the make"[18] is what Becky must fight through on her way up "the social pyramid".

The ticket of admission to such a community is money. The two nations that inhabit it are the haves and the have-nots, and money is the demarcation line between the insiders and the outsiders. Becky has been painfully aware of this barrier since she was "elevated" from her bohemian origin to the garrett room in Miss Pinkerton's Academy. Her penury and wits are for ever pitted against the "ten thousand pounds and an establishment secure" (p. 125) of the Amelias of established society. A recurrent symbol of social superiority is the magnificent family coach. Each time, its separateness is emphasized by the presence of have-nots or hangers- on, which sets off the achievement behind the occupant's hour of triumph, as when Becky rides to court in Sir Pitt's carriage (p. 555). The carriage is, therefore, an important feature in the scene where Becky visits Amelia on the eve of family disaster. Although she has only a rather obscure position as Miss Crawley's companion, who waits in the carriage during Becky's visit, the whole scene nevertheless reflects Becky's rise in the world and Amelia's decline: "Miss Crawley was waiting in her carriage below, her people wondering at the locality in which they found themselves, and gazing upon poor Sambo, the black footman of Bloomsbury, as one of the queer natives of the place" (p. 177).

The carriage also highlights the precarious nature of achieved social position. Amelia, who at the beginning of the novel takes a family coach for granted, is deprived of it when economic forces beyond her ken suddenly remove the ground from under her feet. The coach is, on the other hand, always beyond Becky's reach. Even in her heyday, hers tends to be borrowed splendor: the coach, her fake genealogy and assumed royal manner are all the paraphernalia of an upstart. The moment she seems ready to consolidate her hard-won social position at the expense of Lady Bareacres or Lady Gaunt, she finds that for all its fluidity, the defenses of the "charmed circle",[19] of the aristocratic elite, are strong enough to keep her out.

Becky's major stumbling block is thus money. She may have had counterparts in the young girls with "strong points in the way of beauty or music or conversation" who, according to a contemporary eye-witness, Lady Amberley, beat the insiders despite their own inferior social status. But whereas their success was dependent on their having "the right patronage",[20] in Becky's experience, patronage is a very flimsy basis on which to build a social career. Those who really make it in *Vanity Fair* behave according to the merchant code of thrift and prudent ruthlessness. Making their money breed, they can then, like the Osbornes or the Dobbinses, afford the gentlemanly leisureliness of the aristocracy, the *otium* of the eighteenth-century merchant picaro. Old Osborne is the Regency version of this figure in Defoe or Scott. At the same time, Thackeray's interest in the latent and overt conflict between the aristocracy and the middle class anticipates the emergence of a merchant class that was so wealthy and powerful that it could more than hold its own with the old elite. Meanwhile, the gentlemanly ideal assumes the peculiar ambivalence that it possessed in the Victorian period. On the one hand, it embodies the Puritan-inspired belief in the self-made man who had achieved his success through hard work, thrift, and private enterprise. On the other hand, it still includes the traditional concept of the gentleman with its persistent assumption that trade and manual work are incompatible with the status of gentleman.[21]

Becky's supreme dilemma is that she is a woman who is up against an ideology that sets severe limits on an (especially middle-class) woman's scope of action. She is by definition excluded from the major channels of social advancement; even gambling is beyond reach if she wants to achieve social recognition as a respectable woman. Any *faux pas* is fatal to her because she is a woman. Her career after the Steyne affair shows how impossible it is for a woman whose reputation has been compromised to clear herself of the taint that clings to her. A man, by contrast, is expected to assume a respectable career after he has sown his wild oats. Rawdon Crawley is a case in point. Like Roderick Random, he is rejected by his family and reduced to outcast status. He has acquired the reputation of being wild and dissolute and an inveterate gambler, ready to swindle anybody. Yet, it is Becky who commits the sin that is socially unforgivable. Ironically, her fall occasions his rise. He is reconciled to his family and ends his days as Governor General of a West Indian island through the—admittedly involuntary—good offices of

Lord Steyne, who otherwise escapes all onus by virtue of his social position and wealth.

Becky's great talents are therefore wholly confined by the narrow limits of the woman's sphere. Her restless energy and urge to gain admission are continually pitted against the code of conduct that the passive and docile Amelia embodies. The complementary female image of the merchant-gentleman, Amelia conforms to the portrait Perkin draws of "the 'perfect lady', the Victorian ideal of the completely leisured, completely ornamental, completely helpless and dependent middle-class wife or daughter, with no function besides inspiring admiration and bearing children".[22] Thackeray describes these women as "secret martyrs and victims" (p. 662). He clearly sees their situation as degrading, but his vision of them is at the same time colored by the image which is behind the situation he laments:

> What do men know about women's martyrdoms? We should go mad had we to endure the hundredth part of those daily pains which are meekly borne by many women. Ceaseless slavery meeting with no reward; constant gentleness and kindness met by cruelty as constant; love, labour, patience, watchfulness, without even so much as the acknowledgment of a good word; all this, how many of them have to bear in quiet, and appear abroad with cheerful faces as if they felt nothing (p. 659).

The strategy that determines Becky's behavior both collides with and assumes the social validity of Amelia's code. We have seen how skillfully she exploits the angel-in-the-house role to gain confidence in the social circle she seeks to infiltrate. It is true that Becky, as Gilmour puts it, has the courage to "challenge the fixed hierarchy of English society"[23] in her defiance of Miss Pinkerton and what she stands for, but she, as little as the picaro, has any revolutionary intentions[24]. She may wish to shock from time to time, but her goal is, after all, social admission, as a parasite if necessary. In the latter role, Becky aspires to a place in a community with a power structure in which women are accorded the position of parasites by being purely ornamental, apart from their biological function as mothers. In this sense, Amelia, the perfect lady, is Rebecca's ideal parasite. But Becky is a parasite in a more subversive sense as well. By acquiring perfect lady skills and etiquette, Becky is able to boost her natural talents for social leadership to oust the insiders. She also panders to the other traditional Victorian image of woman: that of courtesan, who in the upper reaches of society might attain a position of influence and affluence through her sexual attraction. Her bohemian background facilitates Becky's entry into this role.

The image of the perfect lady carries pastoral overtones. We have seen that the pastoral mode, with its dream of a simple and secure life, is of considerable importance in many picaresque novels from *Gil Blas* to *Roderick Random*. The picaro may, even in the austere atmosphere of the Spanish prototype, carry with him into the world the picture of a period of comparative happiness before his vicissitudes began. In *Gil Blas* and *Roderick Random,* the happy place is found when the wanderer is well established as a vagabond and then abandoned, but the memory of it forms part of his image of the retreat that materializes at the end of the novel. We have seen that in these novels, notably in *Colonel Jack,* the pastoral ending illustrates the rich eighteenth-century merchant's ambition to retire to the rural mansion he has bought with the wealth acquired by an adventurous, often shady, business career.

The pastoral mode is exploited with great ingenuity in *Vanity Fair,* and it is surrounded by the ambiguity we have detected in so many other contexts in this novel. The pastoral is a major source for the conventional clichés that Becky exploits like grappling irons to scale the social pyramid, but that are also the points in the social facade which the satirical scrutinizer continually exposes as false and hollow.

The glimpses we are given of Becky's childhood lack the flavor of innocence that pastoral pictures of childhood tend to convey. Becky never thinks of "her original humble station" as a happy state because it was humble. On the contrary, when later she thinks back on this period, she considers her present comparatively elevated position as an achievement on her part: she has "raised herself far beyond" her modest beginning (p. 496). Her bohemian childhood nevertheless has a tinge of the pastoral dream for her, representing a carefree alternative to the kind of scheming existence she is forced to lead if she wishes to get to the top. She has had to sacrifice her love of play in her futile struggle for respectability. Characteristically, she has forgotten the time when she was young (p. 496), although her unquenchable high spirits and love of playacting are, as we have seen, evidence of her latent bohemianism. There is a kind of inverted pastoralism in the picture we are given of Becky's power over men. The bohemian strain in her is perhaps the essence of the titillating charm that attracts the men, but it leaves respectable women cold. It could be argued that Becky embodies the male dream of a world of sexual license as an alternative to the Ideal Home—the peaceful but boring earthly paradise of innocence and untainted goodness. The pastoral thus becomes a means of detecting the Victorian male penchant for a double morality—which, in its turn, has formed part of the somewhat prejudiced picture we have of the age.

Although Amelia can create a peaceful haven anywhere, supreme bliss requires, in keeping with the pastoral convention, rural surroundings. Persuaded by his friend Dobbin not to desert Amelia, George Osborne paints this rosy picture of their future residence: "his allowance, with Amelia's settlement, would enable them to take a snug place in the country somewhere, in a good sporting neighbourhood; and he would

hunt a little, and farm a little; and they would be very happy" (p. 160).
The ironical tone of this passage deepens into satire as the portrait of
George as an upstart snob is completed: "He didn't care for himself—not
he; but his dear little girl should take the place in society to which, as his
wife, she was entitled" (p. 160). The falseness of George's pastoral dream
is revealed when it is clear that, if he marries Amelia, he will be disinherited. Poverty is, after all, part of the pastoral mode of life, and also part of
Amelia's romance-colored notions of conjugal happiness: faced with
poverty, George expresses the male notion of male toughness and female
fragility in his remark, " '*I* can rough it well enough; but you, my dear,
how will you bear it?'" Amelia, however, is happy at the news: "The idea
of sharing poverty and privation with the beloved object (...) was
actually pleasant to little Amelia." This is not to George's liking at all.
Again, he strikes a stereotypical male pose, even that of picaro: "'What
vexes me (...) is not *my* misfortune, but yours. ... I don't care for a little
poverty; and I think, without vanity, I've talents enough to make my
own way.'" He ends up by repeating his insistence that she should have
" 'the comforts and station in society which my wife had a right to
expect' " (p. 294). The pastoral is thus exploited as a means of exposing
the rigid role pattern which dominates George's convention-ridden code
of behavior.

The pastoral in *Vanity Fair* is closely linked with Amelia and the
image of woman she embodies. Becky's endeavor to gain admission to
high society—the environment in which "she was formed to shine" (p.
613)—also necessitates her acceptance by the Crawley family, where
Lady Jane is the dominating influence. Through her, Evangelicalism
has invaded Queen's Crawley. The estate has fallen victim to "the moral
revolution" that this movement achieved in the late Regency and early
Victorian periods. Perkin refers to the way "the traditional purtianism
of the English middle ranks" supplanted the relaxed moral atmosphere
of the old aristocracy, working like "a sort of fifth column" within this
class.[25] Amelia's kind of domesticity is a central virtue in this
community, in striking contrast to the splendor and frivolity of high
society.

In her readiness to emulate the domestic ideal, Becky exposes the hypo-
critical element in the new morality. Because its adherents are among the
pillars of society, parasites thrive in the new, as well as in the old, system
and are perhaps less easily detected. The parasite in Becky moves with
ease between the pastoral world of Queen's Crawley and the frivolous
splendor of Lord Steyne's London world, reflecting the old town-
country opposition. Becky returns to Queen's Crawley like a princess in
disguise. She chooses the stage coach rather than a private coach to
emphasize that she is making a pilgrimage to her own humble past, in
itself a pastoral movement. The moment has come for reconciliation
between the two brothers after the death of old Sir Pitt. The welcome and

deference with which Becky is met at the entrance to the estate make her feel that "she was not an impostor any more, and was coming to the home of her ancestors" (p. 486). The stage is set for a pastoral retreat scene—the formula of, for example *Roderick Random,* and this is the light in which it appears to Becky. Her behavior is, as ususal, perfectly adapted to the situation in hand. She echoes Amelia's views of poverty when she asks Lady Jane, " 'What care we for poverty?' " and also voices a traditional pastoral convention. At the same time, she strikes her habitual poor orphan pose: " 'I am used to it from childhood (...)' " (p. 492). The setting is also attuned to the pastoral theme: "One day followed another, and the ladies of the house passed their life in those calm pursuits and amusements which satisfy country ladies" (p. 495). The monotony as well as the precariousness of this kind of paradisaic existence is finely brought out in the following passage. Becky

> sang Handel and Haydn to the family of evenings, and engaged in a large piece of worsted work, as if she had been born to the business, and as if this kind of life was to continue with her until she should sink to the grave in a polite old age, leaving regrets and a great quantity of Consols behind her—as if there were not cares and duns, schemes, shifts, and poverty, waiting outside the park gates, to pounce upon her when she issued into the world again (p. 495).

The passage brings out the unreal character of the Crawley world, as well as its exclusiveness. For Becky, Queen's Crawley is merely an interlude, another opportunity for trying to enter a world that, in the end, proves to be closed to her. Again, Becky is closer to the Spanish type of picaro than to Roderick Random and his eighteenth-century gentlemen-wanderer colleagues who are only temporarily displaced.

The secluded, Arcadian atmosphere at Queen's Crawley is underlined in the reference to the park gates which lead to the world which is Becky's real home ground. As in the opening chapter of the novel, the gates suggest opportunity — a matter of life and death to the picaro — as well as rejection. The pastoral in Becky's case, as in the picaro's, is close to her dream of survival. It is also part of the mechanism by which the insiders keep the outsiders out. One aspect of this mechanism is revealed in the following confrontation scene between Becky and Lady Jane: "Becky came into the room, sneering with green scornful eyes (...) Her [Lady Jane's] simple little fancies shrank away tremulously, as fairies in the story-book before a superior bad angel" (p. 534). Becky's green eyes along with her art as a schemer have made members of the aristocracy refer to her earlier in the novel as " 'that little serpent of a governess' " (p. 303). In this scene, she is explicitly associated with the devil. Becky, as we have seen, is clearly cast in the role of temptress and, as such, is a threat to the new image of domestic fidelity and virtue. But by seeing her as the ser-

pent in the Crawley garden of Eden, Lady Jane also inadvertently diagnoses the threat Becky represents to an exclusive social system and
reveals the rejection mechanism which keeps "the charmed circle" intact
in a period when " 'Society's edge was permanently blurred by the
jostling of the thousands who were trying to get in with the hundreds
who were trying not to be pushed out."[26] Becky's great fall in the Lord
Steyne affair is society's final rejection of a usurper with great natural
talents but without money.

Becky diagnoses her own dilemma during her pastoral interlude at
Queen's Crawley and also puts her finger on the economic basis of the
angel-in-the-house myth. She finds the Crawley way of life boring,
despite its peace and harmony, and reflects that " 'It isn't difficult to be a
country gentleman's wife (...) I think I could be a good woman if I had
five thousand a year' " (p. 495). Becky here refers to the link between
money—the instinct to hoard money, Gilmour's "acquisitive urge"[27]—
and morality that was forged in the wake of the Industrial Revolution.
Thackeray, however, is also reminding us of Defoe's insistence on the
role of Necessity when it comes to socio-moral conduct. Seen against the
unavoidable background of poverty, Thackeray's vision of an alternative career for Becky has a distinctly pastoral flavor: "It may, perhaps,
have struck her that to have been honest and humble, to have done her
duty, and to have marched straightforward on her way, would have
brought her as near happiness as that path by which she was striving to
attain it" (p. 497). The underlying ideology is behind the Victorian
middle-class attitude toward the working classes. Happiness spells
contentment on the social level and acquiscence to the mysterious ways
of God on a religious level. Security, not happiness, however, is Becky's
and the picaro's aim—in addition freedom of social movement.
Happiness is fugitive—inherent in the splendor of the moment.

The contrasting pastoral scene in Amelia's story is her last evening
with her little son before he moves into his grandfather's house.
Appropriately she asks him to read to her the story of Samuel and his
mother on the eve of their parting. Amelia identifies herself with this
woman who is able to thank the Lord for having selected her son for his
service even though this means she has to give him up. Amelia's sorrow
and any trace of rebellion are guided, in accordance with the principle of
endurance and patience with which she has been brought up, into a safe
religious channel: "And he read the song of gratitude which Hannah
sang: and which says, who it is who maketh poor and maketh rich, and
bringeth low and exalteth—how the poor shall be raised up out of the
dust, and how, in his own might, no man shall be strong" (p. 578). In
this very moving scene, the satirical tone has been dropped. The episode
presents God as the power behind the wheel of fortune, which no
member of the community, high or low, can escape. It expresses the
gospel of the unprivileged, denying as it does the permanence of any

system of social classification, and indeed of the whole hierarchical power structure of the community. In the context of the novel and early and mid-Victorian society, it also expresses the middle-class ethos of aquiescence. The passage quoted therefore also points to another aspect of the defense system around the insiders, instilling as it does into the reader the idea of obedience and the futility of human striving, the instinct at the heart of the picaro's fight for suvrival by means of his wits and resourcefulness. Becky's philosophy of action has no room in the religious and social order that Amelia represents and that receives its final sanction in her marriage to Dobbin. She is simply relegated to Bath or Cheltenham, where she "chiefly hangs about," on the fringes of respectable society, forever trying to pry open the door.

The picaresque is one of many strands in the narrative fabric of *Vanity Fair*. In his skillful interweaving of "public" and "private" events, Thackeray draws on the historical novel in the tradition of Scott, which was concerned with the impact of national crises on places and people remote from the main theaters of action. Thackeray's panoramic view of a whole community is different from Fielding's, because Thackeray's historical awareness is stronger, moving as he does not only horizontally through society but also vertically through an epoch. Above all, he seeks to portray the process through which a new social order emerges while the old lingers on. The present chapter has sought to detect ways in which elements in the picaresque formula have been exploited to lay bare the ideological repercussions of this process. We are shown that for all her vitality and kinship to the traditional picaro, Becky has in actual fact less chance of survival than an Amelia, who responds to misfortune as a victim whose only defence is stoic acquiescence. Amelia, unlike the involuntary picaros we have encountered in this study, is never reduced to vagabond existence along the road. She sticks to the course of honest poverty that Colonel Jack chose on his way to Scotland and which in the end led him to prosperity. Becky's dilemma is not only that her lack of money and position prevents her from satisfying the "aquisitive urge" which was such a central force behind the Industrial Revolution, but that, as a woman, she was both behind and ahead of her times. Continually on the move up and down the social scale, Becky is, like the picaro, close to the pulse of the community which is both inhabited and critically examined. She, too, is the child of a somewhat chaotic period in which she appears to have ample scope to practise her art. The gates are, however, also closing in this respect. The picaro's future in the Victorian class-conscious society is not bright: he may find it difficult to find his place as half-outsider in a social system which is more money- and property-oriented than ever.

The picaresque formula thus provided Thackeray with a model for tracing the contours of the process of socio-economic change. The picaresque journey of continual encounters with a nonindustrial environment illuminates the scope and mechanism of social mobility and dramatizes the complementary roles of conformity and defiance in the evolving patterns of social organization. By studying the novel from a picaresque perspective, we are brought face to face with the author's view of the period's ideological climate and with his own ideological bearings.

[1] Percy Lubbock, *The Craft of Fiction* (London: Jonathan Cape, 1957) 93.

[2] Gordon N. Ray, *Thackeray. The Uses of Adversity 1811-1846* (London: Oxford University Press, 1955) 406.

[3] Ray, 395.

[4] Reed, 168.

[5] References, included parenthetically in the text, are to William Makepeace Thackeray, *Vanity Fair* (Harmondsworth: Penguin, 1968)

[6] Barbara Hardy, *The Exposure of Luxury. Radical Themes in Thackeray* (London: Peter Owen, 1972) 28.

[7] Kathleen Tillotson, *Novels of the Eighteen-Forties* (London: Oxford University Press, 1961) 246.

[8] See, for example, Hardy, 24 ff.

[9] Vide supra, p. 15.

[10] Tillotson, 241.

[11] David Cecil, *Early Victorian Novelists* (London: Constable & Co. Ltd., 1957) 80.

[12] David Thomson, *England in the Nineteenth Century (1815-1914)*. The Pelican History of England, vol. 8 (Harmondsworth: Penguin, 1957) 12.

[13] Alfred Lord Tennyson, "The Passing of Arthur", 1. 408.

[14] Arthur Pollard, ed. Introduction, *Vanity Fair. A Casebook* (London: Macmillan, 1978) 15.

[15] Hardy, 20.

[16] Dorothy Van Ghent, *The English Novel. Form and Function* (New York: Harper & Row, 1961) 142.

[17] J. Y. T. Greig, *Thackeray. A Reconsideration* (London: Oxford University Press, 1950) 92.

[18] E. M. W. Tillyard, 119.

[19] Geoffrey Best, *Mid-Victorian Britain 1851-75* (St. Albans: Panther, 1973) 262.

[20] Best, 275.

[21] For further discussion of the permutations of the gentleman ideal under the impact of social changes brought about by the emerging merchant and entrepreneurial class, see Robin Gilmour, *The Idea of the Gentleman in the Victorian Novel* (London: George Allen and Unwin, 1981) 37 and 61-71; Harold Perkin, *The Origins of Modern English Society 1780-1880* (London: Routledge and Kegan Paul, 1969) 273-278 and 431; Best, 268-278.

[22] Perkin, 159.

[23] Gilmour, 61,

[24] Cf. Hardy, 28.

[25] Perkin, 281 and 286.

[26] Best, 262.

[27] Gilmour, 34.

Chapter 6

The Picaresque Formula
and Socio-moral Transformation in
Charles Dickens's *Great Expectations*

> It is wonderful to me how I could have been so easily cast away at
> such an age.... I know I do not exaggerate (...) the scantiness of my
> resources and the difficulties of my life. (...) I know that I worked,
> from morning to night, with common men and boys, a shabby
> child. ... I know that I have lounged about the streets, insufficiently
> and unsatisfactorily fed. I know that, but for the mercy of God, I
> might easily have been, for any care that was taken of me, a little
> robber or a little vagabond.[1]

This quotation is taken from the account Dickens gave his friend and
future biographer, John Forster, of his most painful childood
memory—the time when his father was arrested for debt and taken to the
Marshalsea and his family went with him — except Charles, who had
been provided with a job in a blacking warehouse, although he was only
eleven years old and had to live by himself in lodgings near the prison.
Until 1847, when he made this statement to Forster, he had repressed this
memory. He was now ready to write about it in his autobiographical
novel, *David Copperfield* (1849-50). By that time, Dickens had for many
years enjoyed the wealth and security that his success as England's most
popular and most widely read novelist had afforded him. Yet his success
could not wipe out the stain that he felt this period had put on his life.
" 'From that hour until this,' " he confessed to Forster, " 'no word of that
part of my childhood (...) has passed my lips to any human being. (...) I
never had the courage to go back to the place where my servitude began. I
never saw it. I could not endure to go near it.' "[2]
The vision Dickens has of himself as an abandoned child is close to the
picaresque tale's account of the ejection which starts the picaro's career
of wandering. The loneliness and despair of a Lazarillo infuse Dickens's
sketch. The picaro's traumatic experience of precariousness, of being left
to fend for himself in a hostile environment, is reflected in Dickens's
awareness that the sudden withdrawal of parental care and protection
might well have turned him into "a little robber or a little vagabond."

The passage first quoted might indeed have been taken from a picaro's memoirs, for example, Colonel Jack's. Such a fear might well have inspired the young Dickens to work so hard to establish himself in society; he might equally well see himself as a self-made man who had challenged fortune and worked his way up from nothing. At the same time, he shows throughout his work a fear of the abyss that lies below the social fabric and that threatens to deprive an Oliver Twist or Nicholas Nickleby of the security and position they are entitled to by birth, or to keep a Pip prisoner in the moral noman's-land, which the rags-to-riches formula may entail. Dickens's own career gave him the firm insider status all picaros aspire to, but he never got rid of his fascination for the outcast, for the vagabond he might have been and, therefore, both feared and felt the deepest sympathy for. Twelve years after *David Copperfield,* which presents the story of a young man who makes a successful career after his boyhood confrontation with precariousness, Dickens wrote *Great Expectations,* whose protagonist begins with a low social status, is given a social position he is not entitled to, and then chooses a career that can only offer modest success.

Dickens's financial success as a writer and his preoccupation with the self-made man, in his own career and in his writing, give him the aura of respectability which is such a prominent feature in the Victorian gentleman ideal. At the same time, he was, as Edmund Wilson points out, unwilling to join the governing class. There is a radical strain in him which makes him sceptical of the inherited privileges of class. The social uneasiness of the upstart which he describes so well in his novels, and perhaps with greatest insight in *Great Expectations,* is rooted in his own family background. The blacking warehouse incident cements a social attitude which is latent in his milieu: According to Edmund Wilson, "He had grown up in an uncomfortable position between the upper and lower middle-classes, with a dip into the proletariat and a glimpse of the aristocracy through their trusted upper servants." This was, Wilson adds, an advantage to Dickens as a writer, but "was to leave him rather isolated in English society."[3]

The scope as well as the nature of Dickens's social experience and his underlying personal and family circumstances place him on a wavelength with the picaresque mode and the world it describes. The affinity between this type of novel and Dickens's becomes clear if one quotes part of Geoffrey Thurley's definition of what he calls the Dickens myth: "The child abandoned by feckless or unfortunate parents climbs out of the abyss of poverty and darkness towards security, peace, and light." Thurley sees "the mechanism of the social climb" as the feature which distinguishes the novel from the romance, and he describes *Great Expectations* as a "paradigm novel" because "its narrative action" is derived from the resulting "social and psychological conflict."[4]

In Dickens's early novels, from *Pickwick Papers* and *Oliver Twist* to

Nicholas Nickleby and *The Old Curiosity Shop*, the impact of the
picaresque tradition is quite plain. Even more than Thackeray, Dickens
continues and modifies a mode that had undergone numerous
permutations since its Spanish heyday. His heritage is outlined in the
list of books which comforted David Copperfield in the unhappy days of
his childhood:

> My father had left a small collection of books in a little room
> upstairs, to which I had access (…) and which noboby else in our
> house ever troubled. From that blessed little room, Roderick
> Random, Peregrine Pickle, Humphrey Clinker, Tom Jones, the
> Vicar of Wakefield, Don Quixote, Gil Blas, and Robinson Crusoe,
> came out, a glorious host, to keep me company. They kept alive my
> fancy, and my hope of something beyond that place and time.[5]

David Copperfield shares young Charles's reading interests. The sale of
these books was part of the family disaster which culminated in the
Blacking Warehouse incident,[6] an event that helps to explain the
claustrophobic atmosphere which this incident conveys: Charles's main
imaginative link with a greater world had been cut.

Chandler draws attention to the manner in which Dickens carries on
and modifies the picaresque tradition. Instead of dividing his attention
between the rogue as an individual and his society, Dickens combines
the two interests by "studying rogues as individuals and also as social
phenomena." By doing so, he both draws on the Smollett tradition and
exploits the Godwin/Bulwer school of writers with a "reformative purpose."[7] Dickens's sensitivity to social wrongs is amply shown in *Oliver
Twist* and *Nicholas Nickleby*. The tendency we have followed from
Smollett to Scott to replace the traditional picaro with a protagonist
who is temporarily relegated from his superior social position to a near
proletariat or neutral social status is both repeated and modified in these
two novels. In *Oliver Twist*, the traditional foundling tale is exploited to
highlight the protagonist as the defenseless victim of an oppressive
society. His goodness and incorruptibility, inherited from the decent
upper middle-class family from which he had been removed at birth, are
foils to the endemic cruelty in his environment. Oliver is of the same
family as the sensitive Frank Osbaldistone. He functions as moral touch-
stone and communal conscience. The protagonist in *Nicholas Nickleby*
carries on the dilemma Smollett explores in *Roderick Random:* how can
a respectable, disinherited, and impoverished young man preserve his
honor and integrity? Nicholas is more active than Oliver, but he, too, is
basically a victim. As an intelligent young man who has come down in
the world through his parents' financial misfortunes, he is more explicit
as a vehicle of social protest than Oliver. He is evidence of the survival of
decency and goodness in a corrupt world, but like Oliver he is utterly

dependent on helpers who are firmly established within and at the same time withdrawn from society — an important variation of the pastoral aristocratic retreat theme we have found in the novels we have so far considered.

The passivity that the protagonists of these novels display and their apartness from the society through which they move help to distance them from their picaresque forbears. The colorful and vice-ridden social scene these novels contain is, however, very close to the world of the picaresque novel. The episodic structure of the narratives and the use of the journey to expose social patterns as well as social ills underline the family likeness between Dickens's early fiction and the picaresque tradition.

Great Expectations is more firmly organized than the traditional picaresque tale. Dickens had abandoned its loose episodic structure. The protagonist, however, is, if anything, closer to the picaro and his environment than his colleagues in Dickens's early novels. Pip is the most proletarian of his heroes, closer than any other to the vagabond the author felt he might have become. Pip may be seen as Dickens's double. Through him he makes a vicarious journey through a changing society, drawing on his own social experience as well as that of his fellow countrymen. Aspects of the picaresque formula are exploited to lay bare the dynamics of socio-moral transformation in a period which turned England into the workshop and commercial matrix of the world. In this chapter, we shall examine the manner in which Dickens exploits and expands the resources ot the picaresque mode to fuse the psychological and social concerns which we have seen Chandler detect as one of Dickens's great achievements. Pip, like so many of his picaresque predecessors, acts as social barometer and thermometer. Through him, we are given the feel of moving along the lines betwen classes and between phases of social development. The theme of social climbing implies the traditional precariousness of the rags-to-riches model, but the fear of the abyss is not least the result of clashing social codes: Pip on his journey upward in society is always intensely aware of a complementary journey downwards, even below his humble social origin. Pip is never at ease in the new dispensation — the old always hampers his progress toward the success which is the aim of his climbing.

Great Expectations is the retrospective first-person account of Pip's childhood and early manhood. It thus meets one of Guillén's major requirements for the picaresque novel. The pseudo-autobiographical nature of the novel ensures a unifying "sensiblity," that of the narrator-protagonist. Dickens perfects the method by which life "is at the same time revived and judged, presented and remembered."[8] This double perspective continually invites the reader to identify as well as detach himself from the incident he is being immersed in. The method is particularly valuable in a novel which is so preoccupied with the narrator's emotional odyssey through his past encounters with society.

The opening chapter of *Great Expectations* moves as quickly as the opening of *Lazarillo* or *La Vida del Buscón* to the moment of ejection that terminates the picaro's childhood experience of living in a family. In Pip's case, too, we are provided with genealogical details. His age of innocence is spent in the churchyard, his favourite playground. He is not conscious of separation from his dead family. On the contrary, their tombstones give free rein to his imagination. The first paragraph suggests a sense of pastoral contentment, which is brutally dispelled "on a memorable raw afternoon towards evening" when he discovered "the identity of things" (p. 35).[9] So the process of ejection begins with Pip's realization that he is an orphan, abandoned by his whole family. The churchyard is no longer a happy playground, but a lonely place, in the middle of "the dark flat wilderness" of the surrounding marshes. Pip has discovered his picaro identity: he is friendless and unprotected, fully exposed to the lurking terrors of the place.

It is noteworthy that Pip has made this discovery before the convict's dramatic eruption from among the graves. The pastoral atmosphere of the scene is finally shattered. The actual moment of ejection may be said to take place when the convict turns him upside down, and his confrontation with down-and-out existence changes the whole course of his life. His familiar environment, his recent discovery of his orphan state, and everything that from now on happens to him are ineluctably linked with this meeting in the churchyard. The experience of ejection turns Pip's world upside down. The resulting sense of bewilderment and helpless terror is akin to that of the picaro when he finds himself suddenly deprived of his family and exposed without guidance to the vicissitudes of the road. In the course of his career Pip is shown to be a passive rather than an active hero. The way things are thrust upon him is well illustrated in the convict's brutal demonstration of his complete power over Pip. But despite his paralyzing terror of the ruffian, Pip also exhibits some of the picaro's cunning and resourcefulness in his forage into his sister's pantry to provide food for the convict.

This act in Pip's eyes is sheer robbery. He, like the picaros of old, has been forced by circumstances to start on a road of petty crime which he fears may land him in prison. His discovery of his identity is thus linked with his sense of criminal guilt: he has fallen from innocence and is irrevocably linked with an outcast. He feels as if he has been cast out himself: he has become an outsider in his own environment.

This feeling, however, is ultimately the product of Pip's upbringing. His sister is a strict disciplinarian who in Pip's "words was more than twenty years older than I, and had established a great reputation with herself and the neighbours because she had brought me up 'by hand' " (p. 39). Pip is forever being treated by her and by Uncle Pumblechook as a potential culprit. He is a little boy and consequently in need of discipline. The seeds of Pip's outcast mentality had been sown long before the incident in the churchyard. The friendship that his brother-in-law Joe offers him can give him no protection, only sympathy. Joe is a fellow sufferer rather than a guardian. Continually pestered and tormented by his elders, Pip early develops a sense of resentment along with his sense of guilt. This, too, is part of the picaro's defense mechanism against an oppressive environment. Pip's sense of his own apartness is clearly related to resentment and guilt in the following description of the Christmas dinner the day after his meeting with the convict: "Among this good company I should have felt myself, even if I hadn't robbed the pantry, in a false position. Not because I was squeezed in at an acute angle of the table-cloth (...) nor because I was not allowed to speak (...) nor because I was regaled with the scaly tips of the drumsticks of the fowls. ... No; I should not have minded that, if they would only have left me alone" (p. 56). The very fact that he is a child turns him into an outsider. In Pip's resentment, there is an element of rebelliousness—the tendency Mrs. Joe's upbringing aims at suppressing.

The picaro is ejected into the world because the family can no longer support and protect him. He has to take to the road in order to survive. The road, on the other hand, is the playground of fortune. With luck, the picaro may become a gentleman, although luck is unpredictable and its duration uncertain. There is no steady progress from rags to riches. Riches are often an elusive dream, and the higher the peak of success, the greater the fall.

Pip's first stroke of luck is, in his family's eyes at least, his first visit to Miss Havisham, the rich recluse in Satis House in the neighbouring market town. Pip has reached another turning point in his young life—apparently counterbalancing his meeting with the convict in the churchyard. The occasion is also another turn in the process of ejection. By ordering Pip to attend Miss Havisham, his family removes him from his familiar environment into a strange and unfamiliar world. Mrs. Joe informs her husband that Miss Havisham " 'wants this boy to go and play there. And of course he's going. And he had better play there (...) or I'll work him' " (p. 81). Miss Havisham comes as much out of the blue into Pip's life as the convict, and the link in her case too is cemented with violence. In addition, he is expected to be grateful to his elders for the opportunity he may now be provided for making his fortune through Miss Havisham's patronage: " 'if this boy an't grateful this night, he never will be!' "(p. 81). Mrs. Joe instills gratitude into him even before she informs him what he is meant to be grateful for. Unlike the picaro proper, Pip is not left to fend for himself; he is merely ordered about. He has, however, the picaro's skill at adapting himself no matter how strange the circumstances that confront him are. This ability stands him in good stead when he visits Miss Havisham for the first time and is confronted with a situation that is at least as surrealistic as the one in the churchyard.

In Pip's consciousness, Miss Havisham is from then on as firmly associated with fortune — the state of gentleman — as the convict is with crime. The two form a polaric contrast at the extremes of the rags-to-riches picaresque formula. Like the protagonist in *La Vida del Buscón*, Pip soon comes to reject his own origin. This is evident in the comic scene in which Pip gets his own back on his tormentors by telling them a fantastic story about Miss Havisham, partly because they might not have believed him if had he told them the bizarre truth. Pip's imagination is at least as fertile as that of the picaro. Lying is one of the latter's methods of coping with the world, depending as he does on his wit and cunning, and resorting to tricks whenever he can. By lying, Pip not only distances himself from Mrs. Joe and Uncle Pumblechook, but also from Joe. When Pip confesses to him that his account of Miss Havisham was pure fiction, Joe speaks as the champion of an anti-picaresque mode of humble existence based on truthfulness: " 'There's one thing you may be sure of, Pip (…) namely, that lies is lies. However they come, they didn't ought to come, and they come from the father of lies (…) Don't you tell no more of 'em, Pip. *That* ain't the way to get out of being common, old chap' " (p. 100).

If the convict episode alienates Pip from his sister and what she stands for, the most serious consequence of Pip's visits to Satis House is his alienation from Joe.

Pip is continually made aware that he is fortune's plaything with no say over his own fate. Despite his links with Satis House, he is powerless against the inroads from his criminal connection, as when a man with a file—the passport to the convict's domain—gives him two pounds in the village pub (pp. 106-8). Miss Havisham and, above all, her representative, Estella, instill into him a feeling of inferiority. From the moment he sets foot in Satis House, his sense of being an outsider is reinforced: he is a common laboring boy with coarse hands (pp. 89-91). In the past, the vision of future success for Pip had been confined to Joe's forge. Now, this vision is gradually being replaced by a nightmarish claustrophobic feeling of social confinement. Paradoxically, the shut-in atmosphere of Satis House fans his ambition to achieve the status of gentleman. The fluctuations in the rags-to-riches formula in this phase of *Great Expectations* correspond to Pip's movement between Satis House (riches) and the village (rags). Miss Havisham's sudden decision to apprentice him to Joe — as abrupt as the decision to open Satis House to him, and equally over his head — is the sudden fall from fortune that is always the Damocles sword over the picaro's head. Pip, too, is at the mercy of powers completely beyond his control.

Pip finds it more difficult than the traditional picaro to resign himself to what he considers his misfortunes. Neither is his fall so drastic. He is not reduced to abject poverty, and he is not faced with an unfamiliar environment. On the contrary, it is his bad luck that puts him back in the same milieu where he started. But he has recourse to a means of improving his position which the picaro might also exploit. He, too, uses what his environment offers for social advancement—the village school. It is, however, wholly inadequate, and Pip is reduced to a depressing state of apathy, convinced that he will never be happy at Joe's trade: "I had liked it once, but once was not now" (p. 134)

Miss Havisham rejects Pip after having sown the seeds of ambition and restlessness in his mind. Pip, in his turn, rejects his own class and his home, but can do nothing to alter his circumstances; he can only be ashamed of them. His sense of guilt is deepened by this feeling, and by the circumstances round the assault on his sister. The suspected attacker is Orlick, Joe's workman, but Pip feels responsible because the weapon used is the convict's leg iron, inextricably tied up with what Pip had come to think of as the criminal strain in his heritage. He feels doubly confined: by his narrow environment and by his link with the convict. He feels the secret which connected them "was such an old one now, had so grown into me and become part of myself, that I could not tear it away" (p. 149).

Again Pip's fortune changes abruptly, and this time more dramatically than ever before. Once more Pip has no say, he is merely told about his great expectations by Mr. Jaggers. The legal language used in the announcement must have sounded like a command to Pip:

> "I am instructed to communicate to him (...) that he will come into a handsome property. Further, that it is the desire of the present possessor of that property, that he be immediately removed from his present sphere of life and from this place, and be brought up as a gentleman—in a word, as a young fellow of great expectations" (p. 165).

The old pattern of order and obedience is further underlined in the rest of the decree which forbids Pip to change his name and to ask any questions about the identity of his patron. He is allowed to believe, however, that it is Miss Havisham who has at long last fulfilled his and his family's expectations that she would do something for him: "My dream was out; my wild fancy was surpassed by sober reality;; Miss Havisham was going to make my fortune on a grand scale" (p. 165).

Like a true knight of fortune, Pip travels to London by stage coach. The road is less exploited as a goldmine of adventure in *Great Expectations* than in the picaresque novel proper, and it takes up far less space. Pip travels, however, several times back and forth between London and the town where Miss Havisham lives (and revisits his old village on two occasions). These journeys focus on the rags-to-riches formula, occurring as they do at various points in Pip's ascending and descending career as a gentleman. The stage coach represents a cross-section of society, though Dickens does not make so much out of this feature as do Fielding and Smollett. It expresses the unbridgeable gulf in Pip's social experience: on the one hand, there are the respectable gentlemen passengers to whose company Pip is entitled through his expectations; on the other hand, there are the convicts who might compromise Pip in the eyes of the gentlemen (pp. 248-252). Altogether the stage coach is a vehicle of panoramic social presentation in *Great Expectations,* too, especially when seen in the context of the bustling street scenes at the departure and arrival of the coaches. Dickens presents a view of society which encompasses the lowest as well as the highest rungs on the social ladder. Throughout his changing fortunes, Pip is never allowed to forget how precarious his social foothold is.

Pip's London phase, during which he learns the ways of a gentleman, brings to a head the conflicting strands in his heritage from the past. The moment he arrives in London, he is reminded of the ineradicable stain on his life—his links through the convict with the seamy side of society. The coach terminal is in the vicinity of Newgate prison, and his first visit is to his guardian, whose specialty is criminal law. He arrives with the social uneasiness of the upstart who has not yet learned the language of his new environment. He also has a persistent feeling of uneasiness about his past as a blacksmith's boy, which is both a link with a decent, though humble, profession and an obstacle he has to overcome in his struggle to achieve gentleman status. Pip's outsider complex is hard to overcome.

At the same time, it soon becomes clear that Pip is a quick and willing learner, and he really is very good at adapting himself to circumstances which must at first have appeared frightening and totally bewildering to a green village boy, even making allowance for what he may have picked up of upper middle-class manners at Satis House. Little is made of this in the novel, and there is only passing mention of Pip's hard work as Mr. Pocket's pupil. He soon acquires the necessary skills and accomplishments of a gentleman, such as rowing and social etiquette. He becomes one of the dandies about town, and he acquires expensive habits. He is a parasite in that he only spends money, but he is not the kind of parasite that the moneyless picaro tends to become, and he never has to resort to gambling in order to make both ends meet. His mysterious benefactor is a firm barrier between Pip and the abject poverty that forever threatens to engulf the picaro.

Through his tutors—Herbert Pocket and his father—Pip learns more than social etiquette. They also act as socio-moral examples, who help Pip achieve the gentleness and genuinely refined manner of the true gentleman. He may become a snob, but he is never corrupted by bad company to the extent that many picaros are on their journeys up and down the social scale. Throughout his career as a gentleman with expectations, Pip nevertheless fails to come to terms with Joe and what is most valuable in his heritage.

The test Pip is forever endeavouring to pass is recognition by Miss Havisham and, above all, Estella as a real gentleman. A noteworthy variant of the rise and fall rhythm of the picaresque formula is achieved on the occasion when Pip travels back to the little town in the company of the convicts—in his eyes a stroke of bad luck which makes him feel that he is still chained to the proletariat. This feeling is perhaps reinforced when he arrives at Satis House and finds Orlick there as gatekeeper. Arriving determined to prove himself as a gentleman, Pip feels he is hopelessly slipping back into his past humble position when he sees the beautiful and elegant Estella, the acme of social success. He again feels that he is "the coarse and common boy" (p. 256) he was when he first met her. His feeling of regression is deepened by the fact that she still treats him like a boy, despite her admission that he has changed. However, she rubs salt into Pip's wounded self-respect by leaving Miss Havisham's question, if he is " '[l]ess coarse and common,' " open (p. 257). Although Pip feels she is as inaccessible as ever, he refuses to give up the idea that Miss Havisham has meant them for each other (p. 260), and therefore leaves Satis House with his dream of social advancement intact.

The third and final phase of Pip's fortunes opens as abruptly as the other two. Again, we are confronted with an incident which makes him feel that he is being turned upside down. The return of the convict disillusions Pip as to his great expectations, and he falls from his imagined peak as a gentleman. It is not that he is suddenly deprived of his money—the disaster that would bring a picaro down—but that the money has become unacceptable to him—an idea that would never have occurred to a Lazarillo or Guzmán. He finds Magwitch's behavior as not only his patron but his proprietor revolting. Pip is no longer merely a victim who is ordered about and expected to obey. He shows himself capable of making a choice. Choosing rags rather than riches on what he considers compromising premises, he gradually discovers how illusory the walls between the various worlds he has encountered are. He finds that not only his, but also Miss Havisham's and Estella's pasts, are interwoven with the criminal element. Ironically, it is Joe's world which is unattainable at the end of the novel: there is no way back to the forge. It is also ironic that the money which was the basis for Colonel Jack's success—earned through his work on the plantation—is unacceptable when earned under similar circumstances by Magwitch. The road to economic independence for Pip, on the other hand, lies through his own efforts as a businessman in a foreign country—the source of wealth which enables Colonel Jack to establish himself as a gentleman at the end of Defoe's novel.

The ending of *Great Expectations* is closer to the open ending of the picaresque novel than the closed ending of the happy retreat which the eighteenth-century English novelist tended to prefer and which was also favored by Dickens in his early novels. *Great Expectations* does not end on a happy note with churchbells and happiness forever after, although such an ending is suggested (unlike the earlier version, in which Pip and Estella part without hope of a future union). The village is revisited, and there is a final atmosphere of reconciliation and harmony. Pip has yet a long way to go before he can retire from his business. The penultimate chapter closes on a note of cheerful, but cautious optimism: "We were not in a grand way of business, but we had a good name, and worked for our profits, and did very well" (p. 489).

Pip's career from blacksmith's boy to honest businessman is flanked by that of Herbert, operating within his well-defined upper middle-class perimeter, looking ineffectually about him for an opening (as on page 207), and that of Magwitch, persecuted as a "warmint" by established society. Herbert is ready to fill a responsible position once an opportunity offers itself because he is from the beginning an insider. Magwitch throughout his "career" is an outcast. Ignorant of his origin he is, like the picaro, from the outset left to his own devices.

> "In jail and out of jail, in jail and out of jail, in jail and out of jail (...) I've been done everything to pretty well — except hanged. (...) Tramping, begging, thieving, working sometimes when I could (...) a bit of a poacher, a bit of a labourer, a bit of a waggoner, a bit of a haymaker, a bit of a hawker, a bit of most things that don't pay and lead to trouble, I got to be a man." (pp. 360-361)

In other words, his career has been that of the humbler type of picaro who never moves far above starvation level.

The picaro, like the protagonists of allegory, romance, and the *Bild-ungsroman*–types of narrative that coalesce with the picaresque in *Great Expectations*—passes through a long series of encounters on his journey through society. These encounters teach him the ways of the world and transform him from dupe to resourceful rogue. The encounters develop not only his ability to defend himself, but also his capacity for fellowship. They are stages in his career as social climber, steadily extending his socio-moral awareness. Van Ghent sees Pip as "one more Everyman in the long succession of them that literature has represented,"[10] which seems to relate *Great Expectations* to the allegorical or morality play tradition. The picaresque perspective adds the flavor of concrete human and social plight which emphasizes the protagonist's development as the representative of his class, or as the reflector of a particular phase in the social development of his community. In Q. D. Leavis's view: "Pip, who has been much criticized as weak, uninteresting, tame, and otherwise lacking in spirit and force, was designed for the purpose as representative of the ordinary man, but with greater sensitiveness so that he cannot rest under the load of guilt and shame that other ordinary men managed not to notice."[11] This Everyman quality in Pip and the special nature of his sensitivity emerge in the pattern of encounters that comprise *Great Expectations*. There are two main groups of encounters in the novel, one between Pip and the convict and his representatives, and another between Pip and Miss Havisham/Estella and the world they represent.

The encounter between Pip and the convict in the churchyard replaces a stock-in-trade feature in the traditional traveler's tale, the inevitable hold-up by highwaymen. The suddenness of his appearance among the graves, as well as that of his colleague later on, retain a flavor of the nightmarish terror of such incidents. We have seen how the bond of secrecy which is welded between the two makes Pip abnormally sensitive to criminals and prisons. Later in the novel, it appears at times that only Pip is aware of the sudden inroad of a criminal element into a peaceful and apparently normal society. Pip soon realizes that the hulks, prison, the transport of convicts in the regular stagecoach, criminals frequenting pubs and places of entertainment, crime as an institution—are taken for granted by people in general. Joe may feel compassion for individual convicts, and Herbert may on a particular occasion feel repelled by convicts as "a degraded and vile sight" (p. 248), but the sight of a convict for Pip is immediately felt as a threat to his social aspirations. For him, such a person is more than a "vile sight": he is the embodiment of social degradation.

The picaresque principle of luck manifests itself in its adverse aspect in Pip's encounters with the convict element. On an occasion when he is waiting for Estella to arrive in London, he is taken on a sightseeing expedition to Newgate. In one of his retrospective reflections, Pip the narrator reflects on the mysterious manner in which his life has been linked with crime:

> How strange it was that I should be encompassed by all this taint of prison and crime; that, in my childhood out on our lonely marshes (...) I should have first encountered it; that, it should have reappeared on two occasions, starting out like a stain that was faded but not gone; that, it should in this new way pervade my fortune and advancement (p. 284).

Until the final phase of his journey to manhood Pip is unaware, of course, of the way the underworld, represented by Magwitch, is inextricably interwoven with respectable society, represented by Miss Havisham and Estella. Neither is he aware of the endemic nature of this element in the society he inhabits. Julian Moynahan sees Pip's whole career as vicarious: it "enacts his society's condition of being—its guilt, its sinfulness, and in the end, its helplessness to cleanse itself of a taint 'of prison and crime.' "[12] His extraordinary moral sensitivity predisposes him for such a role.

Until the convict's return as self-made man, Pip sees these encounters with the crime element as puzzling eruptions of what Roderick Random during his career as picaro would have interpreted as the sudden and unpredictable interference of fate, which works in a completely haphazard manner. When Pip recovers from the shock he experienced when Magwitch invaded his existence for the last time, he is no longer merely an ordinary law-abiding citizen whose effort at social advancement is forever thwarted by the outsider element in his background. In contrast to the helpless boy who was turned upside down by the convict, Pip now has friends who can support him, and he has developed a moral integrity which in the end enables him to carve out his own decent career. His final encounter with the convict is also, in the last resort, liberating in that it releases his natural sense of sympathy, first made evident in the churchyard. He recognizes the convict as a human being in need of help, and not merely a fairy tale ogre who keeps on popping up at the various crossroads in Pip's life. Pip realizes that Magwitch has been as much the victim of his environment as he has been. Pip also assumes the role of detective who seeks to piece together a true picture of a world in which he once believed convict and gentleman occupied completely segregated spheres. The final upside down experience liberates Pip from the social uneasiness which has hindered his upstart career. He emerges from his ordeal as a true gentleman, at ease with the world around him.

The contrasting set of encounters with Miss Havisham, Estella, and Satis House is as essential to Pip's moral growth as that with the convict. While his encounters with Magwitch are accidental, those with Satis House and its residents are planned and regulated according to a set procedure. Miss Havisham may invade Pip's life as abruptly as Magwitch, and her behavior may equally remain enigmatic and unpredictable. The great expectations theme and plot depend on Pip's belief that Miss Havisham is the inscrutable, benevolent providence in his life, while the convict is an evil and disgraceful influence. However, once the pattern of the relationship between Pip and Satis House has been established, unpredictability is removed from the daily routine, which follows unalterable rules. Pip invariably arrives at the locked gate and is made to feel like an outsider who may or may not be admitted into a society which does not change. There is also a gatekeeper, to begin with Estella; he is led through deserted corridors, through a neglected garden and past a disused brewery, to Miss Havisham's rooms. Here time has been suspended: the clock has been stopped and everything is left the way it was on the morning when her wedding was to have taken place. His task is to play with Estella while Miss Havisham looks on, and to wheel the latter round the room. At the end of each visit, he is fed by Estella and made to feel his inferior social position.

This regular pattern of encounters and their accompanying routines constitute an area of experience that is sharply demarcated from the village and the marshes which to Pip by then embody his experience with the ominous convict. The two sets of encounters reflect Pip's two kinds of social instinct. The convict encounters create fear of social deterioration and consequently release the mechanism of rejection. Outsider and insider alike fear the abyss beneath them. The set of Miss Havisham encounters, far from scaring Pip, encourages him to associate Satis House with security and harmony, however wretched he may at times be there. His social inferiority complex makes him even more keen to improve his social position. He, therefore, yearns for admission to the world of Satis House and dreams of Miss Havisham as his benefactress. Estella is the catalyzer of Pip's class-consciousness. Ross H. Dabney shows how his "relation with Estella (…) is concerned with (…) class, with status, with habits, occupations, gestures, and language standard in a particular social milieu".[13] She is felt to be beyond his reach, but she is also at the center of a community which provides, as J. Hillis Miller points out, "images of a fixed social order" by which he can be judged "at first as coarse and common, and later as a gentleman".[14] This is a community to which he can be elevated through patronage, the theme of his daydream. Satis House therefore channels Pip's instinctive drive for social improvement. The sudden appearance of the convict stain when he is waiting for Estella in London is consequently a threat to his prospects of achieving social advancement through Estella.

Pip's activities as a detective toward the end of the novel lead to another series of encounters with Miss Havisham. She, too, is shown to be a suffering human being, full of remorse for the misery she has caused other human beings, above all Pip. As in the case of the convict, Pip instinctively responds with compassion. His confrontation with her plight is an essential stage in the humanizing process which Magwitch's revelations started. He realizes that Satis House has been like an enchanted, fossilized fairy-tale palace isolated from life around it:

> That she had done a grievous thing in taking an impressionable child to mould into the form that her wild resentment, spurned affection, and wounded pride, found vengeance in, I knew full well. But that, in shutting out the light of day, she had shut out infinitely more; that, in seclusion, she had secluded herself from a thousand natural and healing influences; that, her mind, brooding solitary,

had grown diseased, as all minds do and must and will that reverse the appointed order of their Maker; I knew equally well. And could I look upon her without compassion (p. 411).

By yearning to inhabit Satis House—a rigidly demarcated social sphere—Pip, too, goes against "the appointed order". His social elevation along these lines not only would have removed him from the abyss, but would have cut him off from his origins, the natural source of his vitality and humanity.

When Satis House is destroyed by fire and Miss Havisham dies, Pip, who had previously rejected Magwitch's money, is left with nothing, except the sum of money Miss Havisham had given him to pay for Herbert's partnership in a firm. But Pip is left a wiser and, as we have seen, gentler person at the end of the novel, bent on making his own way on his own modest income.

The pattern of encounters reinforces the Everyman quality in the novel, while the ambiquity-riddled social landscape is close to that of the picaresque tale. Pip's sensitivity is developed in the course of his wanderings into the socio-moral consciousness which qualifies him as Victorian Everyman. His encounters constitute a series of tests culminating in an ordeal which reminds us of the pattern of traditional allegory and romance. But Pip shares the picaro's dilemma of being an outsider who wants to get in to get on. His ordeal opens his eyes to the falseness of his expectations, but he is as little of a rebel as the traditional picaro. When Pip returns to England "after an eleven-year exile of penitence (…) he returns to honest work within society".[15] Evolution rather than revolution marks Pip's progress through society.

The picaresque formula of unpredictable ups and downs in *Great Expectations* is modified with a back and forth rhythm that underlines the evolution theme. The alternating encounters between Pip and the convict and Pip and Satis House make him feel that he is taking a step back for each step he takes forward. The formula of ups-and-downs is combined with a combative tension between what may be termed socially regressive and progressive forces. Only at the end of his ordeal does Pip realize that he has been engaged in shadow boxing in more ways than one.

By going to play in the churchyard, Pip has in a way made a regressive movement from the village and the rudiments of civilization back into the wilderness with its lurking desolation and violence. The impression we are given of the oppressive atmosphere in his home makes it clear that the churchyard is also a place of refuge to Pip. He goes there to escape from his sister's tyranny. Pip's sudden awareness of the identity of things coincides, as we have seen, with the *Alice in Wonderland* manner in which he is introduced to the convict's world. The process of being turned upside down has a regressive effect, further underlined by the manner in which Magwitch and his desperate situation are associated with the ferocity of beasts of prey. Pip is made to descend to a pre-civilized state of affairs, in which stealing and brute force, and not social organization, are the bulwarks against starvation. By breaking into his sister's larder, he joins the brotherhood of outlaws and places himself beyond the pale of society.

His fear of those who brought him up "by hand" is reinforced by fear of those who are capable of turning him upside down. As a result, Pip, in Robert Barnard's colorful phrase, "soaks up guilt like a sponge",[16] until it is a veritable complex that makes him feel and behave as if he were out of tune with his environment. This predisposes him for the sensitivity we have seen him develop and which, in the end, turns him into the Everyman of a changing society. But we have also seen how this sense of apartness makes him forever fear regression after confrontation with the convict element. When the "stain" reappears, he always has the *Alice in Wonderland* feeling of growing smaller and smaller until he is again the little boy in the forge or out on the marshes, threatened with social expulsion. In Gilmour's words, "Pip is always and only the black-smith's boy, his struggle is to acquire rather than to recover gentility, and he is not allowed to forget or ever truly escape from his rude beginnings".[17]

Pip experiences his own past as a threat; it is as if he were constantly being bought face to face with what he considers his disreputable roots. The protective wall between him and the lurking wilderness that he perceives below the station he is about to secure himself in society is indeed a flimsy structure, and he is in constant fear that it will collapse and leave him where he started. This is the fear behind his allergic reaction to anything smacking of criminals and prisons. It is also behind his odd relationship to Orlick.

Orlick is an enigmatic figure in the novel, and he therefore has received considerable critical attention. The view of him as Pip's double is particularly relevant for the present discussion.[18] H.M. Daleski prefers to see him as "a counterpart of Pip (...) as a man who retains an abiding sense of being unloved".[19] Throughout the novel, Orlick acts as a foil to Pip. He, too, is a blacksmith's boy who wants to get on in the world. His progress, however, is far more limited than Pip's. His expectations are effectively cut short when Pip has him fired from his job as Miss Havisham's gatekeeper. From the beginning Pip sees Orlick as an adversary. If he is to be seen as a double, it may be more relevant perhaps to link him with Joe. He is Joe's complete opposite, in a way, his demon half brother. Pip, at any rate, feels curiously tied to him, and the mysterious link between them is strengthened when Mrs. Joe is assaulted. Pip hates his sister, but it is Orlick who puts his hatred into action. The leg iron is their mutual connection with the criminal underworld, and also the embodiment of their mutual resentment of the tyrant in their community. Their common social ground and their position as rivals are given further emphasis when Pip suspects Orlick of being in love with Biddy, the young woman who is so insolubly tied up with Pip's image of pastoral contentment—and confinement. In this case, too, Orlick is thwarted by Pip, who is otherwise such a passive person.

Thus, Orlick is inextricably mixed up with Pip's whole past, and, like the convict, he erupts from time to time into Pip's career as a gentleman with expectations. It is, however, when Pip has lost his expectations and is still in a kind of no-man's land, that the most dramatic encounter between the two takes place. Orlick emerges as the agent of the regression that Pip has been exposed to throughout his life. Pip is recalled to the village of his origin by the mysterious note he receives when he is still convalescing after his ordeal at Satis House, also a movement back into his past. The place of rendezvous is, appropriately, the old sluice-house out in the marshes. The major regressive episode is thus designed to culminate in an act of complete extinction. Orlick describes in detail how completely his old adversary will be wiped out: " 'I'm a going to have your life! (...) I won't have a rag of you, I won't have a bone of you, left on earth. I'll put your body in the kiln (...) and, let people suppose what they may of you, they shall never know nothing' " (p. 436). He intends to club Pip to death like an animal, but the greatest horror for Pip is that, dissolved in quicklime, he will have been removed from earth with no trace of his ever having existed. Worst of all, people will suspect that he has fled the country and covered all his tracks. Not only his life, but also his good reputation will be lost. He is convinced that if people think he has simply fled, he will be "misremembered after death (...) [and] despised by unborn generations" (p. 436), because he has deserted those who trusted him—Magwitch, Herbert, Joe, and Biddy.

The incident out in the marshes happens in complete isolation from the "normal" world—the village, the little town, and London. It is as if Pip has to withdraw from society in order to get rid of the fear and guilt that have dogged him so long. In the end, it is Orlick who vanishes, while Pip emerges a healthier and more harmonious person when he recovers from the fever that follows his ordeal. Orlick embodies Pip's lifelong fear that he, who, after all, is an orphan without inherited social status, might be forced to share the process of brutalization which turned Magwitch—another outcast orphan—into a criminal. Orlick is linked up with Pip's sense of social precariousness, but he also gives shape to his fear of "the undefined evil" that is such a pervasive element in Dickens's world.[20]

The traditional picaro is a freebooter who gradually develops a chameleonlike ability to fit into any place in society that he has the good or bad luck to occupy at a particular moment. He is the satirical observer of the social hierarchy and the scramble for a place in the sun, but he is also in the thick of the scramble. The loosely organized picture of a chaotic and multifarious society focuses on the flavor of living in such a community, revealing models of social organization and the forces at work behind social behavior. Facets of social experience and its ideological implications are in the foreground. The double perspective of the first-person narrative angle helps to bring about this combination of detachment and involvement. In *Great Expectations,* the mature narrator provides a continuous assessment of Pip's journey from child-hood to manhood and of the social and moral environment through which he passes. We have seen how the English novel is increasingly preoccupied with the protagonist's emotional response to his experience of down-and-out existence, while the Spanish picaro tends to avoid the subjective, internal view. Any pathos the incident may contain is left to speak for itself. In *Great Expectations,* the main interest may be said to be the internal view of Pip's emotional and moral development, the growth and nature of his consciousness. Nevertheless, the picaresque formula does help to bring out the contours of social organization and development which emerge in the course of the novel, raising the more important question of whether Pip's socio-moral transformation coincides with or is at variance with that of his community.

Humphry House claims that *"Great Expectations* is the perfect expression of a phase in English history."[21] The novel derives much of its force from its picture of the process of social evolution and the way it converges on the fortunes of a particular individual. Pip's circumstances and temperament make him the kind of ordinary, yet exceptional individual who could serve as both prototype and vehicle of criticism. Pip, as we have seen, is a Victorian Everyman, which means that he shares with his age certain ideological premises. But his sensitivity is also akin to the ache of modernism which makes some of Hardy's characters deviate from their environment. This quirk in his character is a potential source of social energy, the driving force behind the urge to climb, but, in the close and narrow milieu of the forge as Pip experiences it after his sojourn at Satis House, it leads to a paralysing sense of frustration and apathy. His only outlet is futile day dreaming.

Dickens's picture of Pip's village and his attitude to it are both ambiguous and sympathetic. He shows us that the milieu around the forge was perfect as long as the inhabitants had no ambitions beyond it. At the same time, he also depicts the crippling effect of a narrow environment where nothing happens to a person who is not satisfied with developing his muscles or spending his evenings in front of the kitchen fire or in the pub. Joe's friendship and sympathy make Pip anticipate his future occupation as Joe's apprentice with pleasure, but this is too weak a tie after he is introduced to the world of Satis House and the convict element has created a feeling of unease, which dissolves their old intimacy. The restlessness to which these circumstances lead is rooted in Pip's upbringing. The image of social harmony which the forge represents to Pip later in life is counteracted by an image of disharmony which stems from Mrs. Joe, who is forever harping on her husband's social inferiority and her own special superiority, through her Uncle Pumblechook. As Thurley puts it, "it is she who is so keen for [Pip] to make a good impression on Miss Havisham, and plants in his mind the germ of class-consciousness (...) [and] social discontent."[22]

By making his protagonist a village boy who was born in the early years of the nineteenth-century, Dickens was able to begin his picture of social evolution with a preindustrialized southern English village. Dickens does not give such a detailed account of village structure as George Eliot does in her early novels, but a station–or degree-oriented model is assumed, where each person has his or her place. Joe has a central place in the community because of his craft as blacksmith. He also exemplifies the pre-Industrial Revolution attitude to work. He is proud of his skill and has the integrity of the self-employed artisan who knows the value of hard work. Joe is also typical of the old order in that he is content with his lot and with his station. Later, Pip wonders whether he would have "been happier and better if I had never seen Miss Havisham's face, and had risen to manhood content to be partners with Joe in the honest old forge" (p. 291). However, by the time he receives the news of his great expectations, he and Joe have completely different feelings about the stations they have been born into. Joe is completely devoid of ambition to better himself. Pip, on the other hand, has been bitten by the bug of social unrest that may well be behind his sister's behavior toward both him and her husband. Pip feels by then that the forge is a prison as well as a haven. On his last day at home, he confesses to Joe that he "had always wanted to be a gentleman", and regrets that Joe had not improved his situation by educating himself (p. 174).

Education is the way Pip has imagined he might have gained admission to a higher social station. However, in the narrow milieu of the village, the opportunities for such improvement are extremely limited and might even be discouraged. This is what Joe discovered when he thought of schooling for himself: "'Your sister is given to government.... And she an't over partial to having scholars on the premises (...) and in partickler would not be over partial to my being a scholar, for fear as I might rise. Like a sort of rebel, don't you see?'" (p. 79). In this, she concurs to a prevalent contemporary attitude toward education among the lower classes, a prejudice which was fanned by the efforts of the radical movement in Britain throughout the century to use education as a lever in their struggle for social emancipation. According to "the influential conservative opinion (...) any popular education at all was undesirable and even dangerous".[23] It might lead to subversive activities. Pip's restlessness may be seen as evidence of the danger of introducing a lower class child to matters that are above its station.

While Joe's attitude to society is thus conservative, the result of belonging to a static community, Pip's attitude is potentially disruptive as long as he lives in such an environment, and clearly effects the fraternity between Pip and Joe, which was based on a deep sense of fellowship and equality. The democratic spirit of this relationship appears in sharp contrast to the authoritarian spirit of the household where Mrs. Joe rules supreme. Joe sums up the general principle of arbitrary power which his wife represents, seeing it as a manifestation of the unchangeable, natural social order: " 'On the Rampage, Pip, and off the Rampage, Pip—such is Life!' " (p. 143). In this community, there is a sharp distinction between those who are on the Rampage and those who are victims and expected to submit.

Pip's heritage is thus a contradictory ideology which assumes democratic solidarity as well as division between rulers and ruled, and the accompanying attitudes of domination and submission. The first stage on Pip's road toward his expectations takes him from one pre-industrialized unit to another, from village to market town. In the first place, Pip moves further into the power structure of which he is a slave than out of it. The artisan class dominates the social structure of the village, while trade is at the core of the more complex hierarchical structure of the town, where uncle Pumblechook's business premises are centrally placed in High Street. The street constitutes a closely interrelated commercial chain of being, which is clearly exemplified in the comic sketch of Pip's first view of it from his uncle's shop:

> Mr. Pumblechook appeared to conduct his business by looking across the street at the saddler, who appeared to transact *his* business by keeping his eye on the coach-maker, who appeared to get on in life by putting his hands in his pockets and contemplating the baker, who in his turn folded his arms and stared at the grocer, who stood at his door and yawned at the chemist. The watchmaker, always poring over a little desk with a magnifying glass at his eye, and always inspected by a group of smock-frocks poring over him through the glass of his shop-window, seemed to be about the only person in the High-Street whose trade engaged his attention. (p. 84)

Appropriately, the conversation at his uncle's breakfast table "consisted of nothing but arithmetic" (p. 84), an instrument of oppression used against the defenseless Pip with consummate skill. The closed gates at Satis House therefore make him feel that he has a chance of escaping from his uncle's tyranny and the principle of social advancement by submitting to the will of those who have been placed above him.

Satis House is like the traditional manor house at the summit of the local social pyramid and carefully fenced off from the rest of the community. Pip is an outcast *vis-à-vis* this world, and can only enter it through patronage or by making his own fortune—like another Dick Whittington. When he first goes there, only the first option was imaginable, and this is what occurs to his ambitious sister and uncle. Patronage is at the heart of the preindustrial social system, in keeping with the chain of dependency, which Perkin sees as the principle which both kept people in their places and linked them.[24] Pip may have been commanded to come to Satis House because of Miss Havisham's bizarre plan to wreak revenge on the male sex, but she adopts a well-established procedure when she opens her gates to someone from the bottom of the social hierarchy, carrying on a traditional mode of social invigoration at the top. Her own family had no doubt ascended to the top social level through their success in business, the more common type of upward social movement.

The need for rejuvenation is evident. Satis House suggests a completely self-sufficient social system turned in upon itself and, as a result, going to rack and ruin. The disused brewery and the decaying house and garden are not only a suitable framework for a study of human decay, but, like the stagnation which meets us everywhere, also symptomatic of a process of socio-economic change which has left the house of Havisham in a backwater, completely cut off from a world which is on the threshold of industrial and commercial revolution. Pip clings to the outmoded idea of patronage in his belief that Miss Havisham is behind his great expectations. His dream that she has intended Estella, whom he thinks of as a rich heiress, for him is in keeping with one of the old society's ways of renewing itself without jeopardizing the social equilibrium. However, in his vision of himself as the valiant knight who restores the palace of Sleeping Beauty to life, he embodies the myth of the self-made man who rises from rags to riches in the wake of the process that was to change the socio-economic face of Britain: Pip dreams that Miss Havisham "reserved it for me to restore the desolate house, admit the sunshine into the dark rooms, set the clocks a going and the cold hearths a blazing, tear down the cobwebs, destroy the vermin" (p. 253). Pip is, however, no daring entrepreneur, and Miss Havisham is totally wrapped up in her hallucinations, so Satis House is not transformed, but remains the emblem of a fossilized social structure, cut off from the natural process of socio-economic development.

The sense of guilt that Pip carries with him from his early childhood is deepened by the split he feels in himself between his loyalty to Joe, and what he stands for, and the sense of slavery which his authoritarian upbringing has instilled into him. This feeling is articulated when Pip is apprenticed by Joe—on Miss Havisham's initiative. The integrity of the old artisan and the arrogance of the old lady of the manor are finely expressed in the incident when Miss Havisham offers Joe money for Pip—the customary fee apprenticeship entailed—and Joe's dignified refusal to accept that Pip is a saleable commodity. The lower classes had not yet been reduced to "hands", least of all in the eyes of the artisan class. The same happens when Mr. Jaggers offers Joe compensation so that Pip can be released from his contract as apprentice and begin his career as a gentleman.

By the time Pip is told about his expectations, he has become irrevocably alienated from Joe and his gospel of honest manual work. In the circles to which Pip is admitted in London, unearned income is a must for the gentleman; trade and manual work are far below his dignity. "The word 'expectations'," writes Dabney, "is explicit and appropriate; in the circle of gentility where Pip has been placed one waits for one's destiny and accepts it."[25] Pip therefore finds it very easy to accept the clause in his patron's instructions that "I was not designed for any profession, and that I should be well enough educated for my destiny if I could 'hold my own' with the average of young men in prosperous circumstances" (p. 220). His painful awareness of his origin as a blacksmith's boy is always related to his worship for Estella, and invariably makes him feely guilty of disloyalty to Joe. He nevertheless sees his expectations as a means of becoming worthy of Estella from a social point of view. He may be gratified that he has been elevated from rags to riches, but he has to wage a never-ending struggle to get inside the freemasonry of gentlemen—the natural domain of his friend Herbert and his rival Drummle. Pip has money, and can borrow more, but he never achieves their social ease, which is not dependent on cash. He may see Drummle as a brute, but the latter has inherited the "U"/non-"U" distinction which keeps on defeating Pip. He may have money, but he cannot pretend to "family greatness" (p. 328).

Pip, like Rebecca Sharp, finds himself in a community which is still station-oriented. He is, however, evidence of the trend from station to class which started in the post-Waterloo period. Pip's career exemplifies the role of money in this transformation, but he lacks Becky's skill in exploiting the resulting social fluidity. Pip, however, becomes associated with the process which gradually modified the traditional attitude toward money and what constitutes a gentleman. Herbert may be said to follow a traditional route for a gentleman without capital when he buys himself into a merchant house, but once a patron has helped him with capital, he is left to fend for himself, rather like old Osbaldistone in *Rob Roy*. Banking and commerce are seen as socially acceptable sources of income. This is in itself not very innovatative. We have seen how, for example, Defoe reflects the growth of these activities on an interntional scale in *Colonel Jack*. In *Great Expectations*, however, there is a change of social ideal: idleness is no longer seen as the acme of happiness and respectability. Instead, the ideal gentleman is one who earns money with work. He is the hard-working, self-made man who has acquired social and financial distinction through his own efforts. When Pip rejects his expectations and takes his fate into his own hands, he leaves the thousand-year reign of patronage and joins the age that engineered the Great Exhibition. On the way, he also acquires the social consciousness of the new age. The middle-class ethos, which, as Perkin has shown, usurps the Victorian scene,[26] rejects Joe's belief that everyone should remain happy in his station. Instead, a class-oriented social system is favored which encourages a kind of social obstacle race in which the runners may break their necks, but in which the prize may be a place among the upper echelons of the kingdom. Q. D. Leavis observes that "for Dickens class distinctions were valid since ideally they represented an aspiration towards distinction and fineness".[27]

Pip's sensitivity also makes it obvious that, given the opportunity, Pip would in the end select a modest position, which would allow him to be a gentleman, but which would not expose him to the vicious rat race for power that the self-made man struggling to get to the top has to undergo. *Great Expectations* concludes with a vision of a community in which the social tensions and uneasiness the novel has diagnosed have been released. By the end of the novel Pip can entertain an inclusive view of society and his own social experience. The process of alienation, which had begun in his rigid upbringing according to Evangelical principles,[28] was interrupted during the crisis following the collapse of his great expectations. The new Pip does not return to his social origin, but he is reconciled to it. The return of the convict leads to a renewed and strengthened sense of solidarity which knows no social boundaries, but which does not do away with them either.

This sense of solidarity is physically invigorating.For instance, during the attempt to get Magwitch out of the country, the normally passive Pip adopts some of the picaro's prowess and resourcefulness so he can, like the picaro, circumvent the law. However, it is compassion rather than financial gain which motivates Pip's efforts. The Victorian gentleman's passion for sport and the equally Victorian zest for individual enterprise fuse in the attempt to help one of the victims of the social system. Still, in the end, the law is not circumvented. Magwitch is arrested, brought to trial, and dies a Christian penitent, at peace with himself. Pip's efforts at breaking the law are not the climax of his picaresque criminal career, but the result of his sensitive conscience and recently acquired sense of fellowship with the down-and-outs.

In his hour of need, Pip, in his turn, discovers that a fund of human fellowship is available to him as well. Joe's sense of solidarity takes him to London, a city he detests, when Pip becomes ill after the Orlick incident. Herbert shows how deeply ingrained fellowship is in the image of the true gentleman. Even Trabb's boy, who had chased Pip out of the market town when he was at the height of his career as gentleman apprentice, is ready to help when Pip is attacked by Orlick. The supreme value of the expedition down the river to save Magwitch is the lesson it offers on the value of concerted humanitarian effort. The "lady in distress" whom the three virtuous knights, Pip, Herbert, and Wemmick, are seeking to liberate is not a princess worth half the kingdom, but one who has led a "branded life among men" (p. 352) and whose money has been rejected.

Great Expectations is evidence of the affinity that Dickens's world of fiction has with that of picaresque novels. It expresses his confrontation with worldly success and with a social structure which favored climbing and acquistiveness. In *Great Expectations*, he exploits the protagonist's origin as a picaresque outcast and the possiblities for social mobility to express his mixed feelings about his own society, which stretched from the abyss of destitution to the peak of the Nabobs. Fear of the one is counterbalanced by misgivings about the other. Pip's life and adventures are evidence of the corrupting influence of social climbing, but also show that parasitism is the product of contrasting impulses— the impulse to escape from an outsider status and the impulse to advance to an inside position as high up in society as possible.

Thanks to his patrons, Pip avoids the merciless grappling with fortune at the social borderline, which characterizes the picaro's encounters with the world. On the other hand, his predominant passivity turns him into a sensitive barometer of the process of socio-moral transformation which accompanied Britain on her road to economic dominion. He illustrates the cost of the ruthless cult of the self-made man ideal, as well as the emergence of a social conscience which was far more tender than that of earlier generations. *Great Expectations*, like many picaresque novels, records the pulse of a society in a state of flux. By focusing on the status of a gentleman, Dickens repeats the traditional urge toward insider status of the picaresque novel. But even more important is the effect he achieves by taking the reader to the heart of Victorian society, increasingly dominated by the middle classes, and his ongoing effort to define and redefine the gentleman ideal in accordance with the emerging middle class ideology of hard work and respectability. Pip's sensitivity is in keeping with the growing Victorian uneasiness with the traditional view of the gentleman as idle and aristocratic. Besides, the dream of achieving the status of gentleman is both a question of class and transcendence of class. As Gilmour puts it, "Pip's struggle to become a gentleman is at once a justified aspiration to a better and finer kind of life and an ambition that inevitably gets snarled in the trammels of class."[29] The picaresque formula, implying as it does a rise and fall rhythm according to the law of unpredictability, lends itself to this kind of material. It provides the author with accents and patterns that, according to R. George Thomas, place characters like Magwitch, Estella, and Pip in one category of characters who "are rootless in origins, unlocated in society and free from obligations to the ordinary claims of the average citizen."[30] It is this underlying anarchic strain that most closely links *Great Expectations* to the picaresque novel. It should be added, however, that the picaro does not wish to destroy the society he seeks to enter, but to be assimilated in it. Anarchy is what the insiders fear. And it is this fear of the underworld, universal among the Victorian insiders, that is projected into Pip's experience of contamination through his involvement with the convict. It is also behind Dickens's choice of Pip, the outcast orphan, as his protagonist.

In the last resort, Pip expresses the picaro's urge to get away from his own status. He acquires a conscience that helps him to cover up his tracks as a down-and-out. Dickens carried on the process of aristocratization of the picaro that, as we have seen, had been taking place in the English novel from Defoe and Smollett to Scott. He was also determined to demarcate a niche of middle-class respectability similar to that Robinson Crusoe achieved on his island. In his ideal state of fellowship and respectability, Pip has, however, carved out a place for himself far from the retreats we have been introduced to in the novels we have so far considered.

[1] John Forster, *The Life of Charles Dickens* (London: J.M. Dent & Sons Ltd., 1927) vol. I, 21 and 25.

[2] Forster, 32-33.

[3] Edmund Wilson, *The Wound and the Bow* (London: Methuen, 1961) 43, 45.

[4] Geoffrey Thurley, *The Dickens Myth* (London: Routledge & Kegan Paul, 1976) 18 and 20-21.

[5] Charles Dickens, *David Copperfield* (Harmondsworth: Penguin, 1966) 105.

[6] Forster, 17.

[7] Chandler, 411.

[8] Guillén, *Literature as System*, 81.

[9] Page references, included parenthetically in the text, are to Charles Dickens, *Great Expectations* (Harmondsworth: Penguin, 1972).

[10] Van Ghent, 137.

[11] F. R. and Q. D. Leavis, *Dickens the Novelist* (Harmondsworth: Penguin, 1972) 427.

[12] Julian Moynahan, "The Hero's Guilt: The Case of Great Expectations," *Dickens, Hard Times, Great Expectations, and Our Mutual Friend. A Selection of Critical Essays.* A Casebook, ed. Norman Page (London: Macmillan, 1979) 117-118.

[13] Ross H. Dabney, *Love and Property in the Novels of Dickens* (London: Chatto and Windus, 1967) 134.

[14] J. Hillis Miller, *Charles Dickens. The World of His Novels* (Cambridge, Mass.: Harvard University Press, 1965) 267.

[15] Sylvia Bank Manning, *Dickens as Satirist* (New Haven: Yale University Press, 1971) 197.

[16] Robert Barnard, *Imagery and Theme in the Novels of Dickens* (Bergen: Universitetsforlaget, 1974) 106.

[17] Gilmour, 116.

[18] See Julian Moynahan, 110-111 and Alexander Welsh, *The City of Dickens* (Oxford: Clarendon Press, 1971) 130-131.

[19] H.M. Daleski, *Dickens and the Art of Analogy* (London: Faber and Faber, 1970) 243-244.

[20] Van Ghent, 137.

[21] Humphry House, *The Dickens World* (London: Oxford University Press, 1960) 159.

[22] Thurley, 283-284.

[23] Richard D. Altick, *Victorian People and Ideas* (New York: W.W. Norton & Company, Inc., 1973) 249.

[24] Perkin, 17 ff.

[25] Dabney, 137.

[26] Perkin, chs. VII and VIII.

[27] Leavis, 387.

[28] Leavis, 380.

[29] Gilmour, 12.

[30] R. George Thomas, *Charles Dickens: Great Expectations* (London: Edward Arnold, 1971) 37-38.

Chapter 7

The Picaresque Formula and the Theme of Social Descent in George Orwell's *Down and Out in Paris and London*

In the autobiographical section of *The Road to Wigan Pier* (1937), George Orwell tells us how determined he was to throw up his job in the Imperial Indian Police in Burma when he came home on leave in 1927. He felt he "had been part of an oppressive system" and ""was conscious of an immense weight of guilt that I had got to expiate." To achieve this and to escape from the system altogether, he explains, "I wanted to submerge myself, to get right down among the oppressed, to be one of them and on their side against their tyrants." Then he discovered the English working class and realized that "here in England, down under one's feet, were the submerged working class, suffering miseries which in their different way were as bad as any an Oriental ever knows."[1]

Orwell also stresses his ignorance of the working class and the way he had been conditioned by his middle-class background to share its prejudices and angle of vision, and to associate poverty with social outcasts, "'the lowest of the low'". Thinking that among these people—tramps and beggars—he might "find some way of getting out of the respectable world altogether",[2] he joined them on a number of occasions, dressed as one of them. And it was his greatest triumph when he found that he was accepted by them: "Here I was, among 'the lowest of the low', at the bedrock of the Western world! The class-bar was down, or seemed to be down".[3]

This is the context of *Down and Out in Paris and London* (1933), as he saw it from his social vantage point four years later. Both politically and in terms of social experience more mature, he could then afford to suffuse his account with irony. *The Road to Wigan Pier* is, however, evidence of Orwell's persistent need to escape from his class and descend to what, in relation to the established social hierarchy, was a lower world. At the same time, it suggests that the bedrock he struck was not only the bottom of the ladder, but also classless society, the pastoral haven from which the "system" had ejected man. The title of his first book promises the reader a documentary account of the way the poor live, but it is also an invitation to descend into a world that is out of bounds to the middle-class reader. It is also bait: the reader is made to expect a story of a rogue's progress through a world of petty crime and illicit pleasure—in short, a picaresque tale, in the derogative sense in which this term is often used.

The suggestion of this kind of literary antecedent is probably deliberate. *Down and Out in Paris and London* does offer the kind of titillating material which traditional rogue tales might well contain, for example, the somewhat unsavoury story about Charlie and his exploits in the Paris section. It also has, as George Woodcock points out, a decadent flavor about it in the first part which takes us back to a writer like Oscar Wilde.[4] The 1890s would, on the other hand, for Orwell also be associated with Zola, Gissing, and the early Somerset Maugham, who took their readers into the kind of world Orwell yearned to enter. The disguise and descent theme had also been exploited by Jack London in his novel about East London, *The Abyss,* to prepare himself for which the author in 1902 "submerged himself" in the slum world in a manner that anticipates Orwell.[5] The social realism of these writers and the documentary aspect of their novels naturally appealed to Orwell, who was both conscious of his literary heritage and sceptical of its appropriateness as model for a writer who wanted to expose a social system that he had come to detest as oppressive.[6]

Orwell exploits a number of features in the picaresque formula to deal with his down-and-out experience. The disguise he adopts is close to the picaresque, and so is the view of the world and the rhythm he substitutes for his customary middle-class routine. The picaresque furnishes him with a radical angle from which the social and human condition can be viewed and analyzed. This is the angle from which *Down and Out in Paris and London* will be studied in this chapter.

The idea of descending the social scale is far from the dream of the traditional picaro, to whom middle-class existence is the goal he strives to reach. This is reflected in the retreat which lucky picaros, like Gil Blas and Colonel Jack, achieve at the end of their careers as wanderers. The underworld of social outcasts is the nightmare that a Roderick Random or a Rebecca Sharp experiences as a threat to the safe insider position which Roderick feels entitled to by birth, and Rebecca by her talents. In Pip's case, fear of the abyss is part of his environment and also the result of his own individual confrontation with down-and-out existence. *Great Expectations* offers an interesting modification of the conservative tendency in English novels that exploit aspects of the picaresque formula. Pip is in full keeping with the picaresque tradition in his fear of outcast status and ambition to better his social position. He is, however, an anti-picaro in his rejection of the pursuit of money for its own sake and in his choice of a career which will give him safety but not distinction. *Great Expectations* is thus subversive in its rejection of the selfmade man myth and the cult of unlimited success in business and politics.

The formula of this kind of novel, in which the little rather than the great man is in the foreground, was adopted by H.G. Wells in a manner which may have appealed to Orwell. In novels like *Kipps* (1905) and *Tono-Bungay* (1909), Wells carries on the social realism of the Victorian period, in the Dickensian manner, and he displays a Dickensian interest in the ordinary person's development from a humble origin to a position of wealth and influence. In this manner, he presents a picture of a community in rapid transformation. In *Kipps*, as in *Great Expectations*, however, success is qualified at the end of the novel. Kipps's great expectations dwindle to a small sum of money, which is needed to provide him with the little book shop that is a safe, but unexciting retreat at the end of his career of social elevation. *The History of Mr. Polly* (1910) is of even greater interest in connection with the descent theme in Orwell's work of the 1930s. Mr. Polly is a small shopkeeper who, faced with bankruptcy, sets fire to his shop and "clears out". He chooses the down-and-out, but carefree existence of a tramp—a happy interlude in which he rediscovers his natural environment. The haven he finds at last is a country pub where he settles down to a carefree career as "odd man about the house".

This pattern of rejection is exploited in two of Orwell's novels, *A Clergyman's Daughter* (1935) and *Keep the Apidistra Flying* (1936). Both protagonists express their dissatisfaction with their middle class milieux by adopting for a while down-and-out existence or by refusing to conform to their environment's expectations of a safe career with prospects and a corresponding sense of responsibility. The protagonists' period of rebellion comes in the middle of the books, however, and they eventually return to their middle-class origins. This is also the safe retreat before and after his excursions into down-and-out existence Orwell dramatizes in Down and Out, suffusing the author's social vision with an ambiguity that both baffles and fascinates. Did Orwell see himself as a prince in disguise, who had to experience his people's condition before he could lead them out of the captivity of a caste-riddled society?

Down and Out in Paris and London is the first-person account of Orwell's "endeavour—his undeniable need—to dissociate himself" from his class, which is how Keith Alldritt describes the central theme of the book.[7] The moment of ejection, which in the picaresque novel is marked by the severance of the links between the protagonist and his family, depriving him at an early age of friends and protection, in Orwell's book is an act of dissociation from family, friends, and class which has led the narrator to take up his quarters in a Paris slum. He fends for himself by giving English lessons, but is as ignorant of the ways of the world of which he has become a citizen as the picaro at the outset of his wanderings. The anonymity with which he surrounds himself turns him into an orphan; he is, like the foundling hero of many picaresque tales, removed from his original context, and has, like him, to begin from scratch. The first chapter opens on a harmonious note: we are shown "Orwell"—the "I" of the book—surrounded by his new family—his neighbors. There is a touch of the prelapsarian atmosphere at the outset of *Colonel Jack* in this sketch of his new home:

> My hotel was called the Hôtel des Trois Moineaux. It was a dark, rickety warren of five storeys (...) The rooms were small and inveterately dirty (...) The walls were as thin as matchwood, and to hide the cracks they had been covered with layer after layer of pink paper, which had come loose and housed innumerable bugs. ... It was a dirty place, but homelike, for Madam F. and her husband were good sorts. (p. 6)[8]

In his new surroundings he has not even got a name — he is simply "I". This mask of anonymity is worn throughout his record. "It is as though Blair had disappeared for three months and returned later in the guise of 'I' to tell where he had been."[9]

Lack of work and money starts "I" on the road to his down-and-out existence. As in the case of Gil Blas, his state of innocence and comparative economic ease is brought to an end through an act of robbery: an Italian breaks into his room and steals most of his money: "I was left with just forty-seven francs—that is, seven and tenpence" (p. 15).

The educational aspect of the picaresque formula is exploited with great skill in *Down and Out* by drawing on a well established epic tradition, that of the storyteller whose tales form part of the episodic pattern of the narrative. At the outset of his stay in his "warren", he observes a number of eccentrics in the quarter and diagnoses poverty as the cause of their condition. Soon, he also discovers their skill as storytellers. Above all, they become his guides into the underworld they inhabit. His road to experience consequently takes him through a reality he can see with his own eyes, though it is no simple matter to discard the glasses he has been given by his environment, and a reality which is medi ed through the stories he listens to with such fascination. It is noteworthy how frequently these stories have been fashioned on a picaresque model, or express the essential picaresque situation. Thus Henri works in a sewer, epitomizing down-and-out existence, the "bedrock" to which "I" tries to descend (p. 7). Henri has been reduced to this state from a respectable job with a secure income because he had since been in prison. Charlie, on the other hand, "was a youth of family and education who had run away from home and lived on occasional remittances" in order to lead a disreputable life beyond the pales of "normal" society (pp. 9-14).

More interesting are stories which act as keys to an understanding of the mode of life that "I" has adopted. For instance, the story of a waiter

"I" gets to know at the restaurant where he eventually acquires a job, is
close to the picaresque paradigm:

> He was a comely youth... With his black tail-coat and white tie,
> fresh face and sleek brown hair, he looked just like an Eton boy; yet
> he had earned his living since he was twelve, and worked his way up
> literally from the gutter. Crossing the Italian frontier without a pass-
> port, and selling chestnuts from a barrow on the northern
> boulevards, and being given fifty days' imprisonment in London
> for working without a permit, and being made love to by a rich old
> woman in a hotel, who gave him a diamond ring and afterwards
> accused him of stealing it, were among his experiences (p. 60).

This type of story adds to the panoramic effect of "I"'s account of his
career and helps to widen his social canvas. But it retains some of the
exotic flavor which Henri and Charlie provide. In the case of Boris, we
are given a flamboyant perspective which nevertheless helps to anchor
"I"'s impressions of an unfamiliar world in actual down-and-out
existence. Again we are given a story which conforms with the
picaresque formula. Boris tells "I" about his career in his customary
colorful manner:

> *"Ah, mais, mon ami,* the ups and downs of life! A captain in the
> Russian Army, and then, piff! the Revolution—every penny gone.
> In 1916 I stayed a week at the Hôtel Eduard Sept; in 1920 I was trying
> for a job as night watchman there. I have been night watchman,
> cellarman, floor scrubber, dishwasher, porter, lavatory attendant. I
> have tipped waiters, and I have been tipped by waiters." (p. 22)

Boris is not only one of the eccentrics who enliven the boredom of "I"'s
days, but he also becomes his main helper in the Paris period. He is his
guide, although he is also responsible to a great extent for the somewhat
romanticized, exotic picture we are given of Paris, in sharp contrast to
the dreary atmosphere of the London section. Boris may take "I" into
down-and-out existence, and thus be instrumental in arranging his subterranean experience of life at the bottom—as the meanest of hotel servants—but his temperament also determines "I"'s bearings and marks
the whole of the Paris period. Character and incident are thus set apart
from the analytic assessment which is penned by the narrator in
retrospect.

When in the London section "I" is forced by circumstances to descend
once more into the underworld, he again gains experience via direct
observation and through what his fellow travelers tell him. In a panoramic survey in the manner of Defoe, he shows that his fall to a tramp's
existence has not deprived him of his curiosity:

> All day I loafed in the streets. (...) It was interesting to watch the crowds. The East London women are pretty (...) and Limehouse was sprinkled with Orientals—Chinamen, Chittagonian lascars, Dravidians selling silk scarves, even a few Sikhs (...). Here and there were street meetings. In Whitechapel somebody called the Singing Evangel undertook to save you from hell for the charge of sixpence. In the East India Dock Road the Salvation Army were holding a service (...). On Tower Hill two Mormons were trying to address a meeting. Round their platform struggled a mob of men, shouting and interrupting (p. 120-121).

The London scenes are less exotic than the Paris ones, above all because there is no Boris to give color to them, although in London, "I" too, is met with friendliness among the crowd, and his anonymity is respected: they "asked no questions" (p. 127).

There are fewer tales in the London than in the Paris section. It is as if the tramps and beggars with whom "I" communicates in the former city were too far gone to have the energy to tell stories, or their careers too trivial to qualify them as picaros. From what his tramp friend Paddy, one of his main guides to the world of spikes and mean lodginghouses, says about himself, "I" pieces together a picture of a man who embodies a mode of existence close to the picaro who begins at the bottom of society. Paddy's story is confined to a brief monologue embedded in the narrator's analytic report: "He had two subjects of conversation, the shame and come-down of being a tramp, and the best way of getting a free meal.... 'It's hell bein' on de road, eh? It breaks yer heart goin' into dem bloody spikes. But what's man to do else, eh?' " (p. 134).

There is nothing left of the picaro's resilience and fighting spirit in Paddy's whining complaint, no trace of the wit which is the former's secret weapon. It is as if "I" has come face to face with harsh reality, with no mediating vivid imagination to soften the shock.

Only one tramp appears to have his imagination intact in the London section—Bozo, who becomes his chief mentor. Bozo is a pavement artist, whose downhill journey has taken him from respectability as a house painter, through soldiering, another period of manual work, to a short period of married bliss. Then he is struck by misfortune. His young wife is killed in an accident, and soon after his right foot is "smashed (...) to pulp" after a fall from "a stage on which he was working" (p. 147). He receives only a small compensation, then:

> he returned to England, spent his money in looking for jobs, tried hawking books in Middlesex Street market, then tried selling toys from a tray, and finally settled down as a screever. He had lived from hand to mouth ever since (...) When I knew him he owned nothing but the clothes he stood up in, and his drawing materials and a few books (pp. 147-148).

Unlike Paddy, Bozo has not been degraded by his impoverished situation. On the contrary, "he had neither fear, nor regret, nor shame, nor self-pity" (p. 148). He has the stoic temperament which enables many picaros to endure a miserable life, and he has retained his integrity of character. On the other hand, he parts with the picaro in his rejection of society. He is not, like the picaro, prepared to commit crimes to advance his fortune; he sees crime as an attack on society and considers himself as "the enemy of society" (p. 148). Bozo consequently teaches "I" two lessons: that human dignity and integrity are impervious to money and class barriers, and that descent to the bedrock beneath society is not only a question of understanding and solidarity, but also a process which entails belief in social upheaval.

The stories, "I"'s observations, and his career as a down-and-out create the kind of fluctuating rhythm between ups and downs which characterizes the picaresque plot pattern. As in *Lazarillo*, we rarely move more than a notch above subsistence level, yet the downhill movement and the slight variations in the leeway that luck allows human endeavour are measured with great fidelity. In chapter one, "I" may have enough money to keep going in his "warren" and enjoy the company of the eccentrics with whom the place swarms. However, as his money dwindles and when he loses his job as a private tutor, he is, like the picaro, faced with the struggle for survival. Throughout the book, the survival theme is related to shillings and pence. The narrator charts his downhill movement by counting his stock of money: "My money oozed away—to eight francs, to four francs, to one franc, to twenty-five centimes; and twenty-five centimes is useless, for it will buy nothing except a newspaper. We went several days on dry bread, and then I was two and a half days with nothing to eat whatever" (p. 34).

Inevitably "I" is forced to resort to the pawnshop to boost his dwindling resources. His wardrobe, too, is a measure of the stage he has reached. When he and his friend are reduced to a state of roaming the streets, their spare clothes as well as their money have gone—a serious handicap in their hunt for employment. Down-and-out status is that of the complete outcast, whose sole refuge is a bench in the park or the precarious shelter of the Seine Bridges.

Necessity thus forces "I" to take to the streets. Traveling in *Down and Out* is very much an urban affair. Only in the London section does "I" leave the precincts of the city and venture into the surrounding countryside of Kent. In London, wandering is the only way to keep alive. In Paris, the street is the setting for "I"'s endless search for employment, but also an antidote against boredom, the boon companion of destitution. This is a close-up of Boris and "I" at an early stage of their wandering:

> We again failed to find work the next day ... My two hundred francs saved me from trouble about the rent, but everything else went as

badly as possible. Day after day Boris and I went up and down Paris, drifting at two miles an hour through the crowds, bored and hungry, and finding nothing. One day (...) we crossed the Seine eleven times. We loitered for hours outside service doorways (...) We always got the same answer: they did not want a lame man, nor a man without experience. (p. 29)

As in *Roderick Random*, getting employment is a laborious and futile affair. The outsider in *Down and Out*, too, has the disadvantage of having no friends in influential positions. "I" has cut his moorings in his middle-class environment and therefore is as fully exposed as the picaro to fraud and a haphazard fortune. Bribery may not be the key that will open the necessary doors, but no other key has been provided. In his unquenchable optimism, Boris formulates an important feature in the picaresque formula: " 'Tomorrow we shall find something (...) The luck always changes. Besides, we both have brains—a man with brains can't starve' " (p. 28). This is the picaro's recipe for survival. The book as a whole, however, demonstrates that it does not function among the lowest of the low. The irony of Boris's statement is that luck does change; they are provided with jobs. However, their work in the hotel, "I"'s in particular, only confirms their down-and-out status. They barely earn enough money to keep body and soul together. Their jobs are completely brainless and offer no chance of social advancement—the picaro's dream. They have been reduced to slave-labor status. Thus both luck and the picaro's wit are shown to be confined within very narrow bounds. No openings are offered for a rags-to-riches career.

Luck nevertheless plays an important part in the book. It underlines the precariousness of down-and-out existence, but it also gives scope, however limited, to humankind's natural refusal to despair. So little is needed to make the down-and-out feel that their circumstances have changed for the better. Thus at the nadir of his fortunes in Paris, after sixty hours without food, "I saw a five-sou piece" (p. 38). Luck did not stop here, but got them sixty francs for their shabby clothes at the usually mean pawnbroker's, after which they "ran out, bought bread and wine, a piece of meat and alcohol for the stove, and gorged" (p. 39). At the end of their feasting, they had "eight francs left (...) It was a marvellous change for the better after two bad days" (p. 40).

This type of luck is what makes down-and-out life so unpredictable, but it never lifts them far above starvation level. Luck in *Down and Out*, however, is also akin to the providence which intervenes in *Roderick Random* first, by depriving the protagonist of his inheritance at the beginning of the novel, and then by restoring him to it at the end. In both cases, luck acts as a *deus ex machina*, initiating and terminating at random Ronderick's picaresque career.

In *Down and Out*, providence is a mysterious B. who saves "I" from

more than short intervals of down-and-out existence. The difference is
that it is up to "I" when this resource is to be tapped. The result, as
Edward Thomas says, is that he reader is left with a feeling of "uneasiness" as "B. pops in and out of the story in a bewildering fashion."[10] In
the Paris section, this way out of poverty is left open as long as possible,
but his eventual decision to leave comes as much out of the blue as any
stroke of luck. On the other hand, in the London section, we are given to
understand from the beginning that "I"'s descent into the world of
tramps will be of limited duration, which strengthens our impression of ·
B. as providence, the agent who sets "I" apart from his fellow down-
and-outs.

The resulting feeling that "I"'s hardships are really unnecessary is particularly strong in the London section where we are given the impression that "I" is really only on an excursion. The mood is, nevertheless,
far more gloomy there than in Paris, because the people he meets are in a
worse plight than their Parisian colleagues and are seen with different
eyes. The suggestion of a happy and carefree slum "warren" is absent
from the London pages. In the Paris chapters, the search for work may
seem futile, but work does turn up in the end, however miserable it is.
"I" has, as Woodcock points out, the opportunity to "make the best of his
misfortune" by choosing a job that will give him maximum insight into
down-and-out existence in Paris.[11]

In London, however, "I" is one of an army of people without work
and with no prospect for work. They are not even looking for jobs, but
merely drifting from spike to spike as tramps. After a short stay in a cellar
lodginghouse, "I" has only a halfpenny in his pocket, and is at the mercy
of the London charity system, which provides shelter and a minimum of
food, but forces the tramp to be always on the move. Roaming through
the streets, some of them may pine for work, but there is none to be had,
and the result is growing apathy and loss of self-respect. Boris's belief in
the positions that "brains" will uncover is even more meaningless here,
although "I" finds that unemployment is even harder to bear for the
illiterate man than for somebody with an education. The former, he
finds, "needs work even more than he needs money. An educated man
can put up with enforced idleness, which is one of the worst evils of
poverty" (p. 160).

In this milieu, luck manifests itself mainly in the alternation between
good and bad spikes and through the vagaries of the occupations which
have been left for those who are below organized society: begging,
stealing, the activites of pavement artists or street musicians. In London,
the tramp's profession is wandering—his only way of keeping alive. The
temporary nature of "I"'s career as an outcast puts the interminable
nature of the real down-and-out's wandering existence into perspective.
He is like a caged animal, forever walking round in a circle, with luck as
a miserable bait. Evidence of the survival of the fittest even in this

hopeless milieu comes from the swindlers who feed on the system which keeps the tramps on the move. Although by becoming a swindler, the picaro may be able to move up the social ladder, in *Down and Out,* the swindler is part of the system which keeps the tramps out, and is thus largely beyond their reach.

The open ending of *Down and Out* emphasizes the tramp's place in the English social system. Once a tramp, always a tramp, below the level of the respectable society that "I" can return to when B.'s gentleman is ready to begin his grand tour of Europe, taking "I" along as his tutor, an opening any picaro would be glad to explore. The concluding paragraph focuses on the "I" who has gained maturity and social awareness through his down-and-out interludes. It also demarcates the down-and-outs' territory, the world that had been closed to him before, but which can never be closed again:

> Still I can point to one or two things I have definitely learned by being hard up. I shall never again think that all tramps are drunken scoundrels, nor expect a beggar to be grateful when I give him a penny, nor be surprised if men out of work lack energy, nor subscribe to the Salvation Army, nor pawn my clothes, nor refuse a handbill, nor enjoy a meal at a smart restaurant. That is a beginning. (p. 189)

"I" has come full circle, returning to the class in which he began. A process has been started, however, which refers both to his own social awareness and to forces at work in society at large. The open ending refers to a future which is still in the balance.

In *Down and Out in Paris and London,* Orwell exploits the loose episodic structure of the picaresque novel to achieve a panoramic, half-documentary account of a world below the recognized confines of class society near the end of the 1920s. In what John Atkins calls his "personal search for poverty",[12] he adopted a form which would enable him to focus on the typical, universal aspects of the human condition. The chain of encounters continually bring "I" face to face with what is unfamiliar and strange and with his own middle class idiosyncracies as well. The encounter is thus "I"'s means of gaining access to this closed world, but also a personal challenge: his sensitivity to the lot of the downtrodden and his capacity for understanding and fellowhip are extended and continually tested. The encounters reveal helpers as well as enemies, the former being his concrete environment, the latter the abstract forces which constitute the system within which the down-and-outs are prisoners.

Sympathy and a sense of solidarity may be perceived in this panoramic sketch of the Paris which exists before the respectable citizens are up:

Drowsy men were sweeping the pavements with ten-foot besoms, and ragged families picking over the dustbins. Workmen, and girls with a piece of chocolate in one hand and a *croissant* in the other, were pouring into the Métro stations. Trains, filled with more workmen, boomed gloomily past (p. 80).

"I" is part of this other world; he is one of the crowd:

One hastened down to the station, fought for a place (...) and stood jammed in the swaying mass of passengers, nose to nose with some hideous French face, breathing sour wine and garlic. And then one descended into the labyrinth of the hotel basement, and forgot daylight till two o'clock, when the sun was hot and the town black with people and cars (p. 80).

The impersonal pronoun "one" suggests that "I" is not a sightseer or a sociologist gathering information; he is describing his daily routine as a *plongeur*. As such he belongs to the Paris underworld, which is segregated from the world of affluence that fills the streets, the daylight or midnight world above the *plongeur's* subterranean place of work. The people and cars he leaves behind as he descends into his den are still there when, late in the evening, he again "emerged, sweating, into the cool street. It was lamp-light (...) and beyond the river the Eiffel Tower flashed from top to bottom with zigzag skysigns (...) Streams of cars glided silently to and fro, and women, exquisite-looking in the dim light, strolled up and down the arcade" (pp. 80-81). There is a dreamlike quality about the scene, emphasizing "I"'s discovery of the existence of two worlds in Paris, one, the fashionable world, ignoring the other. The beautiful women "I", as *plongeur*, meets on his way home from work, turn away at the sight of his dirty clothes. The underground cellar where he and his fellows work is an apt symbol of the apartheid system which brands people of the *plongeur* category as social pariahs, out of bounds for respectable middle-class citizens. Appropriately, "I" and his new friends, after their long days in the hotel kitchen, seek relaxation and company in "a little *bistro,* an underground place frequented by Arab navvies" (p. 81). "I"'s friends may tell him stories about their escapades in the higher strata of society, but, by the time he gets to know them, these tales have acquired the flavor of exotic legends and appear to have little basis in reality.

Alan Sandison refers to Orwell's fascination with "a subterranean existence lying enticingly at the feet of the outcast."[13] There is indeed an *Alice in Wonderland* flavor about Orwell's concern with descending into a closed world, which both attracts and repels him. This is even more in evidence in the London section. Again, he is admitted to a world which has been closed to him: "At about a quarter to six the Irishman led me to the spike. It was a grim, smoky yellow cube of brick, standing in a corner of the workhouse grounds. With its rows of tiny, barred windows, and a high wall and iron gates (...) it looked much like a prison" (p. 127). He is invited to join the "long queue of ragged men" (p. 127)—a world which is as effectively shut off from the above-ground world of the surrounding streets as that of the Paris hotel kitchen. "I" finds that it is part of the system to cordon off the tramps and prevent them from settling down anywhere, even on a bench in the park. The police forever keep them on the move, and they are forbidden to come back to the same spike two nights running. Once more a panoramic survey of the scene introduces "I"'s account of his encounters with this world. We are given a careful survey of the men in the queue:

> They were of all kinds and ages, the youngest a fresh-faced boy of sixteen, the oldest a doubled-up, toothless mummy of seventy-five. Some were hardened tramps, recognizable by their sticks and billies and dust-darkened faces; some were factory-hands out of work, some agricultural labourers, one a clerk in collar and tie, two certainly imbeciles. (p. 127)

The canvas "I" paints here represents a cross-section of the community of social outcasts he is about to enter. Each person and category represent a particular place in the social system from which these people have been excluded. We are given a nightmarish version of Vanity Fair.

In the course of his wanderings as a tramp, "I" acquires sociological insight which enables him to give a full report on the life and customs of down-and-outs in Paris and London. He emerges as a latterday Henry Mayhew, the author of *London Labour and the London Poor* (1851).[14] As a sociologist, he seeks to "pierce[the]wall of indifference" which separates his middle-class readers from those "outside the pale"[15] by making them aware of down and out existence. He also aims at diagnosing the social illness of which the down-and-out phenomenon is a symptom.

At the heart of the wretchedness that "I" becomes submerged in during his wanderings is money. A Berlin wall separates the haves from the have-nots. Without money, a person is deprived of food as well as station. We have seen how "I"'s experience denies the picaresque assumption that starvation releases the individual's resourcefulness and thus enables him with luck to survive. As he approaches rock bottom among tramps and vagabonds, "I" finds that he is below the fringe area between the two nations which is the breeding ground of parasites and upstarts. For the London tramp, luck is merely a dream of riches, completely beyond his reach.

Luck is, nevertheless, used with considerable effect to emphasize the

142 THE PICARESQUE IN THE BRITISH NOVEL

arbitrary nature of the two-nation system. Only a thin wall separates the wealthy guests from the army of servants in the Paris hotel:

> Fear of the mob (...) is based on the idea that there is some mysterious, fundamental difference between rich and poor (...) But in reality there is no such difference. The mass of the rich and the poor are differentiated by their incomes and nothing else, and the average millionaire is only the average dishwasher dressed in a new suit. Change places, and handy dandy, which is the justice, which is the thief? (p. 107).

The egalitarian dream which is behind this inversion is illusory in a society which is completely geared to money. The care with which "I" registers his rapidly decreasing stock of ready cash is evidence of the link between money and the individual's sense of security. Precariousness is as prominent a feature in Orwell's book as in *Roderick Random* and *Vanity Fair,* and it is as much a question of shillings and pence. The fear of poverty is part of "I"'s middle-class background. After his "first contact with poverty" in Paris, the narrator reflects that "poverty (...) is the thing you have feared all your life, the thing you knew would happen to you sooner or later" (p. 15). Thomas relates the circumstance that the London section is "so much more painful" reading than the Paris section to Orwell's attention to the humiliating effect of destitution.[16] " 'It seems to me,' " the protagonist says to his tramp mentor, Bozo, " 'that when you take a man's money away he's fit for nothing from that moment' " (p. 147). Bozo has a different view, insisting as he does on the integrity of the individual. The treatment the tramps receive is, however, ample evidence that "I"'s observation is correct. In the eyes of the world, the tramp has lost his dignity.

The Paris hotel and its many restaurants provide a model for a parasitic society in which the rich literally feed on the sweat of the poor. This is a traditional radical view, but in his inside position as *plongeur* "I" discovers for himself how the model works. Also, he finds that the staff is organized in a strictly hierarchical manner. He is, as *plongeur,* at the bottom of a social ladder like that of society at large. *Plongeurs* are the lowest of the low, slaves who cannot escape from the system:

> All that is required of them is to be constantly on the run, and to put up with long hours and a stuffy atmosphere. They have no way of escaping from this life, for they cannot save a penny from their wages, and working from sixty to a hundred hours a week leaves them no time to train for anything else. The best they can hope for is to find a slightly softer job as nightwatchman or lavatory attendant. (pp. 69-70)

The *plongeur* is, like the tramp in London, unable to choose the picaro's means of escaping existence at starvation level. Their dilemma is that they are outsiders within a system whose alpha and omega is money. They have no means of jumping on to the band waggon from which they have been ejected or where they have never been.

The down-and-outs "I" meets illustrate the picaro's ability to adapt, even to the harshest conditions. Although most of them have been reduced to submissiveness through sheer lack of energy, one at least, Bozo, displays the rebel spirit that enables the picaro not only to survive but also to advance in terms of human dignity. The essence of the lesson Bozo teaches "I" is that " 'If you set yourself to it, you can live the same life, rich or poor. You can still keep on with your books and your ideas. You just got to say to yourself, 'I'm a free man in *here*" (...) and you're all right' " (p. 147). Bozo's stand is that of Roderick when he refuses to submit to his tyrant of a captain although he is a helpless prisoner exposed to enemy fire. His mind, too, is free.

Bozo teaches that poverty does not matter in terms of human dignity and integrity. He is thus the major advocate of the egalitarian principle which is the core of the lesson "I" is taught in the course of his down-and-out career. "The implication is," Woodcock writes, "that, having had the courage to descend into the depths, Orwell himself has shed his fear and can recognize the equality of all men."[17] At the same time, he has become aware of the strain life on or below starvation level is both on the individual and on the community of which he is a member.

The protagonist's—and Orwell's—dilemma in *Down and Out* is that they are impelled by circumstances and by inclination to abandon their middle-class background and take up "residence" below the social hierarchy. "I"'s middle-class heritage is exploited throughout the story as foil to the new world he is discovering. It is, above all, evidence of the problem of unlearning what one's whole upbringing has sought to instill into one's character and code of behavior. In other words, Orwell shows how "I"'s ideological basis colors his responses to a community which does not conform to his middle-class expectations. and which he seeks for that very reason. "I"'s record is shot through and through with allusions to his "roots" and their conditioning effect. Again and again he shows, for example, how ingrained he is with the conventional middle-class virtue of cleanliness. It is very difficult for him to feel at home in a filthy and smelly milieu. There is something heroic in his determination to overcome the resulting prejudices and automatic response patterns, like a sense of personal discomfort, for instance, and cliché-like phrases he can hardly control. The result is the ambiguity which Sandison detects in Orwell's attitude to poverty—that is, down-and-out status.[18] His life inside this class liberates him from his narrow background, but also makes his class features surface. We have noticed how he feels both attracted to and repelled by the crowd he joins in the

Métro. The tramps in the spike queue in London release first his automatic reaction that they are "a disgusting sight." Then they appeal to his sympathy: they are "underfed." Finally, he discovers their humanity and their unbiased attitude to other people (p. 127)—in contrast, by implication, to the milieu in which Orwell had grown up.

"I"'s middle-class background colors his whole manner and way of thinking. The struggle to escape from the first clauses in his middle-class code of behavior—thrift, honesty, and plain dealing—is a central feature in the process of maturing he shares with the *Bildungsroman* hero. Thus, when his last *sou* has been spent, he is relieved that his middle-class instinct to provide for the future had made him pay the rent for his room in advance. He therefore avoids the fate of the Paris tramp who is forced to sleep under the Seine bridges. Similarly, when he is faced with poverty in London, he safeguards himself against complete destitution by hiding away his best suit when he goes to pawn his wardrobe. The door to respectability is left ajar. "I" thus hesitates to let go of his middle-class world. The supreme evidence of this is the link he maintains with his benefactor, B. On the other hand, he soon finds that despite his precautions, he has to surrender some of his inherited notions about human intercourse if he is to survive—even if only temporarily. Such a surrender is also a precondition for admission to insider status in down-and-out society. When he has been offered work as a *plongeur,* he hesitates to accept the job because his middle-class respect for the idea of a contract makes him hesitate about the terms. He has to promise to stay in the job for a month, while he knows that he might have to take another job any day. Boris is fuming, while "I" objects that " 'it seemed more honest to say that I might have to leave.' " Boris retorts with the crucial question, " 'Do you think a *plongeur* can afford a sense of honour?' " (p. 53). If "I" had not been prepared to compromise his deep-rooted sense of honor, he would not have got the job and the unique chance it offered for admission to a world that had been closed to him.

One of "I"'s greatest difficulties is to shed his class characteristic of reserve in order to feel at ease in his new environment. The idea of the proletariat as an open and friendly community beyond the pale of order and respectability suffuses the Paris section with a pastoral aura which is reminiscent of the freebooter community Gil Blas encounters and the gypsy society Tom Jones is invited to join. "I," too, is invited to join a brotherhood in which moral and social status is of no account. He finds that fellowship is the password to this community. Solidarity is the main lesson he is taught during his career as *plongeur.* One of the effects of B.'s interference is that "I" has to begin all over again when he descends to the London tramp world. Again, he is invited to join after having been through the test of initiation. When he has donned his tramp's outfit, he recalls,

I dared not speak to anyone, imagining they must notice a disparity
between my accent and my clothes.... My new clothes had put me
instantly into a new world. Everyone's demeanour seemed to have
changed abruptly. I helped a hawker pick up a barrow he had upset.
"Thanks, mate," he said with a grin. No one had called me mate
before in my life. (p. 115)

As in Paris, "I" has to unlearn his middle-class ideology, and this is a
slow process. But he feels he has been admitted to the company of tramps
through incidents like this, and he soon has his own mate, Paddy. When
he first meets him, "I" responds with the kind of ambiguity he finds, as
we have seen, so hard to avoid. Seen with his middle-class eyes, Paddy
has "the regular character of a tramp—abject, envious, a jackal's
character." At the same time, he is a supreme exponent of the
proletariat's innate sense of solidarity: "Nevertheless, he was a good
fellow, generous by nature and capable of sharing his last crust with a
friend; indeed, he did literally share his last crust with me more than
once" (p. 136). Squeamishness and appreciation are finely mixed in this
account of the final act of solidarity in the book, which occurs during
"I"'s excursion into Kent:

"Here y'are, mate," he [a tramp] said cordially. "I owe you some fag
ends. You stood me a smoke yesterday. The Tramp Major give me
back my box of fag ends when we come out this morning. One good
turn deserves another — here y'are."
And he put four sodden, debauched, loathly cigarette ends into my
hands. (p. 177)

The world of the down-and-outs and that of the upper middle-class
are continually juxtaposed in *Down and Out*. Orwell is indeed bent on
"shocking his middle class reader"[19] by insisting on rubbing in details
that she or he will reject as offensive. At the same time, he builds up a
picture of a hidden society, which as "I" comes to realize, represents
values which cannot thrive in a convention-ridden community, geared
to property and money.
It is, however, clear that "I"'s journey from ignorance to social
awareness is, above all, a personal journey in which the protagonist has
come to terms with his own dilemma of being the prisoner of a world he
wishes to reject. To achieve liberation, he adopts the picaro's *persona*,
but reverses the direction of his quest. Instead of seeking insider status in
the upper reaches of the social pyramid, "I"'s aim is insider status below
the bottom rung of the ladder which the picaro yearns to ascend. The upside down perspective which is so dominant in *Great Expectations* is behind the *Alice in Wonderland* element in *Down and Out*, too. Paradoxi-

cally, "I" has to go down in order to come up. In the process, he has come to terms with the burden of guilt and self-consciousness which has dogged him through Paris and London, and he has been able to question and give new meaning to terms like *down and out, outcast, the lowest of the low, bottom*—words which are firmly associated with the abyss of the protagonists' nightmares from *Roderick Random* to *Great Expectations.*

By the time Orwell wrote *The Road to Wigan Pier,* he had come to realize that "unfortunately you do not solve the class problem by making friends with tramps. At most you get rid of some of your own class-prejudice by doing so."[20] He had discovered that between the tramp and his middle-class vantage point comes the working class—which it is the object of *The Road to Wigan Pier* to explore. But by then not only did Orwell have a fuller knowledge of the social system of contemporary Britain, he also had achieved a clearer picture of the cure for a society which is riddled with the disease of class division. The cure was an Orwellian brand of socialism which would bring about a revolutionary transformation of society and bring equality, liberty, and justice to the fore—and, above all, solidarity. However, although the cure may not have been spelled out, the picaresque formula—turned upside down—helps us to perceive the contours of the new society in *Down and Out.*

[1] George Orwell, *The Road to Wigan Pier* (Harmondsworth: Penguin, 1974) 129-130.

[2] Orwell, 131.

[3] Orwell, 134.

[4] See George Woodcock, *The Crystal Spirit* (London: Jonathan Cape, 1967) 93-95.

[5] See Bernard Crick, *George Orwell. A Life* (London: Secker and Warburg, 1981) 109-110.

[6] Alex Zwerdling notes that Orwell had great respect for writers like Dickens, Zola, Tolstoy, Conrad, while he shared the left-wing distrust of fiction in the thirties. *Orwell and the Left* (New Haven: Yale University Press, 1974) 146 and 160.

[7] Keith Alldritt, *The Making of George Orwell. An Essay in Literary History* (London: Edward Arnold, 1969) 49.

[8] References, included parenthetically in the text, are to George Orwell, *Down and Out in Paris and London,* (Harmondsworth: Penguin, 1974).

[9] Peter Stansky and William Abrahams, *The Unknown Orwell* (Frogmore, St. Albans: Paladin, 1974) 222.

[10] Edward M. Thomas, *Orwell* (Edinburgh: Oliver and Boyd, 1971) 20. See also Christopher Hollis, *A Study of George Orwell. The Man and His Work* (London: Hollis and Carter, 1956) 47.

[11] Woocock, 97.

[12] John Atkins, *George Orwell* (London: John Calder, 1954) 84.

[13] Alan Sandison, *The Last Man in Europe. An Essay on George Orwell* (London: Macmillan, 1974) 63.

[14] Peter Lewis, *George Orwell. The Road to 1984* (London: Heinemann, 1981) 26.

[15] Zwerdling, 138.

[16] Edward Thomas, 18.

[17] Woodcock, 99-100.

[18] Sandison, 60.

[19] Alldritt, 48.

[20] Orwell, *The Road to Wigan Pier,* 135.

Chapter 8

The Reverse Movement of the Picaresque Rhythm in John Wain's *Hurry On Down*

In his recent book *A Short History of English Literature,* Robert Barnard refers to the new generation of writers who, in the mid-1950s, "achieved a decisive re-orientation of the novel downwards socially, and they created a kind of novel that was light, freewheeling, with something of the zest of the old picaresque tradition."[1] This generation of writers, referred to as "Angry Young Men" after John Osborne's *Look Back in Anger* (1956), or as the "Movement," were antiestablishment and highly sceptical of the previous generation of writers' interest in modernism and experimentation. The novel that, alongside Kingsley Amis's *Lucky Jim* (1954), was generally heralded as the harbinger of a new era in literature was John Wain's *Hurry On Down.* This novel, according to the first, highly critical historian of this group of writers, Kenneth Allsop, has "always been placed in the list by trend-charters as a significant and major work."[2] This perspective has faded over the years. The reader is struck, however, by the manner in which Wain deliberately exploits the picaresque formula to reverse the aim of the picaro—to achieve social elevation—as the title of the novel suggests. In his downward movement, the hero reveals his affinity with Orwell's brood, but his aim is different. Charles Lumley's dream is not the status of an insider in the proletariat, which "I" struggles so hard to win in *Down and Out.* He tries to achieve instead some sort of outsider's status, not only *vis-a-vis* his own middle-class origins, but in relation to the whole social system.

The deliberate use of the picaresque formula—ranging from satire to such stocks-in-trade as the loose episodic structure, sudden and often violent reversals of fortune, coincidence, and slapstick humor—lends to the story the zest that Barnard identifies as a prime characteristic of the picaresque tradition. It is the aim of this chapter to explore the manner in which Wain draws on the perennial social interest of the picaresque formula, along with its appeal as entertainment, to come to grips with the pressures of the age in which he was living. Like his predecessors in such novels as *Lazarillo, Gúzman,* and *Colonel Jack,* Charles Lumley is rootless, but not because he has been left out in the cold by the social system. Nor has he been disinherited, like Roderick Random, or deprived of his expectations, like Pip. On the contrary, the protagonist in *Hurry on Down* has been well served by his benefactor, the welfare state, which has provided him with a university degree and a social security system.

Charles Lumley and his colleagues, however, rebel because they feel they are being forced into narrow grooves — in terms of profession, class, and moral convention. In the course of his career, Charles Lumley also finds that affluence has not done away with the fringe areas in which crooks and knights of fortune have traditionally flourished. In other words, the picaro need not become a museum piece, nor an entertainer at a folklore festival. *Hurry On Down* is evidence of the vitality of the picaresque mode as well as of the way it adapts itself to changes in social and literary focus.

In *Hurry On Down*, Wain abandons the picaresque formula's favored first-person narrative stance and adopts a third-person point of view. The satirical thrust is sharpened at the expense of the irony with which a first-person narrative is fraught: the third-person narrator, after all, can speak with greater detachment and his awareness is apt to be greater than that of the first–person, whose understanding of his own situation tends to be deliberately toned down.

Allsop sees *Hurry On Down* as "the iliad of a modern displaced person."[3] The opening episode in the novel indeed focuses on Charles Lumley's displaced situation; gradually we realize that he is the author of it himself. If Allsop had the siege that was central to Homer's poem in mind, he might have quoted the initial confrontation between Charles and his irate landlady as evidence that the young man not only has distanced himself from his origin, but is virtually besieged by the representatives of the establishement from which he seeks to escape. When Charles gives notice without giving specific reasons his landlady bombards him with questions which assume that one must be both straightforward and polite when one gives notice, as if it were an act governed by contract as well as etiquette. Similarly, she is both puzzled and annoyed when he hesitates to tell her where he works and what exactly he is doing. Charles Lumley does not live up to the code she expects her lodgers to observe: " 'I've never had any lodger here but what I've known he was respectable, yes, and in a steady job too' " (p. 8).[4] Her parting reference is to his credibility — " '*if* it's true what you're saying' " (p. 9)—another axiomatic assumption of the middle class to which she belongs.

The opening of *Hurry On Down* differs from the traditional picaresque novel as well as from *Down and Out*. The picaresque formula assumes an opening situation which focuses on the picaro as a child, about to be ejected into a hostile environment. In *Down and Out*, the protagonist has been adopted by the environment he had chosen in deliberate preference to his own family and friends. Far from being rejected by his new environment "I" is being initiated into it, a ceremony which counterbalances his own rejection of his heritage. Charles Lumley and his landlady are involved in a confrontation which implies mutual rejection. In *Hurry On Down*, the ceremony of ejection, which is such a characteristic feature in the picaresque novel, is in the foreground of the picture we are given of Charles the following morning: "Suitcase in hand, Charles stumbled next morning over the greasy hall mat for the last time, and lurched out into the July sunshine" (p. 10). It is as if he were thrown out of a milieu he is expected to inhabit, as a result of his class and education. He has displaced himself by refusing to conform.

The opening episode closes the first phase of Charles's career as wanderer. In a flashback, we are told how he had refused to apply for a job on leaving the university. Instead, he had simply stuck a pin into a list of towns he had drawn up, appropriately, "at random" (p. 10). He then got on the first train without making any further preparations, and without leaving any address behind—the first middle-class rule that he flaunts: "Full of hope, he had scurried across country to this dingy huddle of streets and factories, only to spend his precious weeks in nail-biting indecision. Nothing had been settled, not even the obvious and simple question of a trade" (p. 11).

Charles's first venture into the unknown thus turns out to be a failure. He had been unable to solve his "predicament" (p. 11), which is left undefined, beyond a vague feeling of being "hemmed about" (p. 11). The main culprit is singled out: his fragmentary university education, "three years' random and shapeless cramming" (p. 11). Charles's second venture takes him back to his home town. Spending his last pound on the railway ticket, he goes to see his fiancée, but instead gets involved in a confrontation with his class, represented by his prospective brother-in-law, Robert Tharkles, and his wife. From then on, Tharkles is the incarnation of the middle-class ethos that Charles is determined to escape. We are given another scene of mutual rejection, but one in which the representative of the establishment is ultimately seen as the ejector and Charles as the ejected. He can refuse to conform, and he may fight back, but he is bound to lose, being up against the aggressive potential of a whole class.

Tharkles, like the landlady, attacks Charles who has acted against the middle-class notion of common decency, from the premises of class:

> "I met your parents the other day.... I think you ought to realize there's a pretty widespread dissatisfaction with the way you're going on. For one thing the way you just disappeared after taking your finals. Your father told me you hadn't even given them your address.

They had absolutely no means of getting in touch with you. I must
say I think that's pretty shabby." (p. 17)

A violent quarrel follows, which culminates in a fight in the slapstick,
mock-epic, comic tradition reminiscent of Fielding's novels, but which
harks back to the earliest picaresque tales. Charles grabs the washing
bowl and "with a tremendous sense of release, he swung it round" (p. 19),
emptying its contents over Tharkles and his wife. As in the incident
with the landlady, Charles's act of rejection is accompanied by
suggestions of ejection from the milieu to which he refuses to conform:
the bowl "had hardly landed before Charles clawed open the back door
and rushed out.... the gate clicked shut behind him, and he stumbled
forward into the road" (p. 20).
   Charles seeks refuge in a pub where the majority of the customers are
working class. He finds that this is a closed world to a person like him,
who is "imprisoned in his class" (p. 25). He is, like the picaro, a
gatecrasher; not even alcohol can make him acceptable in the new
milieu. Drunk, he becomes "the cause of a disturbance" (p. 27), which is
usually out of character for a person of his background and upbringing.
Again there is a mixture of gestures suggesting rejection and ejction at
the end of the incident. He is, in his drunken state, immune to shouts
from the customers—" 'throw the clumsy bastard out!' "—and "the
menacing approach of the landlord":

> Instead of quailing before the hailstorm of abuse that swept at him
> from behind the bar, he merely blinked benignly (...) at the
> landlord's whirling face (...) and then, turning coolly on his heel,
> calmly opened the door and went out, to be greeted by the warm
> silence of the summer night, and the village street opening and
> closing like a huge oyster shell. (p. 27)

After this three-tier process of ejection—from his respectable
lodgings, from his family and background, and from the working-class
pub—stages on his journey downwards in the social system—he finds
himself in the street, like the picaro at the start of his wanderings: "He
had nowhere to go, no money and no plans" (p. 27). His situation is not,
however, one of despair. In his drunken state, he merely notices that the
night is warm, as he walks along in a state of excitement. He feels
liberated from his class and is conscious of a process akin to the second
birth, which is what Wicks suggests that ejection is for the picaro.[5] After
each of the incidents, which terminate so violently, there is a suggestion
of a new beginning. First of all, he displays the picaro's skill in falling
on his feet and adjusting himself to his altered circumstances. Then "he
felt a new elation, a new freedom" (p. 29). Retching, he wonders, "could
he not, just as easily, cast up and be rid of his class, his *milieu*, his

insufferable load of presuppositions and reflexes? (...) Why should it not end here, and he be reborn, entering the world anew" (p. 30).

The next phase does indeed suggest that Charles has been reborn as a social individual. His job as a window cleaner sends him scurrying down the social ladder from his middle-class origins. On the other hand, it is a step up the ladder in relation to the picaro's down-and-out beginning, close to starvation level. As a drunk Charles has adopted the basic picaresque condition of precariousness, which is underlined by his temporary lodgings in a YMCA hostel. As a window cleaner, he moves in a fringe area beyond the confines of class. He is able to retain his individuality and can remain completely anonymous, like "I" among the down-and-outs in Paris and London. He has company, but both he and his new friends avoid any ties that will commit them. Charles shares lodgings with a bohemian novelist and his mistress and is lucky enough to get a partner who can protect him, but theirs is a simple contractual relationship. His protector does not ask any questions and does not invite any. He does not even know Charles's address. We are given another rejection-ejection incident when Charles offers his services as window cleaner to the headmaster of his old school. Again, he barely escapes being thrown out. His behavior is interpreted as insulting, in revenge for some grudge he has against his old school. Charles realizes that one is not supposed to step out of the niche in the class hierarchy into which one has been born and which one has been educated to fill. Jobs earmarked for the lower orders are out of bounds for people like him.

His new "profession" gives Charles a sense of security and ease. The fact of working with his own hands and earning the money he needs with his own sweat gives him a pastoral feeling of contentment. He is completely without ambition, can enjoy his Sunday mornings off, and has no anxiety about tomorrow. After work, he returns to his loft, where he "lean[s] back in utter contentment, a glass of beer at his elbow (...) taking life as it came" (p. 49). "Wheeling his cart out every morning, Charles felt solid, respectable, and habit-ridden" (p. 70). After a while, he decides that he could do with a change. To celebrate his independence and his new prosperity, he dons "the uniform of the class he had renounced" and goes to spend a night at the Grand Hotel, "determined to live at the rate of a thousand a year for the next few hours" (p. 73).

In his careless determination to spend rather than hoard his hard-earned money, Charles behaves like a true picaro. The visit to the hotel, however, takes him away from his pastoral environment and introduces him to the kind of milieu that is traditionally the hunting ground for knights of fortune. The event that leads to Charles's fall from innocence is his falling in love with Veronica, a girl he sees in the hotel. She is completely beyond reach for a window cleaner: "she clearly moved in circles that demanded money as a condition of entry—money, good clothes, social position" (p. 77).

His work and his pastoral haven in the loft enable him to return to a state of near contentment. However, he has been bitten by the money bug. Charles finds an outlet for his new restlessness in his habit of roaming around the countryside at random on his bicycle. Feeling unsettled and vaguely dreaming about future prospects, he is nearly run over by a car driven by Robert Tharkles. His passenger is Betty, the novelist's mistress, with whom Charles shares lodgings. To his horror, Charles realizes that she is a prostitute and that both he and the novelist had been living on her earnings. This discovery marks the end of his sojourn in his bohemian paradise. What shocks him most is that his attempt to break away from the Tharkles world has proved futile. He has, on the contrary, through Betty entered "his name on the Tharkles payroll.... He had become a parasite on the world he detested" (p. 81).

Charles decides to quit his lodgings, and again his act of rejection fuses with the complementary act of ejection. Finding the novelist in a sulky and somewhat aggressive mood, Charles decides to "fade out", that is, leave without notice. Then "lock, stock, and barrel; he hitched the cart behind his bicycle and pedalled away from the home that had become unbearably sullied (...) That episode was over" (p. 85). The ejection motif is strengthened in the twin episode of his partner's arrest. The latter disappears into prison, as a consequence of his activities in a world that is both unknown and closed to Charles. The police warn him off, intimating that he has been under surveillance. His partner's landlord displays even more of the ejector's mentality. He gives Charles the note the prisoner had left for him, but refuses to be involved in any way. When Charles asks him where his partner is going, the landlord answers, " 'It's where *you're* going that interests me (...) Outside' ". Again Charles finds himself at the bottom of society: "Charles picked up his bicycle and, too dispirited to mount, wheeled it aimlessly away" (p. 88). He resumes his residence in the YMCA, where the warden "received [him] back without comment or question." In keeping with the picaresque formula the end of this phase in Charles's career marks his fall to a lower social position. The precariousness of the picaro's lot is echoed in the remark that "His foundations had been knocked from under him" (p. 88).

Attending the trial against his partner, Charles first feels "another vacuum inside him" caused by the termination of his link with his partner. He realizes that what had brought them together was their "shared predicament" of being on the run from their pasts (p. 90). He then makes up his mind to seek entry into the world to which his partner had belonged. Taken on as Export Express driver, Charles has for the first time a steady weekly wage, and has climbed at least one rung higher on the social ladder. With plenty of money to frequent bars and restaurants, he is ready to enter the glamorous world in which Veronica moves. Indeed, she is behind his decision to change his profession.

Charles's new world is one in which the picaro thrives. In this twilight area between unearned riches and respectable work, crooks and parasites of all descriptions flourish, with more than a dash of violence and crime. Like the picaro of old, Charles in his passage from innocence to experience moves through a milieu in which he can hardly escape contamination. He becomes a drug pedlar, a career which acquaints him with a wide range of picaresque clientele. This phase represents the highlight of adventure and fast living in the novel. With his wallet brimful of money, Charles discovers that Veronica is within his reach. He now moves in her circles.

As in the window-cleaning phase, Charles experiences an interlude of pastoral calm when he cultivates his affair with Veronica. The climax of this "magic spell" (p. 131) is their excursion to his old university, where they become lovers. But this is only a passing ray and the violence which is rife in Charles's underground environment soon extinguishes it. This central episode in the book follows the pattern established in the previous phase of an abrupt, new birthlike beginning, followed by pastoral contentment, which leads on to a period of growing restlessness and violence, and the final catastrophe. Charles ends his career as drug pedlar pursued by the police, his conscience troubled by the memory of the brutal murder of a journalist who was tracking down a good story for his paper. Suddenly deciding to reject his criminal career, he tries to stop the car in which he is a passenger, but is instead thrown out and left unconscious in the road.

This is the most dramatic of the ejection incidents in the novel. In his feverish fantasies in the hospital, Charles experiences the same elation he felt after he had walked out of the working class pub. Both literally and in his dreams, he hovers between life and death: "During the few minutes that followed Charles died, was born again, lived whole lifetimes of pain and fever" (p. 152). Recovering, he feels that the past "was a former life, over and done with, something he had forgotten about. Since then he had died and been reborn a score of times" (p. 156). Again, he wishes to cut his moorings in the past completely. Veronica, he now disovers, is the mistress of a rich business tycoon, his benefactor, and she and her world become repulsive to him, linked as they are to money and the network of fraud and crime from which he had just escaped.

At the end of his hospital stay, he starts all over again, at the bottom of the social pyramid. As a hospital orderly, he is soon up against his middle class background's resentment of his refusal to follow the rules of the game and stay put in his own class. The violence with which he has previously been ejected from his milieu recurs at a medical students' party, when he is literally thrown down the stairs after he refuses to conform, insisting on defying the system. A pastoral interlude follows in which he appears to be happy in his lowly occupation. He becomes engaged to a working class girl, through whom he seems assured of admission to the class which was so hostile to him in the pub. Again Charles feels he has landed on his feet. Although he may be fortune's plaything, forever experiencing violent and unpredictable ups and downs, he has acquired the stoic view of the picaro who believes " 'something reasonable always turns up once you've abandoned the idea that one particular job is the only one you're cut out for' " (p. 178)—the view of the class he has rejected.

Such a view in the picaro's case, however, is linked with a spirit of restlessness which makes it difficult to settle down to one particular job or relationship. Charles very soon realizes that he cannot contemplate a lifetime of tranquillity with Rosa. When he is fully recovered from his nearly fatal clash with the underworld, his "itch" (p. 190) flares up once again. When luck puts a position as a chauffeur for a rich patient in his way, he welcomes it as a chance of getting away. The violent rejection-ejection incident which terminates this episode—one long pastoral interlude—occurs when he breaks with Rosa and is nearly thrown out by the staff nurse: " 'Well go on, get out (...) Get out and do some work, even if it is your last night,' " she says in answer to Charles's information that he is leaving (p. 197).

Charles thus keeps to the formula with which he leaves one and enters another phase. As a chauffeur to a rich man, Charles enters the Tharkles world again, in one of the picaro's favourite disguises, as a parasite. He has become a " 'louse on the scalp of society' " (p. 205). His niche is one rung up from that of hospital orderly, but as a member of the servant class, he is still well below that of his origin. In the eyes of his former fellow student, Hutchins, who has been employed by Charles's new benefactor as tutor, Charles must be "down on [his] luck" (p. 205). The job is, in other words, out of bounds for somebody with Charles's social background and upbringing.

Charles is given a false sense of contentment and security during his Sussex period—a state of mind that he tends to be in during his pastoral interludes. His room over the garage, facing the luxurious beauty of the Sussex countryside, inspires him with the detached happiness that he has always sought by withdrawing from his class. As before, however, he cannot maintain his detachment for long. Hutchins is a potential threat to his tranquillity, and his employer's son, whose one interest is racing cars, gets him involved in his experiments, much against this will. Once more Charles moves from one phase to another abruptly and violently. The collision between the racing car that the young boy has built and the Daimler that Charles has been hired to look after propels Charles out of the society he had increasingly come to reject as fake. Without waiting for his dismissal, he leaves abruptly for London, leaving behind him his completely ruined reputation. (He is also suspected of having stolen some jewelry, a crime Hutchins had committed.)

Again, Charles is reduced to down-and-out status. He even has to sleep on a bench in a park. His experience as tramp, however, is of short duration. Pursued by the police—the ejecting agents in this "community"—Charles runs into the arms of Mr. Blearney, a rich gentleman in the rather shady entertainment business who had befriended Charles when he was an Export Express driver. Blearney gives his friend a job as bouncer in an underground night club that he owns. Charles is in the picaresque position of being just above starvation level, and there is no question of pastoral contentment this time. Anyway, his night club phase is so short that Charles really only has time to give further evidence of his eerie gift of landing on his feet. The rejection-ejection formula is again at work. The abrupt beginning of the episode suggests the customary point of departure of a new birth. He is soon deprived of his innocence when he learns that the club is actually a den of vice. In the end, he acts as his own bouncer. Going over to deal with a difficult customer, he finds that the person is his old friend and fellow lodger, the bohemian novelist, who is now working for a radio entertainer. Charles is offered a job in his team, and leaves the niche he is occupying with his usual abruptness—in the company of the person he was meant to dispel.

Charles discovers that he has finally hit upon a career that can offer him both excitement and contentment. His ready wit, which he has tended to use as a means of provoking others, he now exploits to amuse a nationwide audience—and earn good money at the same time. Charles is a far cry from Lazarillo, whose wit is his lifeline. Above all, he will not have to sacrifice his individuality, since in this job, eccentricity is a gold mine. His contract with the radio company gives Charles the kind of permanence and security he can accept. He is finally impervious to class restrictions—or so he thinks.

However, *Hurry On Down*, like the traditional picaresque novel, ends with a question mark. Veronica turns up again, and Charles initially seems to reject her, but she remains a source of temptation, the Eve who might entice him out of his new found paradise:

> If an animal who was tame, or born in captivity, went back to what should have been its natural surroundings, it never survived. (…) Here was his cage, a fine new one (…) And she had snapped the lock and was calling him into the waving jungle. When he got there, he would die. (p. 251)

On the other hand, "she was beautiful, and he loved her, and to accept her with death and catastrophe in the same packet would be no trouble at all" (p. 251). By implication, another phase would emerge, like the Phoenix out of the ashes of the old one. The final words of the novel, "They looked at each other, baffled and inquiring" (p. 252), may herald another rebirth—but they also anticipate the termination of the current happy spell. The ending focuses on "their predicament" (p. 252) rather than on their possible future bliss. They are indeed a well-matched pair of rogues, given emphasis by Veronica's assumption of the name of Defoe's picara, Moll Flanders (p. 250).

Hurry On Down presents a panoramic picture of English society in the early fifties. The welfare state had been established, but Sir Winston Churchill's return to power did not according to Martin Green entail an unqualified "happy return to old traditions; indeed there was a general call for England to give up its political reliance on 'gentlemen' "[6] The underlying shift in social emphasis is part of the energy and frustration that send Charles hurrying down the established English social hierarchy. In the course of his multifarious career Charles discovers how class-ridden the community still is. No matter where he goes or what job he takes, he knocks his head against the class barrier in the society which surrounds him, and inside himself. In retrospect, Charles sees himself as a student, "bowed over books, listening to instruction, submitting to correction, being endlessly moulded and shaped" (p. 28)—to man the *HMS Britain*. Blake Morrison traces the popularity of John Wain's first novel and the work of his fellow writers in "the Movement" to the reading public's feeling that these writers represented the "'coming' class. They were identified with a spirit of change in post-war British society, and were felt to be representative of shifts in power and social structure."[7]

Charles Lumley is a typical product of a section of the middle class which the welfare state brought into prominence and on which it depended—those who were meant to take over from the "gentlemen", the "predominantly lower-middle-class group struggling to assert itself." At 23, with a university degree to his credit, Charles is, as we have seen, expected to settle down in one of the professional grooves for which he has been trained. The question confronting him is one he shares with a host of other young people: "There was only one question: how to use the first twenty-two years of his life as a foundation for the next fifty." The apocalyptic perspective he includes in his picture of the future is also one he shares with his contemporaries: "If, indeed, there was to be a next fifty; and the mushroom-shaped cloud that lived perpetually in a cave at the back of his mind moved forward for a moment to blot out everything else" (p. 29). Although usually suppressed, this anxiety is an important ingredient in Charles's sense of precariousness. In this respect, too, he is on a wavelength with his generation and the Movement's response to the horrors of nuclear war. They subscribed to Charles's laconic view that "still, one must behave as if there was going to be [another fifty years]." (p. 29)[9]

Survival in *Hurry On Down* is not primarily a matter of finding enough to eat, as it is in the Spanish picaresque novel of the seventeenth century. If he had put as much energy into job-hunting as he did in finding a way down in society, he probably would have succeeded in finding a profession in which he could have done reasonably well. The spectre of unemployment seemed, after all, to have been vanquished— one of the achievements of the welfare state. The ingenuity Charles displays during his career presumably would have stood him in good stead if his goal had been professional success. Survival for Charles is, in addition to the context of collective security, a question of the status and integrity of the individual, which he feels are threatened by an environment which expects the individual to adapt and conform to a national code of behavior á la 1984. The reason that he wishes to "hurry on down" in society is his belief that only by freeing himself form his class can he survive as an individual. Frederick R. Karl sees "reaction to class stratification [as] (...) the key to Lumley, as it is to Amis's Jim."[10] This also means rejecting the profession he had been taught to enter.

Charles soon finds that an individual on his own, cut loose from his environment, is as much at a disadvantage as the ragged picaro at the outset of his wanderings. He may be even worse off, for he has never had to fight for the crumbs in the gutter. He is too sensitive and too lacking in the roughness of manner that is required to survive as the fittest. Ejected from the Tharkles world, he finds to his dismay that he is unfit for the working class world he meets in the pub:

> This establishment (...) was predominantly working class in atmosphere; consequently it was peopled by raw, angular personalities who had been encouraged by life to develop their sharp edges. His sharp edges, on the other hand, had been systematically blunted by his upbringing and education.... He had been equipped with an upbringing devised to meet the needs of a more fortunate age, and then thrust into the jungle of the nineteen-fifties. (p. 25)

His sensitivity has made it equally impossible for him to pursue the goal of success embodied by his own background. On his train journey to his home town after his first attempt to de-class himself, he meets the parents of George Hutchins. George is a typical upstart, and, as such, he follows the course opposite to Charles's. His ambition is to make his way up the social pyramid, and throughout the novel he is presented as a rather odious character. He is condemned by Charles, oddly enough because he has rejected his parents, represented as honest, decent working-class people, of the kind Orwell portrays in Coming Up for Air (1939). Charles, who has rejected his own parents, takes to them for their simple virtuousness, while his reaction to George is colored by his class-determined dislike of snobs (p. 13). (Charles reacts in a similar manner to Rose's parents, and to her upstart brother, Stan.) George is first and foremost a hard-headed careerist, bent on making the most of the education and professional qualifications he has gained through hard work and ruthlessness. He lives, according to Charles, by the "raw cult of success" (p. 14).

We have seen how physical and above all, psychological violence is endemic in every section of the community Charls encounters on his journey. He is subjected to or threatened by physical violence when he crashes into the working-class pub. He meets violence in its most brutal shape when he tries to bypass the trade union as a window cleaner, and when he works as an Export Express driver. His job as a bouncer also implies confrontation with violence. Psychological violence is rife in the milieu he is seeking to escape from. Like the picaro, he moves through areas which are infested with thugs and gangsters. The picaro, however, learns to fend for himself through cunning, sheer strength, or skill in the use of weapons. For Charles, on the other hand, there is never any question of using personal strength or weapons to defend himself. He is either helped by people who know the ways of the world, or the art of fighting (like his partner in the window-cleaning business), or he simply resorts to his arsenal of words. He also has a habit of making himself scarce the moment the other party prepares to strike. The only time he is the victim of raw violence is when he is shoved out of the car at the end of his drug-peddling phase.

On this occasion, Charles is saved by a representative of the upper reaches of the Tharkles world. This is doubly ironic because, first, his benefactor is Veronica's wealthy lover; and second, he represents the essence of what Charles wants to get away from. Besides, the rich businessman who pays for his treatment in a private ward in the hospital is one of the modern pillars of society as well as part of the shady world Charles moves into as Export Express driver.

Charles's wish to "hurry on down" from the Tharkles world and the resulting activities may at first glance seem subversive. But he is not bent on carving out a down-and-out existence for himself. It is made quite clear that he is not like the writers of the thirties (Auden and Orwell, for example), who rejected their own class in favor of the proletariat, "the People." Charles speaks contemptuously about "the expensive young men of the thirties" whose rejection of their own class "was moved by the desire to enter, and be at one with, a vaguely conceived People, whose minds and lives they could not even begin to imagine" (pp. 37-38). Charles may be forced by circumstances to seek shelter in a YMCA hostel, but he is not there to find and show solidarity. On the contrary, he fears that "he had already drifted dangerously close to the dreaded state of becoming a member of [the] community" the hostel constitutes. He therefore decides to go somewhere else. With a strong touch of Orwell, Charles turns down a number of alternatives because they offend his middle-class notions of decent accommodation: "others had been merely squalid, and Charles shared the general human attitude towards squalor—he enjoyed his own but disliked other people's" (p. 38).

Charles sees class as a prison house. The history of his career reveals his endless struggle to escape from the "cage" (p. 251) and leap free of class. He is so happy in his job as radio entertainer because he at long last has acquired the state of nothingness he saw as his goal at the end of his working-class interlude (p. 193): "Neutrality; he had found it at last," he says (p. 250). It is, however, no easy matter to achieve classlessness. "Throughout his wanderings," Dale Salwak writes, "Lumley maintains that his aim is to escape all identification with class. Ironically, each of his jobs is involved with society and carries some sort of class identification."[11] It is easy enough to change his hair style, the "only class badge he was wearing" (p. 73), or to adopt the "uniform" of the class of which he is a temporary member. There are, however, elements in his heritage which are almost ineradicable, for example, his accent, which Orwell found was no barrier after all. During his window-cleaning phase, Charles is painfully aware of the labeling effect of accent. His situation is like that of escaped prisoners-of-war who have to keep their mouths shut to avoid detection. His own case, he feels, is a "close parallel (...) for his accent would have given him away even if he had made a serious attempt to pass for a "typical" window-cleaner; and ultimately, converstation would have led to arrest and a closer detention in the prison camp. The way to stay outside the barbed wire was to keep his mouth shut" (p. 39). It is even more difficult for Charles to free himself from the manners, idiom, and general code of behavior of the class he has left. He wages a running battle against middle-class notions of proper, gentlemanly behavior. Thus he demon-strates how he has unlearned what has been instilled in him by not getting up when he is introduced to a lady (p. 55), by spitting into the fire (p. 186), and by draining his tea immediately, instead of sipping it slowly (p. 58). These are comic incidents in his odyssey toward social anonymity.

More serious is the evidence we are given of the indelible stamp of class. His exaggerated individualism is rooted in middle-class ideology. Behind Charles's race down the social scale is his allergic sensitivity to personal contact of any kind, which makes him yearn for neutrality and detachment as the ideal mode of life. We have seen how Orwell's protagonist in *Down and Out* fails to shed his middle-class identity no matter how desperate he is to achieve a state of social metamorphosis. He longs for communion with down-and-out society because its values are anti-individualistic. The community and the accompanying social virtues of solidarity and fellow-feeling are in the foreground in the Paris and London underworld. Down-and-out status in *Hurry On Down* is diametrically different. It enables the individual to withdraw into a cocoon that isolates him from the world of responsibility and social obligation. Thus in the loft he shares with the Bohemian writer and his mistress, he is able to discard "the relics of his upbringing," for example, his inherited image of the home (p. 49). The acme of happiness for him during this period, are his evenings: "Charles was physically tired and contented (...) and was (...) full of thoughts which neither of his companions would have understood or wished to share" (p. 49).

The middle-class dream of solitary bliss, in which the individual is not only able to nurse his sensibility, but is also left to his own resources, is at the heart of the ironic vision which surrounds the Sussex episode. As the rich man's chauffeur, Charles believes he has found a perfect island in the Sussex countryside. He is left completely to himself. There are no fellow servants, and he knows no one in the vicinity. "He was a Crusoe with no need to look for footprints in the sand" (p. 199). A Colonel Jack and a Roderick Random arrive at a paradise of inactivity at the end of their wanderings. *Otium* is the emblem of the status and wealth they have achieved. They are Crusoes returned from their solitary, but successful travels. But Charles reverses the progress that they typify of going from a state of nothing, and by thrift, business acumen, and luck arriving at a final state of idleness. In Charles's case, the blessed state of non-achievement is the result of refusing to play the game of his class. The repeated use of the ejection-rebirth formula underlines the idea of complete reversal as a means of escaping from a class-bound social system, while it also serves to "defamiliarize" the ideology which keeps Charles in thrall. The epiphanic experience which tends to herald a new phase in Charles's career is embodied in language denoting the pioneer's discovery of a new land, or the religious mystic's experience of a new beginning. This is the way he responds to his career as windowcleaner for instance:

> His life had only really begun a week ago. Until then he had merely been an offshoot, an appendage, a post-script, to the lives of several other people. This new life was really his own…. With one bound he had leapt clear of the tradition of his class and type. (pp. 31-32).

The irony is that this kind of bliss does not last. It is not true that his perfect island is without footprints. He soon discovers that there are other people about. He is dogged, for example, by his own former fellow students who represent careers and social attitudes he rejects. Above all, he is haunted, as we have seen, by his own middle-class *persona*. There is, as Karl points out, a strong element of anti-social egotism in Charles's quest for the solitary state.[12] At the extreme end of the middle-class cult of individualism, this stance may be taken as a conservative feature. The latent reactionary tendency is perceived, above all, in the isolationist impule which implies withdrawal from the historical process of socio-political change, an attitude which, according to Morrison, was common among the writers of the Movement.[13]

There is, nevertheless, a radical element in Charles's rejection of his middle-class-dominated society. Morrison shows how their contemporaries attributed a "socialist perspective" to the Movement, and he finds that they "to some degree did so."[14] Charles's determination to free himself from class distinctions has a socialist flavor, as does his rebellion against the middle-class view of a socially determined hierarchy of occupations. Solidarity in Charles's milieu means conforming to society's expectations. Deviation is letting one's class down—high treason in the eyes of the middle-class establishment. When Charles refuses to come to heel at the medical students' party, he is, as we have seen, kicked out. He thus makes the painful discovery that the two-nation social model is still in operation: "The outsider was outside, and they were inside" (p. 176). Charles, like his picaro ancestors, are up against an insurmountable barrier.

This barrier is made even more formidable by the manner in which the Tharkles world had infiltrated the whole of society. There is a pronounced socialist perspective in the analysis of the way their main weapon, money, is used to divide people into categories segregated from each other according to their function as exploiters and exploited. The shock of discovering that he had been living on Tharkles's money through Betty gives Charles insight into the role of money in this system:

> Money. The network everywhere: no, a web, sticky and cunningly arranged. You were either a spider, sitting comfortably in the middle or waiting with malicious joy in hiding, or you were a fly, struggling amid the clinging threads.... His contempt for the spider remained genuine and sustaining even while his wings were being pulled off, even while he was being eaten. But the classification did not work. Which was Betty, a spider or a fly? And which, oh which, was the girl in the Oak Lounge?
>
> ...
>
> He remembered reading about spiders. Sometimes the web caught a wasp by mistake. Then the spider had to dismantle the web. The wasp had to be let go, because it was dangerous.
> It seemed as if the wasps had the right idea. (p. 84)

One of the picaro's most sought after routes up the social hierarchy is marriage to an heiress, which is normally bound to prove a *cul de sac*. In *Hurry on Down*, Veronica functions as picaresque decoy by representing the customary strategy for social elevation in the picaresque novel, at the same time that she lures Charles away from his downward path. Does the wasp image also suggest that through her he may regain the sting of which, we have previously been told, his upbringing has deprived him (p. 25)?

One way in which he may compensate for this loss is by being a parasite on the hated organism. This is again one of the picaro's favorite disguises, enabling him as it does to infiltrate the society he wishes to enter. In Charles's case, however, parasitism is surrounded by ambiguity. As an Express Export driver, for example, he makes plenty of money on the vice and depravity which riddle the Tharkles world. But he is also given insight into the nature of this disease, which, like prostitution in Shaw's *Mrs. Warren's Profession,* is seen as the very principle upon which the money-grabbing and class-divided capitalistic society is founded. His own career as a parasite gives Charles an intense moral experience, that culminates in his being thrown out of the car. Prior to this action, he feels his moral sensibility suddenly come alive again. He has the eerie experience of waking up from a nightmare:

> Whole areas of his mind that had for months been frozen or jammed, freed themselves now with a succession of violent jerks. He felt like a man waking from a drugged sleep (...) one question flared before his eyes: what was he doing here? (...) Sitting beside a tall, thin crook (...) being driven in a stolen car, pursued by the police, wanted for dope-smuggling and murder, was this he, Charles Lumley? (p. 149).

The subsequent phases in his career see Charles trying to disentangle himself from the Tharkles world and its corrupting influence, although his brief spells as private chauffeur and night club bouncer demonstrate the perennial temptation of parasitism to those who are at loose ends. The recurrent emphasis on the death-rebirth cycle in the story of Charles's adventures also has a moral undertone of spiritual decay and renewal. From the beginning, Charles is intensely aware of the threat of emotional stagnation and sterility which solitary confinement within his class involves. By adopting the picaro's mode of life, he is also able to "irrigate his life a little" (p. 73). The irrigation the phrase refers to is the visit to Grand Hotel which releases the drug-peddling chain of events, further evidence of the ambiguity with which every strand in Charles's experience is surrounded. Characteristically, neutrality and parasitism are fused in the "happy" ending of the novel, which, we have seen, leaves one with the impression that Charles is still baffled about his future: will he remain free—neutral—or be put back into the cage by relapsing to the role of parasite?

In *Hurry On Down,* the picaresque formula is used to explore the predicament of a raw, sensitive, and well-educated young man of the middle-class, who, in Wain's words, is "'pitchforked out into the world,'"[15] that is, English society of the early 1950s. Behind his refusal to adapt himself to the milieu he is expected to serve is his lack of the traditional background of civil servant. He comes from the provinces and from a lower rung on the middle-class social ladder than the public-shool-educated young men in the past who became the gentlemen who ruled England. Charles is thus typical of a new generation of university graduates who feel that they are strangers in the land they are meant to serve, and consequently ill at ease. They feel, according to Allsop, "unassimilated. They are a new rootless, faithless, classless class (...) becalmed in the social sea (...) They are acutely conscious of lacking the arrogant composure of the ruling-class line."[16]

We have seen how Charles, like the picaro, repeatedly feels his status as an outsider. The paradox is that his main object after his rejection of the middle class and all it stands for is his unpicaresque determination to acquire outsider status, or, better, to cease worrying about the insider-outsider distinction at all. However, right through the novel he fights in vain to escape from it. Toward the end, he ruefully admits to his friend and benefactor Blearney that "I never rebelled against ordinary life: it just never admitted me (...) I never got into it" (p. 248). Ordinary life is presumably also the kind of "steady, humdrum life" he says he had turned down (p. 248), including a conventional career.

The issue Blearney and Charles discuss is whether Charles is "typical." Blearney first claims that Charles is typical in his insistence that luck, or "a freak of chance," has given him his job on the radio team (p. 247). He thus resorts to the picaro's favorite way of explaining the vicissitudes of fortune. Charles interprets "typical" as meaning average: "ordinary life," and so forth, is that of "normal" young people. However, Blearney then makes it clear that by "typical" he refers to the kind of person who joins the world of entertainment—his world: " 'It's the type who wants neutrality who comes into our racket. Doesn't want to take sides in all the silly pettiness that goes on. Doesn't want to spend his time scratching and being scratched. Wants to live his own life' " (p. 248). It is this kind of typicality that made the reading public of the 1950s herald Charles as one of the angry young men, although we may feel that his anger is rather feeble. The withdrawal instinct he displays seems, at first glance, remote from the picaro's ceaseless social energy whose aim is upward. But the picaro, too, is neutral in his readiness to adapt himself to any climate of opinion in order to get in. He certainly would not have understood the rejection of the "scratching and being schratched" principle.

The picaro would, on the other hand, have been in his right element in the kind of community in which Charles is thought to be typical on another occasion. Charles is, as we have seen, always chary of opening his mouth in case his accent should give away his true identity. When this happens during his Export Express driver phase, his new acquaintance feels bewildered, accustomed as he is to thinking of accent as the badge of class as well as profession:

> "Dear, dear, oh dear, the world's moving too fast for poor old Arthur. Here was I trying to size you up, and failing because you didn't fit into any type I knew, and now it turns out you've got a job I'd never even heard of. And what kind of job might that be? One of these new kind of jobs (...) where you couldn't rightly say whether a fella was a workman or an office stool percher or a manager. It's all upside down these days." (p. 99)

The picaro would have exploited this kind of fluid environment to carve out a niche for himself, and Charles, too, at times benefits from the collapse of the old class-bound professional hierarchy. In this case, too, the opposite direction that his wandering follows is striking. His formula is the picaresque formula turned upside down: failing "to take root in the cliff-side of a shattered bourgeoisie," he "had tried manual work, he had tried crime, he had tried being a servant" (p. 233), and at the moment, he is a down-and-out who has to be rescued by Blearney. All his efforts have been directed at getting out of the clutches of class, while the picaro would have striven to use these openings as stepping stones into the class system.

His concern with the typical links Wain to the tradition of satirical-social realism in the novel, which has favored aspects of the picaresque mode. With its focus on the universal aspects of human behavior and on the human condition, the picaresque frequently shows kinship to the allegorical tradition. The didactic element in novels such as *Gúzman* and *Colonel Jack* also connects the two modes. In *Hurry On Down*, considerable attention is paid to Charles's moral development—the way his moral sensitivity is first blunted by the environment through which he moves and then revives. The death-rebirth formula which shapes every phase of his career helps to highlight his moral growth. Toward the end of the novel, Charles presents a universalized summary of his pilgrim's progress in mock-allegorical terms:

> The young man (Hopeless) breaks out of the prison of Social and Economic Maladjustment; he carries on his back a hundredweight of granite known as Education. After a skirmish with the dragon Sex, in which he is aided by a false friend, Giant Crime, he comes to the illusory citadel called Renunciation of Ambition. And so on. What an allegory it would make! (pp. 233-234)

The tone is facetious, but there is an undertone of seriousness in the passage which originates in the sketch we are given of Charles's abnormal state of mind when he has his "vision": "With uncanny vividness, derived partly from fatigue, his consciousness freed itself from his body, sitting here at the table, and watched the scene, cleverly picking out the allegorical elements" (p. 233). Charles reveals here his acute sense of the significance of what is happening to him and of the pattern in the apparently haphazard concatenation of incidents. We have also seen how Charles tends to experience a kind of epiphany each time he is ejected from one phase into another.

Charles displays a self-consciousness and degree of introversion which are unusual in the picaresque novel. The traditional picaro tends to be very reticent about his own emotional state and is apt to speak about himself and others in a very laconic manner, regardless of the nature of the recorded experience. An exception is Gúzman d'Alfarache. He is not only observer and narrator but also critical commentator who, in the course of the long novel, diagnoses the disease from which his society suffers and also sketches out an alternative society. At the end of *Hurry On Down*, Charles is not, like Gúzman, a galley slave. On the contrary, we have seen that he has eventually found his niche—or drifted into it. But he, too, has been given social insight in the course of his wanderings and a clear picture of a sick society with "disabled" inhabitants (on page 171, for example). However, it is part of the dilemma of the 1950s that the alternative society is only vaguely perceived and that it is surrounded by contradictions. Characteristically, the open ending gives way to a sense of bafflement. From beginning to end in *Hurry On Down*, the picaresque formula is exploited to tell a tale of the times. In the process, we have come full circle; we have hurried on down to the individual and his Sisyphean struggle with his insider-oriented environment—the picaro's perennial situation.

¹ Robert Barnard, *A Short History of English Literature for Foeign Students* (Tromsø: Universitetsforlaget, 1984) 196.

² Kenneth Allsop, *The Angry Decade. A Survey of the Cultural Revolt of the Nineteen-fifties* (London: Peter Owen Limited, 1964) 72.

³ Allsop, 73.

⁴ References, included parenthetically in the text, are to John Wain, *Hurry On Down* (Harmondsworth: Penguin, 1977).

⁵ Wicks, 247. Vide supra, p. 14.

⁶ Martin Green, *Children of the Sun. A Narrative of "Decadence" in England After 1918* (New York: Basic Books, Inc., Publishers, 1976) 386.

⁷ Blake Morrison, *The Movement. English Poetry and Fiction in the 1950s* (Oxford: Oxford University Press, 1980) 57.

⁸ Morrison, 84.

⁹ Morrison, 89-90.

¹⁰ Frederick R. Karl, *A Reader's Guide to the Contemporary English Novel* (New York: Farrar, Straus and Giroux, 1972) 224.

¹¹ Dale Salwak, *John Wain* (Boston: Twayne Publishers, 1981) 34.

¹² Karl, 228.

¹³ Morrison, 91-98.

¹⁴ Morrison, 84.

¹⁵ Wain, as quoted in Allsop, 68.

¹⁶ Allsop, 27.

Bibliography

Alldritt, Keith, *The Making of George Orwell. An Essay in Literary History*. London: Edward Arnold, 1966.

Alemán, Mateo, *The Rogue or the Life of Guzmán de Alfarache*. Trans. James Mabbe, New York: AMS Press, Inc., 1967.

Allsop, Kenneth, *The Angry Decade. A Survey of the Cultural Revolt of the Mid-Fifties*. London: Peter Owen Limited, 1964.

Alpert, Michael, trans. *Lazarillo de Tormes*. In *Two Spanish Picaresque Novels*. Harmondsworth: Penguin, 1975.

Alter, Robert, *Rogue's Progress. Studies in the Picaresque Novel*. Cambridge, Mass.: Harvard University Press, 1964.

Altick, Richard D. *Victorian People and Ideas. A Companion for the Modern Reader of Victorian Literature*. New York: W.W. Norton & Company Inc., 1973.

Ashton, T.S. *Economic Fluctuations in England 1700-1800*. Oxford: Clarendon Press, 1959.

Atkins, John, *George Orwell. A Literary Study*. London: John Calder, 1954.

Barnard, Robert, *A Short History of English Literature for Foreign Students*. Tromsø: Universitetsforlaget, 1984.

Imagery and Theme in the Novels of Dickens. Bergen: Universitetsforlaget, 1974.

Best, Geoffrey, *Mid-Victorian Britain 1851-1875*. Frogmore, St. Albans: Panther, 1973.

Bjornson, Richard, "Victimization and Vindication in Smollett's *Roderick Random*." *Studies in Scottish Literature*, XIII 1978.

Blackburn, Alexander, *The Myth of the Picaro. Continuity and Transformation of the Picaresque Novel 1554-1954*. Chapel Hill: University of North Carolina Press, 1979.

Blewett, David, *Defoe's Art of Fiction. Robinson Crusoe, Moll Flanders, Colonel Jack and Roxana*. Toronto: University of Toronto Press, 1979.

Boucé, Paul-Gabriel, *The Novels of Tobias Smollett*. London: Longman, 1976.

Cecil, David, *Early Victorian Novelists. Essays in Revaluation*. London: Constable & Co., Ltd., 1957.

Chandler, Frank Wadleigh, *The Literature of Roguery*. New York: Burt Franklin Reprints, Lenox Hill Pub. & Dist., Co. 1974.'

Cockshut, A.O.J. *The Achievement of Walter Scott*. London: Collins, 1969.

Crick, Bernard, *George Orwell*. London: Secker & Warburg, 1981.

Dabney, Ross H. *Love and Property in the Novels of Dickens*. London: Chatto & Windus, 1967.

Daiches, David, *Literary Essays*. Edinburgh: Oliver and Boyd, 1956.

Daleski, H. M. *Dickens and the Art of Analogy*. London: Faber and Faber, 1970.

Defoe, Daniel, *The History and Remarkable Life of the Truly Honourable Col. Jacque Commonly Call'd Col. Jack*. London: Oxford University Press, 1970.

Devine, T. M. "The Scottish Merchant Community, 1680-1740", *The Origins and Nature of The Scottish Enlightenment*. Eds. R. H. Campbell and Andrew S. Skinner, Edinburgh: John Donald Publishers Ltd., 1982.

Dickens, Charles, *David Copperfield*. Harmondsworth: Penguin, 1966.

Great Expectations. Harmondsworth: Penguin, 1972.

Earle, Peter, *The World of Defoe*. London: Weidenfeld and Nicolson, 1976.

Fleishman, Avrom, *The English Historical Novel. Walter Scott to Virginia Woolf*. Baltimore: The John Hopkins University Press, 1971.

Forbes, Duncan, "The Rationalism of Sir Walter Scott." *Cambridge Journal*, 7, 1953.

Forster, John, *The Life of Charles Dickens*. London: J.M. Dent & Sons Ltd., 1927.

Fredman, Alice Green, "The Picaresque in Decline: Smollett's First Novel." *English Writers of the Eighteenth Century*. Ed. John H. Middendorf, New York: Columbia University Press, 1971.

169

Freedman, Ralph, "The Possibility of a Theory of the Novel." *The Disciplines of Criticism*. Eds. Peter Demetz, et al., New Haven: Yale University Press, 1967.

Frye, Northrop, *The Secular Scripture. A Study of the Structure of Romance*. Cambridge, Mass.: Harvard University Press, 1976.

George, M. Dorothy, *England in Transition. Life and Work in the Eighteenth Century*. London: Penguin, 1953.

Giddings, Robert, *The Tradition of Smollett*. London: Methuen & Co. Ltd., 1967.

Gilmour, Robin, *The Idea of the Gentleman in the Victorian Novel*. London: George Allen & Unwin, 1981.

Goldberg, M. A. *Smollett and the Scottish School. Studies in Eighteenth Century Thought*. Albuquerque: University of New Mexico Press, 1959.

Green, Martin, *Children of the Sun. A Narrative of "Decadence" in England After 1918*. New York: Basic Books, Inc., Publishers, 1976.

Greig, J. Y. T. *Thackeray. A Reconsideration*. London: Oxford University Press, 1950.

Guillén, Claudio, *Literature as System. Essays Toward the Theory of Literary History*. Princeton University Press, 1971.

"Toward a Definition of the Picaresque." In *Proceedings of the Third Congress of the International Comparative Literature Association*. Utrecht: Mouton, 1962.

Hall, John, *The Sociology of Literature*. London: Longman, 1979.

Hamilton, Henry, *The Industrial Revolution in Scotland*. London: Frank Cass & Co. Ltd., 1966.

Hardy, Barbara, *The Exposure Of Luxury. Radical Themes in Thackeray*. London: Peter Owen, 1972.

The Moral Art of Dickens. London: Athlone Press of the University of London, 1970.

Harvie, Christopher, *Scotland and Nationalism. Scottish Society and Politics, 1707-1977*. London: George Allen & Unwin, 1977.

Hill, Christopher, *1530-1780. Reformation to Industrial Revolution*. The Pelican Economic History of Britain, vol. 2. Harmondsworth: Penguin, 1978.

Hollis, Christopher, *A Study of George Orwell. The Man and His Works*. London: Hollis and Carter, 1956.

House, Humphrey, *The Dickens World*. London: Oxford University Press, 1960.

Kahrl, George M. *Tobias Smollett. Traveler-Novelist*. Chicago: University of Chicago Press, 1945.

Karl, Frederick R. *A Reader's Guide to the Contemporary English Novel*. New York: Farrar, Straus and Giroux, 1972.

Knapp, Lewis M. *Tobias Smollett. Doctor of Men and Manners*. Princeton: Princeton University Press, 1949.

Leavis, F. R. and Q. D. *Dickens the Novelist*. Harmondsworth: Penguin, 1972.

Lesage, *The Adventures of Gil Blas of Santillane*. Trans. Tobias Smollett, London: Walker and Co., 1823.

Lewis, Peter, *George Orwell. The Road to 1984*. London: Heinemann, 1981.

Lubbock, Percy, *The Craft of Fiction*. London: Jonathan Cape, 1957.

Lukács, Georg, *The Historical Novel*. London: Merlin Press, 1965.

Mackie, J. D. *A History of Scotland*. Harmondsworth: Penguin, 1979.

Manning, Sylvia Bank, *Dickens as Satirist. Yale Studies in English*, vol. 176. New Haven: Yale University Press, 1971.

Marshall, Dorothy, *Eighteenth Century England*. London: Longman, 1974.

Miller, J. Hillis, *Charles Dickens. The World of his Novels*. Cambridge, Mass.: Harvard University Press, 1965.

Morrison, Blake, *The Movement. English Poetry and Fiction of the 1950s*. Oxford: Oxford University Press, 1980.

Moynahan, Julian, "The Hero's Guilt — The Case of *Great Expectations.*" In *Hard Times, Great Expectations, and Our Mutual Friend. A Casebook.* Ed. Norman Page, London: Macmillan, 1979.

Myers, Douglas, "Scottish Schoolmasters in the Nineteenth Century: Professionalism and Politics." *Scottish Culture and Scottish Education, 1800-1980.* Eds. Walter M. Humes and Hamish M. Paterson, Edinburgh: John Donald Publishers Ltd., 1983.

Novak, Maximillian E. *Defoe and the Nature of Man.* London: Oxford University Press, 1963.

Orwell, George, *Down and Out in Paris and London.* Harmondsworth: Penguin, 1974. *The Road to Wigan Pier.* Harmondsworth: Penguin, 1974.

Owen, John B. *The Eighteenth Century, 1714-1815.* London: Nelson, 1974.

Parker, Alexander A. *Literature and the Delinquent. The Picaresque Novel in Spain and Europe, 1599-1753.* Edinburgh: The University Press, 1977.

Perkin, Harold, *The Origins of Modern English Society, 1780-1880.* London: Routledge & Kegan Paul, 1969.

Plumb, J. H. *England in the Eighteenth Century.* The Pelican History of England, vol. 7. Harmondsworth: Penguin, 1972.

Pollard, Arthur, ed. *Thackeray. Vanity Fair. A Casebook.* London: Macmillan, 1978.

Prebble, John, *The Lion in the North. A Personal View of Scotland's History.* Harmondsworth: Penguin, 1973.

Quevedo, F. de, *La Vida del Buscón (The Swindler).* In *Two Spanish* Picaresque Novels, trans. Michael Alpert, Harmondsworth: Penguin, 1975.

Ray, Gordon N. *Thackeray. The Uses of Adversity (1811-1846).* London: Oxford University Press, 1955.

Reed, Walter L. *An Exemplary History of the Novel. The Quixotic Versus the Picaresque.* Chicago: University of Chicago Press, 1981.

Richetti, John J. *Defoe's Narratives. Situations and Structures.* Oxford: Oxford University Press, 1975.

Rogers, Pat, *The Augustan Vision.* London: Methuen & Co. Ltd., 1978.

Salwak, Dale, *John Wain.* Twayne's English Authors Series, vol. 316. Boston: Twayne Publishers, 1981.

Sandison, Alan, *The Last Man in Europe. An Essay on George Orwell.* London: Macmillan, 1974.

Scholes, Robert, *Structuralism in Literature. An Introduction.* New Haven: Yale University Press, 1974.

Scott, Sir Walter, *Rob Roy.* London: Dent. Everyman's Library, 1976.

Sieber, Harry, *The Picaresque.* The Critical Idiom Series. London: Methuen & Co. Ltd., 1977.

Smollett, Tobias, *Roderick Random.* London: Dent. Everyman's Library, 1975.

Smout, T. C. *A History of the Scottish People, 1560-1830.* Glasgow: Collins, 1975.

Speck, W. A. *Stability and Strife. England 1714-1760.* The New History of England, vol. 6. London: Edward Arnold, 1977.

Stansky, Peter and Abrahams, William, *The Unknown Orwell.* Frogmore, St. Albans: Paladin, 1974.

Starr, G. A. *Defoe. Spiritual Autobiography.* Princeton: Princeton University Press, 1965.

Sutherland, James, *Daniel Defoe. A Critical Study.* Cambridge, Mass.: Harvard University Press, 1971.

Thackeray, William Makepeace, *Vanity Fair.* Harmondsworth: Penguin, 1968.

Thomas, Edward M. *Orwell.* Edinburgh: Oliver and Boyd, 1971.

Thomas, R. George, *Charles Dickens: Great Expectations. Studies in English Literature,* no. 19. London: Edward Arnold, 1971.

Thomson, David, *England in the Nineteenth Century (1815-1914)*. The Pelican History of England, vol. 8. Harmondsworth: Penguin, 1957.

Thurley, Geoffrey, *The Dickens Myth. Its Genesis and Structure*. London: Routledge & Kegan Paul, 1976.

Tillotson, Kathleen, *Novels of the Eighteenth-Forties*. London: Oxford University Press, 1961.

Tillyard, E. M. W. *The Epic Strain in the English Novel*. London: Chatto & Windus, 1958.

Van Ghent, Dorothy, *The English Novel. Form and Function*. New York: Harper & Row, Publishers, 1961.

Wain, John, *Hurry On Down*. Harmondsworth: Penguin, 1977.

Watt, Ian, *The Rise of the Novel. Studies in Defoe, Richardson, and Fielding*. Harmondsworth: Penguin, 1963.

Welsh, Alexander, *The City of Dickens*. Oxford: Clarendon Press, 1971.

Wicks, Ulrich, "The Nature of Picaresque Narrative: A Modal Approach." *PMLA*, 89, 1974.

Willey, Basil, *The Eighteenth Century Background. Studies on the Idea of Nature in the Thought of the Period*. Harmondsworth: Penguin, 1962.

Williams, Basil, *The Whig Supremacy, 1714-1760*. The Oxford History of England, vol. XI. Oxford: Clarendon Press, 1962.

Williams, E.N. *Life in Georgian England*. London: B. T. Batsford Ltd., 1963.

Wilson, A.N. *The Laird of Abbotsford. A View of Sir Walter Scott*. Oxford: Oxford University Press, 1980.

Wilson, Edmund, *The Wound and the Bow. Seven Studies in Literature*. London: Methuen, 1961.

Woodcock, George, *The Crystal Spirit. A Study of George Orwell*. London: Jonathan Cape, 1967.

Zwerdling, Alex, *Orwell and the Left*. New Haven: Yale University Press, 1974.